DEALING
WITH
RELATIVES
(EVEN IF YOU CAN'T STAND THEM)

**Also by
Dr. Rick Brinkman and Dr. Rick Kirschner**

Dealing with People You Can't Stand

*Life by Design:
Making Wise Choices in a Mixed Up World*

DEALING WITH RELATIVES

(EVEN IF YOU CAN'T STAND THEM)

Bringing Out the Best in Families at Their Worst

Dr. Rick Brinkman
Dr. Rick Kirschner

McGraw-Hill

New York   Chicago   San Francisco   Lisbon   London
Madrid   Mexico City   Milan   New Delhi   San Juan
Seoul   Singapore   Sydney   Toronto

Library of Congress Cataloging-in-Publication Data

Brinkman, Rick.
  Dealing with relatives (—even if you can't stand them) : bringing out
the best in families at their worst / By Rick Brinkman and Rick
Kirschner.
     p. cm.
  ISBN 0-07-137738-7
  1. Family.   2. Interpersonal relations.   3. Communication in the
family.   I. Kirschner, Rick.   II. Title.
  HQ734 .B8156 2002
  306.85—dc21   2002013131

1 2 3 4 5 6 7 8 9 0 AGM/AGM   0 9 8 7 6 5 4 3 2

ISBN 0-07-137738-7

We dedicate this book to the family of humanity.
Behold what goodness and pleasure we experience
when we join together in peace.

Contents

Part I:
Meet the Relatives

A Lens of Understanding on why they act the way they do

Part II:
Family Camp
A learning environment for essential skills

Your reactions to relatives are a group of powerful associations that give you the leverage to change your world!

Eight Strategies: Create Neutral Turf . . . Create a New Dynamic . . . Find a New Environment . . . Gain a New Perspective . . . Reverse the Roles . . . Find the Right Time . . . Change Your Mode of Communication . . . Change from the Inside Out

Part III:
Family Gatherings, Get-Togethers, Show-Ups, and Showdowns at the Not-OK Corral

These numbers can mean the difference between having a good time that strengthens your family relationships and having an awful time that damages relationships to the detriment of family.

Geography . . . Frequency . . . Time . . . Magic Number Worksheet

To help you go from "have to" to "don't have to" to "don't want to" or "really want to!" we offer you this pre-obligation checklist. While you don't have to use it, you may want to give it a try.

Pre-Obligation Checklist

There are three stages to family events: before, during, and after. Giving and getting meaningful support can be an important aspect of each of them.

The Before Stage . . . The During Stage . . . The After Stage

If you decide to go to an event and you choose not to suffer, then you can go with a different attitude, or go with a different attitude and behavior. To avail yourself of one or both of these two choices, we offer you the following four rules.

Decide in Advance . . . Plan for Sore Subjects . . . Keep Your Perspective . . . Use Reminders

Part IV:
Bringing Out the Best in Relatives
at Their Worst

*Specific options for dealing
with the Eight by Fate*

20. The Martyr   199

The Martyr is a needy giver, giving gifts whether you want them or not. Each gift comes with an obligation.

Fable: The Three Bears . . . Understanding the Martyr . . . Dealing with the Martyr . . . Options with the Martyr . . . Fable Finale: The Three Bears

21. The Mystery   215

When those who feel like an outsider get far enough outside, they become a Mystery to those on the inside.

Fable: The Ant and the Grasshopper . . . Understanding the Mystery . . . Dealing with the Mystery . . . Options with the Mystery . . . Fable Finale: The Ant and the Grasshopper

22. The Rebel   229

Rebels hold others responsible for their own feelings of insignificance.

Fable: The Black Sheep . . . Understanding the Rebel . . . Dealing with the Rebel . . . Options with the Rebel . . . Fable Finale: The Black Sheep

23. The Dimension of Greatness:
Top 10 Qualities of Great Relatives   245

What follows are the top 10 composite responses about what constitutes a great relative, in descending order of frequency.

A Great Relative: Values Communication . . . Loves Unconditionally . . . Is Accepting and Respectful . . . Offers Support . . . Is Helpful . . . Keeps in Touch . . . Is Wise with Money . . . Is Also a Friend . . . Doesn't Hold On to the Past . . . Is Fun, Optimistic, and a Positive Influence

Appendix   251

Resources for dealing with serious family pathology.

Resources . . . Organizations . . . Peer Counseling Groups

An Invitation from the Authors   253

Acknowledgments

We are deeply grateful to the following people for their help and support on this project: Our family members who, like us, are never difficult to deal with; our children, Aden and Carle, who have given us our deepest understanding of the meaning, value and purpose of family; our wives, Lindea K and Lisa B, whose advice, encouragement, suggestions, insights and endless patience made this book happen; our parents, without whom none of the majesty and miracles in our lives would have been possible, and whose question "How's the book coming?" helped us hold the focus to get it done; the many people who let us interview them, and openly shared their stories of triumph and travail with us in the preparation of this material.

Introduction

Loved, liked, or despised, everybody has relatives and everybody has to deal with them. You may not choose them, but you never really lose them, because family is family for life. The label of "relative" covers a wide range of relationships—from parents, siblings, and offspring, to aunts, uncles, nieces, nephews, cousins, and in-laws. Whether they are melded, welded, or only marginally attached to your family, they are your relatives nonetheless.

As a result, behavior in a family can be incredibly diverse. Some of your relatives may be cautious, whereas others are carefree. Some are only there when you want them, while others are never there when you need them. Some may be offensive, while others are easily offended. Some may take great pains to make sure you know they are suffering on your behalf, while others may come and go like the wind and never notice the mess they leave behind. How do you sort it out and make sense of it all? What can be done when relatives behave badly?

In writing this book, we were faced with a humbling fact. Family is a subject of great scope and complexity! In order to be successful in having worthwhile and fulfilling relationships with your relatives, you need insights and skills that work reliably through time, and a way to organize them so that you can learn them, refer to them, and use them when something more is required. Since the best advice needs a consistent organizing framework, we strove to design a simple model with simple steps that can explain why people act the way they do and what you can do about it.

Such was our task and our intention. To accomplish it, we followed a similar organizational model to the one in our book, *Dealing with People You Can't Stand*. We encourage you to consider that book as a companion volume to this one, a useful supplement with even more choices for influencing relationships.

This book has four parts. In Part One, we introduce the "Eight by Fate," the eight behaviors that make for great relatives or difficult ones, and provide a Lens of Understanding to help you make sense out of why your relatives act the way they do (and why you act the way you do too!) In Part Two, you're invited to "Family Camp," a learning environment for the basic set of communication skills you'll need to interact with your family members in a constructive and creative way. In Part Three, we provide you with material that relates specifically to the special case of family gatherings. We call it "Showdown at the Not-OK Corral." This section can serve you as a useful reference in preparing for holidays and reunions. Part Four returns to the Eight by Fate behaviors and provides you with a set of options for dealing with each of them, based on the skills you acquired in Part Two. We conclude the book with "The Dimension of Greatness: The Top 10 Qualities of an Ideal

Relative." If you've ever wanted to let your relatives know what you want from them, or you have ever aspired to be a great relative yourself, these are the most desirable characteristics of great relatives according to the people we interviewed for this book.

You may be wondering who we are and how we came to write this book. You can find an extensive bio in our first book or on our website www.TheRicks.com. Suffice it to say that we are Rick and Rick, twin sons of different mothers. We met while students at a naturopathic medical school, and our friendship and partnership has endured for well over two decades. (To learn more about naturopathic medicine and the states in which it is licensed, visit the American Association of Naturopathic Physicians at www.naturopathic.org.) We live parallel lives in many ways. We are both married to women whose names start with the letter "'L.'" We each have one child, a daughter. Our daughters are the same age apart as we are. We once unknowingly bought the same Armani suit fifteen hundred miles apart on the same day, and discovered the fact when we showed up for a video taping wearing identical suits. We are both physicians, we both live in Oregon, and we both speak to audiences all over the world. Together, we have studied health from the point of view that thoughts and emotions play a significant role in well-being. We are both students of human nature and have arrived individually at the shared point of view that working things out works better than getting worked up and that it is possible to work things out even when one party doesn't necessarily want to! We are convinced that relationships improve when people know what to do and then do it. And we both agree that you always have a choice about what you do with the circumstances of your life. You can suffer and complain about what is wrong and who is wrong and what can't be done and why it can't be done, or you can apply your time and energy to making things better for others in their dealings with you and for yourself in your dealings with others.

This book is not intended as a reference text for dealing with mental illness and serious family pathology. Such work is best handled with appropriate support and services (see Appendix.) But it is designed to help you improve the quality of your family relationships when your approach has been clouded with stress, anger, fear, and frustration. In preparing to write this book, we conducted hundreds of interviews with people from a wide range of cultures and backgrounds. The stories in this book, including the fables and fairy tales, are about real people. The names and circumstances have been changed to protect both the innocent and the guilty. The people with whom we spoke were open and honest about the difficulties they faced with their relatives and the solutions they developed to overcome those difficulties. With their help and insight, we were able to find out the best of what works to bring out the best in relatives at their worst. We've written this book to pass this information on to you.

Without further ado, it's time for you to meet the relatives!

Part I

Meet the Relatives
A Lens of Understanding on Why They Act the Way They Do

Chapter 1

Family Fables by the Doctors Rick

Your family members may agree or disagree with you about which of your relatives are the most difficult to deal with or the most badly behaved. Yet most of the people we have interviewed on this subject seem to have similar problems with similar kinds of behavior. With their help, we identified eight patterns that commonly occur when family members make each other crazy. Apparently, eight is enough, since these eight patterns in all their variety seem to describe the lion's share of difficulties. They are: the General, Judge, Pleaser, VIP, Meddler, Martyr, Rebel, and Mystery.

Some of your relatives may engage in two, three, four, or more of these eight behaviors at different times. And any one of these behaviors can lead to difficult behavior in others. The good thing about bad behavior is that all behavior is fluid by nature, changing from moment to moment, situation to situation, and person to person. It is possible for you to have a good influence on bad behavior. The first step to gaining that influence is to recognize and understand what you're dealing with. To that end we offer you these eight fables.

The General: The Family Trip

Joe barked orders as he drove down the long stretch of highway in the middle of the desert. "Communications officer, use your communicator to contact our next base. Tell them we will be arriving late. Number one? Do you have that navigation report yet? I need it ASAP!"

In the passenger seat beside him, Joe's wife Mina fumbled with the map. She turned it first one way, then completely flipped it around the other way, then back the first way again.

"Is anyone listening to me?" Joe called out with frustration.

"I'm listening to you, Captain!" exclaimed Tommy from the backseat. "But Darla can't hear you because she's got headphones on. Do you want me to disintegrate her with my space blaster?"

Joe glanced in the rearview mirror to see his daughter's head bobbing to a beat that only she could hear. "Tommy, get her attention now."

Tommy slugged Darla in the arm. Darla immediately slugged him back. In no time at all they were going at it in the backseat.

"Hey, you kids!!" Joe yelled as he held the wheel with one hand and tried to whack someone in the back with the other. Unfortunately, his hand was an unguided missile and he only succeeded in whacking the side of the baby's chair. This woke Mary up, and she immediately began to cry. Aw, for crying out loud! Joe thought. The baby had just fallen asleep fifteen minutes earlier. Joe looked forward to the day when she was old enough to be ordered to stop crying.

Mina put down the map and reached back to attend to the crying baby.

Joe ordered his wife, "Number one, do that later! I need those navigational coordinates and I need them now!"

Mina rolled her eyes. "Earth to Joseph. We are in the middle of the desert and this is the only road. There is not another road connecting with this one for about 25 miles. So unless you plan on driving at hyper-light speed, which by the way you can't, because as I recall when we were at the car dealer, you passed on that option, I think I probably have time to attend to Mary."

Darla put her music player on pause and helped her mom get Mary out of the baby seat.

If he couldn't control his wife, Joe told himself, at least he could control his kids. "Communications Officer Darla!" he commanded. "Get on subspace and contact our next starbase to let them know we will be arriving late."

"I can't do that, Dad."

"Call me 'Captain.'"

"Why?"

"Because I said so."

"Well, Captain Dad," she said, voice dripping with sarcasm as she mentally counted her blessings that none of her friends were here to witness this, "I have some bad news for you. Subspace communications are out."

"What do you mean, subspace communications are out?" Joe snapped.

"I mean the cell phone has no battery power."

"What? Why not?"

"Because I used it up during the first hour of this stupid trip, talking to my friends back home."

Before Joe could react, his wife delivered some more bad news. "We are really going to have to stop soon. I need to change Mary."

"Yeah, let's stop, I want a milk shake," Darla piped in.

"Yeah, let's stop someplace where they have giant snakes!" Tommy chimed in.

"We are not stopping until after we hit the interstate." Joe said with finality.

"Joe, we need to take a break." Mina said softly.

"We need to keep going, number one," Joe countered. "And don't countermand my orders in front of the crew."

"Why do you keep calling me number one?"

"Because you are my first officer."

"Then as first officer, Captain Bligh, I am telling you to lighten up and take a break, or there will be a mutiny on this ship."

"Fine," Joe fumed. "We'll stop."

The kids cheered in unison.

"But only for five minutes to use the bathroom. And no large drinks! I don't want your bladders filling up again. We'll have to make up for the lost time."

The Judge: The Real Story of Jack, the Giant, and the Bean Stalk

The Giant dreaded his mother's visits because she criticized or complained about everything. Last visit, he put her in the tower, because it had the best view, but she whined about having to walk up all the stairs. The time before, he gave her a ground floor room, and she said, "What? I'm not special enough for a tower room?" So far, this visit was proving to be no different.

"Look at the way you're dressed! A sloppy schlump! How can you expect people to fear you?"

"But, Ma, it's not easy to find size extra-extra-extra-extra-large shirts."

"Are you too lazy to do what you must to look scary? Yes, you are! Look at this place. You certainly haven't done any yard work since I was here last. How can you let that unsightly giant bean stalk grow in your front yard? And don't tell me you can't clean up once in a while! Why, fee fi fo fum, it smells like the blood of an Englishman! Well, at least I hope you have taken good care of my dear goose."

As his mom went into the castle to find her goose, the Giant rolled his big eyes, then plopped down onto the stone steps. He slumped sadly, feeling so incredibly small.

That's when Jack emerged from his hiding place behind the beanstalk and approached the Giant. "Hey, Giant, whatsup?" he inquired pleasantly.

The Giant just shrugged and looked away.

"It's tough when relatives are so critical." Jack said sympathetically.

"Hmph. Tell me about it," the Giant muttered.

Jack went on, "I know, because my mom's like that too."

"For real?" The Giant turned to look at Jack for the first time.

Jack went on, "Yeah, nothing is ever good enough. And if anything goes wrong, she immediately blames me! Like, she tells me to sell the cow because we need food, right? Well, I meet this dude with magic beans—"

The Giant's eyes opened wide. "Magic beans? Cool!"

"Yeah, I thought so too! He says he'll trade me the beans for the cow."

"Sucka!" The Giant laughed.

"For sure! But when I bring home the beans, my mom is all over me about how I never get things right. Then she throws the beans out the window!"

"Bummer," the Giant sympathized.

"Not!" Jack smiled. "Overnight, it grows into this bodaciously huge bean stalk!"

The Giant's eyes were wide with surprise. "Too cool! Guess what? I also have a giant bean stalk in my front yard!"

"I know, dude! That's how I got here," Jack replied.

"No way!!"

"Way!" Jack sat down next to the Giant. They sat in silent rapport for a while, staring at the beanstalk, until the Giant broke the silence. "You got any pets?"

"Naa. I mean, I had the cow, but now she's gone. You?" Jack asked.

"Just my mom's stupid goose! It drives me crazy! It honks all night long and it leaves golden eggs everywhere that I have to pick up. I wish she'd take it with her when she leaves."

Jack's eyes opened wide, "Golden eggs! Why would you not want golden eggs? Where I come from, gold is everything!"

The Giant started to shake, and then burst out laughing. "Around here, that's just what comes out the back of a goose." Then he looked thoughtful, and said, "I've got an idea! Since you like gold so much, how about I hook you up with the goose that lays the golden eggs? You can take it with you!"

Jack's jaw dropped in shock, "Dude, you're kidding!"

"No, dude, really. My mom wants me to be scary, so I'll give her scary. Here's the plan. I give you the goose. You act scared and make a run for it, like you're stealing it. I come after you. I'll do some fe-fi-fo-fumming, which will sound really terrifying, but just know that we're cool. Maybe I can impress my mom and get rid of that stupid goose in one fell swoop!"

"I'm down with that!" Jack agreed. "I'll go tearing back to the bean stalk like you are the biggest, baddest thing I have *ever* seen!"

And with that, Jack high-fived the Giant (really high!), while the Giant low-fived Jack (really low!). And the rest was history.

The Pleaser: Leave It to Pleasers

As June Pleaser vacuumed the rug, she thought about what else needed doing. I'll finish the cleaning, she thought, then plan the Cub Scout meeting, make those centerpieces for the PTA fund-raising dinner, and prepare a nice dinner for my husband and the boys.

Just then, June's youngest son, Woodchuck, came in with his friend Filbert. "Hi, Mom," he said. "Any of those chocolate chip cookies left?"

"Oh no, I am afraid they're all gone."

In unison the boys said, "Awwww!"

To which Mrs. Pleaser replied, "Well, I'd be happy to bake you some fresh ones."

"Gee, thanks, Mom!" Woodchuck exclaimed.

"Thanks, Mrs. Pleaser!" Filbert said.

And they ran upstairs.

Before she could get to the kitchen, the phone rang. It was her husband. "Hi, honey," she greeted him.

"Say, dear," he said. "I have a very important business associate in town. Instead of taking him out to a restaurant, wouldn't it be so much nicer to bring him to our house for one of your delicious home-cooked dinners?"

June Pleaser thought, Oh dear, but to her husband she simply said, "Yes, it would."

"Great! I also told him about your fresh bread and homemade pies, and he can't wait to try them!"

June Pleaser looked at the clock and hesitated. But when he said, "Can you do it, honey?" she quickly replied: "Of course, dear."

As she hung up the phone, her older son Rollie walked in the front door with his buddy, Freddie Hassel.

"Hello, Rollie. Hi, Freddie," she said cheerfully.

"Hi, Mom."

"Hello, Mrs. Pleaser. I must say, you are looking exceptionally attractive today. What a lovely dress!"

"Why, thank you, Freddie."

"I wish I looked that nice, but I lost a button from my jacket and now it isn't right."

Mrs. Pleaser quickly offered, "If you give me your jacket, I'll sew a new button on for you."

"Oh, Mrs. Pleaser, that is so nice of you. But I really don't want to impose."

"Don't be silly, Freddie, it is no imposition at all."

So Mrs. Pleaser got the sewing done, then the baking and the cooking, and their dinner guest was quite pleased when she volunteered to bake 50 pies for his charity event.

Later that night, Rollie and Woodchuck were in their room getting ready for bed. While Rollie checked out his complexion in the mirror, Woodchuck sat on his bed, tossing a ball into his baseball glove. "Hey, Rollie," he said, "can I ask you something?"

"Sure, squirt."

"Just today, Filbert said he didn't get all his homework done, and he didn't know what he was going to do, because if he got in trouble one more time at school he was done for."

"Yeah, so?"

"Well, I gave him my homework, so he wouldn't get in trouble, and instead I got in trouble! I didn't even think about it. I just did it. But I don't understand why I did it."

"Well, Woodchuck, sometimes, when people are trying to be nice and stuff, they do things that they don't want to do, or even have time to do, because they want to please the other person. Did you ever notice that Mom does that a lot? Maybe you learned it from her."

Woodchuck looked thoughtfully at his baseball glove and said, "Gee."

"Yeah, squirt," his brother continued, "and sometimes, late at night, I bet when Mom is taking off her makeup and junk, she probably cries to herself and wonders why nobody considers her needs."

"Gee, Rollie. Do you think Dad knows?"

"Well, squirt, maybe. But we are living in a late `50s patriarchal family, where the man earns the money and the woman stays home and takes care of everybody. So he may not mean to take advantage of her, but even a nice guy like Dad probably winds up doing it anyway."

"Gee, Rollie, what should we do?"

"Well, I don't know about you, squirt, but I have a big date tomorrow and my car is a mess. So tomorrow I am going to casually mention the dirt to Mom. I bet I get a free car wash."

The VIP: Bonaparte Family Reunion

Joseph Bonaparte's words dripped with sarcasm: "I suppose now we are going to have to spend the entire evening hearing about the latest victory of my great younger brother, the Emperor Napoleon!"

Louis Bonaparte rolled his eyes. "Or perhaps we are going to have to hear for the 100th time about how you were passed up in the line of succession." He is such a bore, Louis thought.

Joseph scowled. "I was King of Naples!" He shook his fist defiantly.

Louis sneered. "Oh, pardon! For two short years only, and you did it so badly that Napoleon demoted you to King of Spain." Louis let the insult do its poisonous work, then delivered his coup de grace: "And, I must say, you were such a pathetic king that you lost your crown during the Peninsular War!"

"Well, *mon frère*," Joseph countered, "ees it not also true that when Napoleon called on you to abdicate your throne in Holland, you came out like the whipped dog that you are?"

At that moment Pauline, their middle sister, appeared in the doorway. She was a radiant vision of loveliness in swirling skirts. Indeed, she knew she looked good, and she knew how to use her looks. Had she not used her charms to snag General Leclerc as her husband? When he died, had she not captivated Borghese, the Roman noble? They could not resist her! As she glided over to them, she said, "Now, boys, boys, boys. I think we are all *en famille* Bonaparte, and our loyalty must be to each other."

"So easy for you to say," said Joseph, covering his nose with his hand silk. "Everyone knows that it is you who ees Napoleon's favorite sibling."

"Yes," said Pauline, matter-of-factly, "that is true." And she swirled away, nose up, head held high.

Meanwhile, Napoleon's ambitious younger sister Caroline was holding court on the far side of the room. "As Queen of Naples," she was saying, "I stimulated the arts and letters and of course brought about the recovery of the classical treasure of Pompeii and Naples. But someday, when my son takes over as Emperor of France, you will see what is possible."

Elisa sighed silently, allowing her youngest sister to go on and on. She didn't really care to compete with her. She was smart enough to know there was more to life than this foolish Bonaparte family tradition of oneupsmanship. Besides, she had more than enough to occupy her attention as administrator of Tuscany. But she felt it only fair to give Caroline the news: "Sister, I hate to be the one to tell you this, but Napoleon has produced an heir. There go your hopes to have your son succeed him as Emperor."

Caroline Bonaparte's breath caught in her throat. She felt as if she had been kicked in the stomach. Plots and contingencies began to swirl in her head.

Meanwhile, Joseph and Louis were now joined by their brother Lucien. In no time they were bragging and bickering again, while the youngest Bonaparte, Jerome, stood and watched in silence, keeping his thoughts to himself.

Lucien proclaimed, "Who was the first prominent president of the Council of 500? It was I! During the Coup of 18 Brumaire, when Napoleon had lost his nerve and the council was ready to make him an outlaw, who harangued the troops and dispersed the council? Again, it was I! Why, if not for me, Lucien, our dear brother Napoleon would have come to nothing!" He ended with a flourish.

Jerome was nine years Lucien's junior, 15 years and 16 years younger than his brothers Napoleon and Joseph, respectively. He didn't understand the competition between his older brothers. He just thought it was way cool to have a big shot older brother who was both Emperor and a general. And the perks were awesome! Napoleon had hooked him up as King of Westphalia, and it wasn't every 23-year-old that got to be King of

Westphalia. Not to mention that Napoleon also set him up with a hot royal babe, Catherine of Württemberg. And she rocked! Ah, *oui,* Jerome was down with all that.

Then the trumpets blared and the soldiers snapped to attention. With hand tucked in his midriff, head held high, and seeming taller than anyone in the room, the Emperor Napoleon Bonaparte arrived at his family reunion.

The Meddler: Interference from Olympus

Daphne stood up, surprised to see her future mother-in-law. "Hera, how nice of you to drop by! To what do I owe this honor?"

"Daphne, my future daughter-in-law." Hera took hold of both Daphne's shoulders, leaned back, and eyed her up and down. "I have come to help you dress. Let us begin, because much work will be required."

Before Daphne could utter a word, Hera breezed by her, walked through the columned entrance and into her apartment. Daphne chased after her. "Sorry, Hera, this isn't exactly a good time. I haven't had a chance to pick up." But as she arrived in the main living space, Hera was nowhere to be seen. "Hera?" she called out.

"In here," came Hera's voice from Daphne's bedroom.

From my bedroom! How dare she! Daphne thought. She walked into the bedroom and was about to say something when again she was stunned into silence. Hera was going through her closet like a whirlwind. Some outfits were thrown on the floor, others on the bed, and Hera had something to say about each in turn.

"Trash. Trash. This one you can wear on your honeymoon. This one, forget it, you'll never fit into it. This one . . . "

Caught between her outrage and her desire to not offend her future mother-in-law, Daphne silently simmered. And as Hera went through her closet, Zeus's head appeared out of nowhere and hovered in the center of the room, surrounded by roiling clouds. Oh, my god! Daphne thought. He's as invasive as she is!

Daphne assumed Zeus had appeared in order to speak with Hera, but Zeus, apparently reading her mind, spoke to her instead. "It is time we had a talk," he said. "I have a great career planned for you, young lady. I have decided to put you into the Victory business. There is always a demand for Victory. Nike has done quite well with it, you know, but she doesn't have as much time as she used to, what with her success in athletic gear. I've given this a lot of thought, and I think Victory is the best place for you, because . . . well, let's face it, my dear, you're no Aphrodite." Zeus then laughed so hard that the curtains and wall hangings billowed. "I must head out," he said, chuckling at his pun, "but please tell Apollo when he gets home that I have some direction for his career as well. I have work for him in prophecy, medicine, music, and hunting." And with that, Zeus's head faded away. Hera finished rifling through the closet, and satisfied with her handiwork, departed shortly thereafter.

That evening, when Apollo came to visit, Daphne delivered Zeus's message, and a whole lot more. "I can't believe it!" she yelled, stamping her foot for emphasis. "She comes in here, starts going through my closet and actually telling me what I should and shouldn't wear. And your father, telling me he has a 'destiny' for me. I mean, what gives them the right to think they can play gods in our lives?"

"Well, actually," Apollo replied, "Hera is the goddess of marriage and women, and—"

"Don't 'actually' me, mister. Is this something I have to deal with in you as well? Next, you'll be prancing around here telling me you're the son of a god. . . ."

"Well, actually, I am the sun god," Apollo interrupted, trying to be funny.

But it didn't work. "Well, Mr. Sun God, if you or your mother thinks—"

Apollo interrupted, "Actually, Hera is not my mother, but she is sort of my stepmother. My real mother was Leto, but Hera turned her into a swan. She's over at the lake in the park, if you'd like to meet her. Bring her some bread, and she'll be crazy about you."

Daphne stared at Apollo with her mouth open for what seemed like an eternity and then said, "All right, Apollo. Marriage is a big commitment. Before we proceed any further, I think you need to sit right down here and tell me more about your family."

The Martyr: The Night Before Christmas

"Ho ho ho," Santa laughed. "Well, Pinky, it's one week before the big night, and we seem to be ahead of schedule! I am delighted."

Pinky, the head elf, was always cautious about getting overly optimistic. But even he had to admit things were in great shape. He replied, "Yes, this is the first year in a century that I can remember having elves standing around at this time of the season."

Santa smiled, leaned back in his chair, and prepared to light a celebratory pipe. At just that moment Mrs. Claus appeared at the door, with the phone in her hand. "Dear, I have my mother on the line. She is inviting us to come down to the South Pole for Christmas Eve dinner."

Santa almost swallowed his pipe. "Christmas Eve dinner?" he sputtered. "But—But—"

Mrs. Claus continued, "She has been baking for a week, and she plans to have the penguins all lined up to give you a 21 flipper salute."

Santa put his pipe down, took a deep breath, and said, "You well know, my dear, that I have to work on Christmas Eve."

Mrs Claus pulled the phone away from her ear, and Santa could hear his mother-in-law starting to whine: "Don't tell me he can't stop by for a dinner! He has to eat, doesn't he? He certainly looks like he eats. And who told him to do everything in one night anyway? Not to mention that it was I who gave him the down payment on that magic sled and those reindeer in the first place. That's why he's able to be such a big shot! If not for my sacrifices on his behalf, he would still be a fat old man delivering presents in a small village in Sweden."

Santa put his head in his hands and shook his head slowly from side to side as he muttered to no one in particular, "That was 800 years ago! Do I still have to hear about it after all this time? I knew I never should have taken that money."

Meanwhile, his mother-in-law continued dejectedly, "Oh, well, if he's too important to come to the South Pole, I suppose I can understand. Just because I've been working with 1500 penguins for the last week to get them to march in formation isn't so important. And even though I did cook all his favorite foods, which I don't particularly like, and it took a lot of work. But if he has more important things to do, don't worry about me, I'll just sit here by myself in the dark, since there won't be any point in turning the lights on."

Mrs. Claus covered the mouthpiece of the phone and said, "Come on, Santa, she went to all that trouble for you. You can't let her sit there alone on Christmas Eve!"

Santa sputtered, "I didn't ask for her to do any of that! It's the night before Christmas, for heaven's sake, and she knows full well that this is my busy season."

Mrs. Claus glared at him. "I find it hard to believe that you can't find a little time for her. She's my mother!"

Santa crinkled his face in frustration and ran his hand first through his beard, then his hair, then across his forehead, then through his beard again. Meanwhile, Pinky the Elf was slowly backing out of the room. But Santa noticed and said, "Oh no you don't! If I have to go, you have to go!" Then he looked at Mrs. Claus, took a deep breath, and said, "Tell her we'll be there, but we can't stay long."

Then he heard his mother-in-law say, "I hope he wears the blue suit I made for him. That red one makes him look fat."

Santa just shrank into a chair, looked down and muttered, "Over the river and through the woods to the Grand Martyr's house we go."

The Rebel: The Pirate Convention

Blackbeard pounded his fist for quiet and then bellowed from the podium: "Quiet down, ye louts. Two of our panelists today are the most

famous female pirates ever to sail the seas. Renowned fighters, each more
ferocious than any man, we have the infamous Anne Bonny and Mary
Read!"

As Anne and Mary scanned the crowd, the mostly male audience broke
into raucous applause. Each person feared not to be seen applauding. The
legends about Anne and Mary were all too real.

Blackbeard pounded his fist again, then continued, "Our third panelist
today hardly needs any introduction; it's none other . . . than our very own
Captain Kidd!"

There was scattered applause, punctuated with sneers and mumbling.
It seemed that some of the pirates had an issue with Kidd, who tried to
stay "legal" by first getting the King of England's "blessing" to raid
Britain's enemies.

"All righty, me hearties, let's hear yer questions for the panelists."

A few hands went up. Blackbeard pointed with his sword. "Aye, you in
the third row with the red bandana and eye patch."

A gangly fellow stood up and said, "This question is for . . . Mary Read.
Um, why do you dress like a man?"

Mary Read bolted out of her chair and reached for her sword, "Why
shouldn't I? Ye have a problem with that?"

Fellow panelist and shipmate Anne Bonny grabbed Mary's sword hand
and restrained her. "Easy there, Mary. It's only a question in a panel discussion now, isn't it?"

Mary made herself sit back down. "Oh, yes, a panel question. Then I'll
answer ye. Well, it was a bad life for a woman in the 1670s. My father died
while me mother was pregnant with me. Then me infant brother Mark
died. He was the legal heir according to that stupid, patriarchal primogen-
iture system. Since a woman couldn't own anything, me mother had me
dress like a man and take me brother's place." Her voice was rising. "Why
should a woman accept misery and poverty because of the rules made by a
bunch of men?" Again she was out of her chair, shaking her fist at the
audience. "What right do ye have to tell a woman what to do, how to live,
how to die!"

Blackbeard cleared his throat. "Good point, Mary. Aaarrrggh, next
question."

A young man wearing a horizontally striped shirt raised his right hook.
"Aye, this question is for Mr. Kidd, and for Anne Bonny as well. What led
ya to a life of piracy?"

Kidd stood, slowly and proudly. He was well-educated, and fancied
himself an orator. "I was borrrn in Greenock, Scotland, around 1645. My
fatherr was a Presbyterian minister and a strict Calvinist. He had rules
for everrrything! There was a rrright way to pray, and a rrright way to eat,
and a rrright way to rrrelieve oneself. I could barely breathe in the midst
of so much contrrrol and judgment. I used to sit on the hill and gaze at the

many ships coming from every corner of the world on their way to and from Glasgow. And when I saw those ships, I saw frrreedom. So when I was 15, I got aboarrrd one of those ships, and I have neverrr looked back." He bowed and ceremoniously gestured toward Anne.

Anne remained seated. "I hail from a plantation in Charleston, South Carolina," she began. "My daddy had this whole plan for my life. I was supposed to be some sweet, subservient girl who did what she was told. That was no life for me, so I found a way out. In my teens, I married a renegade seaman by the name of James Bonny. I didn't really love him and he was a bit of a cad, but it sure made my daddy mad. Of course, then my daddy tried to control me by disowning me, so I burned down his plantation. I'll not be controlled by any man! I'll decide how I will live my life!"

The crowd cheered. Some of the men waved their sabers in the air while others stomped their wooden legs. Blackbeard interrupted, pounding on the podium to restore order, "All righty, then. Before we break, a few more announcements. Tonight's cocktail party will be a no host bar, so bring yer doubloons or yer own rum. And tomorrow the rowboats will be leaving sharply at midday. Anyone not there on time will miss the annual pillaging of the town. Thanks to our sponsor, the Columbia Cannonball Company, everyone who survives will receive a Jolly Roger T-shirt!" He then banged his fist on the podium one last time, spat in the audience's direction, and said, "This here meeting is adjourned!"

The Mystery: The Mystery of the Missing Man

It was a dark and misty night, and I was in my office. The humidity was killing me. Outside, the rain kept falling, like an ocean emptying into the mean streets of this metropolis.

My name is Rick. Rick Stranger, P.I. The P stands for private. I stay undercover. It's what I do. The I stands for me. I'm an investigator. My job? I find missing people.

I was thumbing through the stack of paper on my desk, looking for the crossword puzzle I'd started the night before. I spend a lot of time in this office, and I don't get a lot of calls. Something to do with being undercover, I suppose. I could barely see in the light of the solitary bulb dangling from the ceiling that dimly lit the office. Then I saw her. I don't know how long she'd been standing in that dark doorway. The gleam in her eyes pierced the darkness. She was crying. I hate it when dames cry.

"You have to help me!" she cried. She dabbed at her eyes with her handkerchief.

I said, "Go on."

"My brother never said much. No one knew what was happening in his life. He left home many years ago. Then he stopped coming to family events, and eventually he didn't even call. Now, no one has seen him in years and everyone seems to just accept the mystery of it. Everyone except me, that is."

I wanted to say "Let him go if he doesn't want to be found. Maybe he has judgments about the family. Maybe he feels if you don't have something nice to say, don't say anything at all. Maybe he doesn't like the family's judgments of him." Instead I asked, "Why the big push to find him now?"

"Isn't it enough that I miss him? We all miss him."

I could tell she needed to talk, so I acted like I was listening.

"You've got to help me," she pleaded, and I wanted to. "I don't know what else to do."

"All right, but I only work undercover." I emptied the stale coffee from my cup into the trash, then refilled it from the pot of bitter black stuff. No wonder my office smelled like old coffee. It was all over the floor around the trash can. "I get half my fee in advance. The rest if I find him." She opened her bag and handed me money. Our relationship was off to a good start. Why did she seem so familiar? "Coffee?" I offered.

She nodded.

I handed her a cup as I asked, "What does he look like?"

She clasped the cup with both hands, as if to warm herself. "Last I saw him, he was about your height, similar features."

I asked if there were any distinguishing marks.

"I'm not sure." She spoke hesitantly. She was fighting back tears, but her tears were winning. "I did find this, though." She reached into her handbag and handed me a piece of paper.

Something was written on it, but I couldn't make out the words in the dim light. I pulled out my lighter, flicked it open. I waved the flame across the paper. I knew these words! I wrote these words that day I left home! How did this dame get my letter? Why did she seem so familiar? Could she be my . . . Some questions need an answer. Some questions are better left unanswered.

I got up suddenly and walked her out the door. "Lady, if anything turns up, I'll let you know. But I can't be seen with you right now. It would blow my cover. Watch that first step on your way out."

As I watched her disappear down the dark stairwell, I wondered how, out of all the offices in all the buildings in this godforsaken town, she had to come to this one. I'd heard this story before. I knew it well. I'm not trying to be mysterious. But I'm a private investigator. That's who I am. It's what I do. I poured myself another cup of stale joe, sat down, put my feet up, and pulled my fedora over my eyes. I had some investigating to do. Privately.

The Five Choices

Everyone has family that is sometimes difficult to deal with. But if you've had it with the criticism and rudeness, if you're fed up with interference, tired of taking orders, unwilling to be taken advantage of, or frustrated with egotism, don't despair. Remember, you always have a choice. In fact, you have five choices:

1. Suffer and complain

If you want things to remain the same, and you're satisfied to be right about what's wrong while doing nothing about it, this is your best choice. It's a complete waste of time, but it's your time to waste!

2. Go away

If you won't make the effort to work it out, or you made the effort and got nowhere, you can create the boundary of time and distance to protect yourself from the pain. This a very common choice. But before you walk away, consider your other choices:

3. Accept them the way they are

Even if they never change at all, you can change the way you see them, listen to them, and how you feel around them. A change of attitude can set you free from negative reactions to problem behaviors.

4. Love yourself when they're around

Overcoming negative and mixed messages from others requires a more loving relationship with yourself. When you give yourself the love and acceptance that you can't get from them, you stop being needy and change the dynamic of the relationship.

5. Exercise your influence

Just as some people bring out the best in you, and some people bring out the worst, you have this same ability with others. There is a behavioral balance in relationships, and it can be shifted with intentional behavior. When you shift what you're doing, your relative will have to shift what he or she is doing too.

Since you've read this far, we assume that you have decided not to waste your time on suffering about your relatives, and you're at least considering the possibility that you don't have to avoid them or leave them behind. Read on, to find out why they behave the way they do, and what your options are for bringing out the best in relatives . . . even at their worst!

Chapter 2
The Lens of Understanding: The Normal Zone

You and your relatives—now that's a relationship worth understanding! This chapter is about understanding how and why your relatives behave the way they do.

As we did in our first book, *Dealing with People You Can't Stand*, we again refer to four positive intents. In the case of family, these four intents represent four interpretations of the word "behave." To understand these four intentions, we need to construct our grid.

As you focus your lens of understanding on behavior within your family, pay attention to each person's general level of *Engagement*. It should be fairly easy for you to identify everyone's relative comfort zone on the *Engagement* line. Notice that the range of self-expression goes from *Restrained* to *Uninhibited*. A restrained person can be yielding or submissive, or may withdraw from others completely. An uninhibited person can be determined, dominating, or intimidating and hostile.

We all respond to different situations and different people with different degrees of engagement. In times of challenge, difficulty, and stress, people tend to become insecure, and move out of their normal zone. When that happens, they become either more restrained or more uninhibited than when they feel secure.

The second line in our lens is *Focus of Attention*. There are predictable patterns for how people pay attention to each other. Sometimes you or your relative may be more aware of the situation you find yourself in, whether the setting is a public place or private place. Other times, attention is drawn more to feelings and emotions. When attention is focused almost exclusively on a situation, we call that a *Situational Focus*. When attention is focused almost exlusively on the emotional tone and feelings surrounding relationships, we call that a *People Focus*.

Within this range and depending on the situation, behavior can quickly go from one extreme to another. During times of challenge, difficulty, or stress, most people in families tend to focus with greater exclusiveness on either the *Situation* or the *People*, than they would in their normal mode of operation. To discern a person's *Focus of Attention*, you must listen closely. When someone is *Situation*-focused, their word choices reflect where their attention is. "Is your room clean?" "Did you make the reservations?" "How long before we get there?" When someone is *People*-focused, their word choices reflect that. "Hey, what's up? How was your weekend? How's the knee? How's life?"

Let's put all of this together. For each of your family members, and for yourself, there is a zone of normal—or best—behavior, and exaggerated—or worst—behavior. A person can focus on people uninhibitedly (attack), normally (engaged), or with restraint (submission). A person can focus on a situation without restraint (dominance), normally (engaged), or with inhibitions (withdrawal).

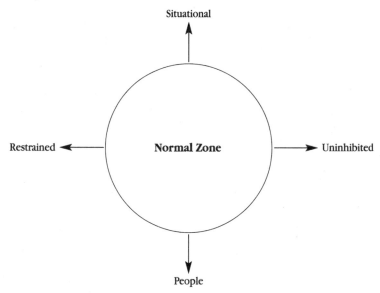

Figure 2-1

What Determines Focus and Engagement?

To account for these interesting differences, we've organized our understanding of behavior around four "positive" motives or intentions, and their negative corollaries.

Be Responsible/Don't be irresponsible
Be Appropriate/Don't be inappropriate
Be Considerate/Don't be inconsiderate
Be Significant/Don't be insignificant

Each of these intentions can be the primary motivation for a somewhat predictable range of behavior.

Where do these intentions come from? Parents (and other authority figures) give children numerous messages regarding their behavior. Since families are concerned with survival, support, and social standing in the larger community, it stands to reason that any behaviors that strengthen a family's overall success in these areas are going to be encouraged. Behaviors that negatively impact on these areas are going to be discouraged. Over time, you learn about family power centers, family traditions, what is expected of you, and what the consequences are if you fail or succeed in measuring up to those expectations. If you spent some or all of your childhood in an institution, you learned about yourself in relation to that institution in much the same way.

During childhood, parents and other authority figures attempt to help children define and recognize various boundaries. They tell children to "behave" themselves and then devote an extraordinary amount of time trying to explain what "behave yourself" actually means. The "big" people use their size and position of authority to deliver conditional "if-then" messages to the smaller people, and most children get the message that the love they desire is dependent on their behaving as they've been told. They also get the message, stated or implied, that if they fail to behave in the desired way, love will be withdrawn. Since a core desire of every child is to be loved and to belong, children listen to all this input with great determination, and these messages carry a lot of weight. As a result, children develop strong subconscious intentions to behave in ways that get the love, or not behave in ways that lose it.

The authority figures in our lives were once children too, and they learned to "behave" in the same way that their children do, from people who also happened to be busy and burdened, and not necessarily wise or articulate. If parents lack clarity, send mixed messages (and most do!), put children into intentional or unintentional double binds (whether you talk back or keep quiet, YOU are in trouble!), or otherwise impose their own emotional turmoil into the environment, this interference and obstruction makes a child's understanding of just how one is supposed to "behave" all the more difficult. Is it any wonder, then, that family members behave in such difficult ways?

Strong intentions are strong motivators, and families reinforce them through repetition, ritual, story, and custom. For better or worse, conditioned behaviors become the norm in families. When you visit with your own relatives, or in some cases, just think about them, you can see what condition your condition is in. And so everybody's conditions can make for better or worse conditions for everybody else, into the future.

We don't want to oversimplify the complexities of family relationships. We are not claiming that these four intentions are the only intentions that motivate behavior in families. But they can serve as a coherent frame of reference for understanding a wide range of difficult behaviors and problems with relatives. And for that purpose, four intentions are enough.

Just as you choose what to wear from a variety of clothing styles (formal-wear, daily wear, underwear, etc.) your behavioral choices also de-pend on the situation and the relationship. Your behavior changes as your priorities and intentions change. Like a familiar T-shirt, sweater, or pair of jeans, you have well-worn patterns of behavior and intention with certain relatives in certain kinds of situations. Identify these four intentions in yourself, and you'll be better able to recognize them in your relatives. See Figure 2-2.

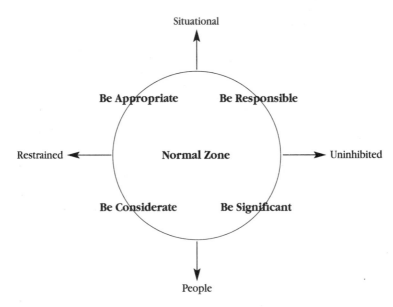

Figure 2-2

Be Responsible

Have you ever felt the future (of something) resting on your shoulders? Have you ever known that the fate of others was somehow up to you, or that you would be held accountable if something went wrong? Did you ever swear that it wasn't your fault?

Lack of trust, whether justified or not, is a major cause of arguments between parents and children, and, later, between relatives. Responsibility breeds trust. So if you want others in your family to have confidence in you, then you had better *be responsible.*

The way to make sure something happens is to take charge and make it happen. The way to prevent something from happening is to take charge before it happens. If it has already occurred and it's a bad thing, take charge and stop it from happening. And if you are concerned about something happening or not happening again, take charge and stay in charge until you are convinced the problem is solved and the situation resolved.

When you feel responsible, you need an overview of the situation. Paradoxically, your awareness of people may be limited to those you deem necessary. You prefer action to deliberation because missing the moment is inexcusable. You may give others directives instead of making suggestions, because there is no time to waste. You must be strong and compensate for the weakness or unwillingness that you find around you. Since you must build confidence and avoid interference, you may not want to show weakness. Your communication is likely to be direct and to the point. *"Bottom line: Here's how it is going to be."*

But the intention to *be responsible* isn't the only motivator for behavior in families. Sometimes it is more important to to *be appropriate* or *not be inappropriate,* depending of course on the most appropriate or least inappropriate response to the situation.

Be Appropriate

Have you ever wanted to fit in, or somehow avoid standing out? Were you told repeatedly to "be sensible" or "act your age" or "be on your best behavior," in order to fit in with your family? Have you ever tried to keep your head down and your mouth shut in the presence of a family problem, or become obsessed with details in order to make sure that nothing goes wrong? However it happens, the desire to *be appropriate* can produce a constant background anxiety about measuring up, fitting in, or avoiding expulsion.

Hardly anyone likes to be left out, and if you want to fit in and have a family accept and include you, then you'd better *be appropriate* when you're with them. Each family has its own culture. Some people learn about their family's culture in an environment of acceptance and inclusion. Others learn in an environment of rewards and punishment. And still others never learn, suffering only disapproval and disdain for their failed efforts to fit in.

Apply the intention to *be appropriate* to the way you live your life, and you can participate with others in shared activities and environments.

If you apply the intention to *be appropriate* to problem solving, you get critical thinking, a necessary skill for avoiding delusions when going along with the crowd. If you fail to apply the intention to *be appropriate,* you get criticized.

When the intention to *be appropriate* is your highest priority, you can't help but notice the details. You know that "fools rush in," and that fools are often excluded, so you will probably take a good, long look before leaping, if you ever leap at all. If no one else leaps, you'll be right there beside them as the wisdom of leaping is discussed. And you may refuse to do something because of a particular doubt about whether it is fitting under the circumstance. Discretion, after all, is the better part of valor, or so they say.

Be Considerate

Have you ever cared about what other people think? Have you ever wanted others to be happy with the way something turned out? Have you ever tried to help someone by opening a door or picking up something that someone you cared about had dropped? If so, then you know what it's like to *be considerate* of others.

The intention to *be considerate* is cultivated in families where concerns about humility and selflessness are promoted. And it is an important drive when you want others to care about you or consider your feelings. But it can become a case of too much of a good thing. That's because there is an inherent danger in putting others first. If you're not careful, it can leave you with an empty cup and nothing left to give.

When *being considerate* is your highest consideration, you consider the needs of others over your own. You hesitate to speak or act until you are certain that others are taken care of, and you watch their faces closely for signals of approval or rejection. Your feelings are the likely barometer by which you measure your success. An innocent "How are you?" may make you the captive audience of someone in your family who apparently really needed to talk to somebody.

If someone says to you, "Can you do me a favor?" and you're wanting to *be considerate*, you might reply "Sure! How can I help?" If they are also in a considerate mode, they might see your behavior as considerate and then feel inconsiderate about having asked it of you. That's when they say, "You know, never mind, I can take care of it. But thank you all the same." To which you might reply, "No, it's no problem at all, I'm happy to help!" without even knowing what it was you were going to be asked to do or were so willing and eager to agree to!

Sometimes, however, standing tall around people and being recognized by them is a higher priority than pleasing them.

Be Significant

When you were a child, did you have someone constantly telling you what you were going to be when you grew up? Did you ever have a relative who always called you by someone else's name, or couldn't even remember your name? Or, worse yet, a parent who called you by your sibling's name? Remember how insignificant that made you feel? If you have ever had the desire to be somebody, to make an impression, or make your mark, or just wanted a little special treatment, then you know what this positive intention is all about.

To be recognized for your individuality, you must *be significant.* While some shy away from significance (the considerate ones), some share in it (the appropriate ones), and still others acquire it without necessarily wanting it (the responsible ones), some people just have a deeper need than others to *be significant.*

Being significant can obviously mean something different to everyone, since everyone is different. Yet for the person who does not know the fundamental truth of his or her own specialness, the desire to fulfill the intention to *be significant* can be so intense that he or she will take serious risks, with money, health, and life itself, just to gain the admiration of others that they are unable to give to themselves. Their behavior may be perceived by others as needing to be the center of attention. A driving intent to *be significant* often occurs in large families, where getting noticed is difficult at best and absent at worst.

If this intent is your highest priority, you are likely to speak up when you have something to say. Your communication will be direct, enthusiastic, and hard to ignore. You may sound confident to others, because of the significance you find in what you have to say. Your part of a conversation with relatives may sound something like this: "My life is going great! Let me tell you about it." When asked for your help, you may quickly agree and then use the time it takes to help as time to talk about what you've done and what you're going to do. And you may embellish what you say just to hold the spotlight on yourself a little longer.

It's a Question of Balance

These four positive intentions can best be understood and appreciated when taken together as a whole. To completely fulfill any one requires that, to some degree, you fulfill them all. A functional person takes responsibility for themselves and for their situation, because they realize they have the power and ability to make tomorrow different from today. This requires that appropriate choices be made. To increase certainty about those choices, the feedback of others, as well as their needs and interests, must be considered.

Believing it significant to do so makes it all possible. Though the priority of these social intents can shift from moment to moment, and all can be present in some degree or other, the circle (Figure 2-2, page 20) represents the normal condition of balance in us all.

As Intent Changes, So Does Behavior

Consider the following situations to observe how behavior changes with intent:

Tommy comes home from college for his two-week vacation, moves his stuff into his room, and settles in. The first few days, he wants to be appropriate, to learn how things have changed since he was here last. He also wants to be able to do this again if and when it's necessary, so he is considerate of the interests and needs of his parents and younger siblings. One day, his parents invite him to accompany them to social event at a restaurant in town. "How should I dress?" he inquires. "It doesn't matter to me," his father replies. Mom says "Just wear something nice." Tommy, lacking any clear idea of what is required of him, spends 20 minutes staring into the blackness of his duffel bag and sorting through the pile of clothes in the corner, which consists mostly of old sports jerseys, worn-out pants, socks with holes, and T-shirts with odd slogans and logos. He tries on two different shirts with tan pants, four ties, a polo shirt with shorts, and a sweater with dark pants. Where do you think he is within the lens of understanding?

Obviously his social intent is to *be appropriate*. He slows down the decision-making process, hesitant because he wants to make sure he fits in at the unknown event. Finally, he settles on the sweater and dark pants. Yet when he arrives at the event, he sees his cousin dressed in worn-out jeans and a sweatshirt. His aunt and uncle look like they're going golfing. His mom and dad are wearing matching shirts. And he realizes that anything would have sufficed.

It is the weekend now, and Tommy is working away at his computer, doing a job and housing search for his next year at college. His little sister comes in and says, "Tommy, Tommy, come look! I made a pretty picture of a birdie in my room!" Tommy abandons his search and spends the rest of the day with his kid sister. That night, the parents ask Tommy what he wants to do while he's home this summer. "Whatever you guys want to do." At dinner, Mom says "Tommy, will you have time to clean out and organize our shed?" Tommy thinks of his housing and job search, knows that this really needs his attention, but heck, they could use a hand and he does have carpentry skills. "Okay, sure thing." Where is he now?

Obviously, *be considerate* is Tommy's primary intent. He puts his own needs aside to please the people he cares about. His job and housing search becomes secondary to getting along with family, so he decides it can wait.

The next day, Tommy gets in the shed, pulls out all the boxes, recycles the cardboard, and while he is in there, he goes ahead and builds those shelves Dad always meant to build but never got around to. And he creates an organizational scheme for miscellaneous items, with everything labeled. At last, it is done, and Tommy's chest swells with pride. He's certain his parents will be thrilled. But when Mom returns home from running her errands, she is hungry and wants to make something to eat. Tommy insists that she come out to the shed first and see what he's done. Where in the lens is Tommy now?

If you recognize that, after all his effort, he would like to *be significant*, you've made an important choice. Had he been in a *be considerate* mode when his mom returned home, he probably would have waited until she'd had a bite to eat. Instead, he couldn't wait to show her what he had done.

Days turn into weeks, and Tommy is running out of time to line up a job and housing. School begins in just over a week, and his deadline is at hand. He's making calls, searching the web, and posting on messageboards. His little sister comes in and asks him to come play with her in her room. "C'mon," she pleads. "Me, me, me, me," she chants until Tommy gets angry. "Stop distracting me and leave me alone," he says, as he shows her the door and closes it behind her. A little later his mom knocks on his door and tells him dinner is on the table. Without looking up from the computer, he says, "I'm not hungry." She asks if he would like her to put his dinner in the fridge and heat it up later. "Whatever!" he says distractedly. "Tommy, you open this door right now, young man!" says Mom. Fists tightened, face in a grimace, he opens the door, stares witheringly into his mother's eyes, and bluntly says, "Look, I don't have time for this! Can't you see that I'm busy?" then abruptly closes the door, turns back to his computer, and thinks, "Nuts! The best rents are gone! I'm going to need two jobs to pay for housing!"

Now where is Tommy?

If you're thinking "In the doghouse!" you're probably right. But *be responsible* is the answer we're looking for. Under the pressure of his obligations, Tommy becomes more situationally focused and is not willing to take time for the people in his family. His communications are more direct and to the point. He is now considering added responsibilities, something that had been unthinkable a few weeks earlier, when he had the luxury of time to hang out with his sister and help out with the storage shed.

Notice how Tommy's behavior changes according to what is most important to him in a particular situation and time. Changes in behavior are based on changes in our internal primary directives in any moment of time.

Assuming you could recognize at least a little of yourself in these four positive intentions, do you now have some insight into how different people in the same family can get on each other's nerves and get into problems with each other?

Of course, life is rarely this simple and easy to understand. But mark our words: When trouble starts, that's the time to look for intent instead of getting hung up in reaction to the difficult behavior. Fail to notice what's really going on and the situation may become much more difficult to deal with (though what is going on may become increasingly obvious.)

What's that, you say? The situation is already much more difficult to deal with? Emotions are already out of control? Then fear not, and do read on, because in the next chapter, we'll describe how relationships go from good to bad, and from bad to worse, and how to begin the process of bringing out the best in relatives at their worst.

Chapter 3

The Either/Or Zone:
Greatness or Danger

Just outside of the *Normal Zone* lies a gray area where unfulfilled intentions require a choice between aspiration or fear, between a positive response or a negative reaction. The *Either/Or Zone* is a fork in the road.

Take the road less traveled and you find yourself in the *Dimension of Greatness*. When people manifest the greatest aspect of their intentions, they bring the other intentions into balance to produce the best possible outcome. All intentions work together to fulfill each of them, providing a synergistic effect where the whole is truly greater than the sum of its parts. Behavioral choices are constructive, and communication facilitates understanding and positive change.

Take the low road, however, and you find yourself in the *Danger Zone,* where family problems reinforce each other in a relentless cycle of reaction. The range of difficult behavior is a broad one, so the *Danger Zone* is a vast wasteland of squandered hopes, broken dreams, obstructed desire, and endless frustration.

The farther your relatives stumble into the *Danger Zone,* the less likely they are to use their innate intelligence and creativity to get out of it. Before long, their behavior is based on conditioning alone as they struggle to resolve a problem they don't understand.

Thwarted and Projected Intentions

What would cause a person to venture into such a terribly limiting place as the *Danger Zone?* What fog could so blind a person to true fulfillment of their best intentions? For simplicity's sake, let's call it conditioning, through repetition and reinforcement. Once blinded by conditioning, a person can enter the *Danger Zone* through the fear of threatened intent or projected intent. Family members may feel threatened by their own sense of failure around their good intentions. Then they fight their fear by overcompensating for it, or succumb to it by underestimating themselves and others. Or they may project their own shortcomings and failures onto someone else, and thus guarantee their own failure.

Projections in families can be the hardest problems to solve. That's because the person *with* the problem is the one who *has* the problem. Peer through the fog of your own conditioning to see how it works. A parent who lives with shame wants his or her child not to be a source of embarrassment. Siblings who grow up feeling out of place fixate on the failure of others to fit in. The disrespectful child demands to be treated with respect. The person of low self-esteem is unable to recognize the value in another.

You can see how confusing this must be for the one on whom the projection falls, for it makes no sense. Family members try to defend themselves, yet nothing changes. Worse still, their defense may be to offer up their own projections. As each member tries to resolve his or her own fears of failure through the others, the relationship can only get worse.

What happens when people who won't take responsibility for their own behavior demand that others be held accountable? When people who never notice their own shortcomings make it their job to point out the shortcomings of others? When a person rudely insists that others be considerate? When a person who neglects opportunities for self-improvement decides to put others down for failing to take initiative? Typically, the result is that people feel angry, confused, resentful, and frustrated because they're receiving mixed messages.

A Closer Look

Examine the four intentions in these two ways— threatened intent and projected intent— to get a better understanding of how they work against you and your relatives. See Figure 3-1.

Be Responsible

When people want to *be responsible* and events seem to be tumbling out of control, their conditioned reaction is to take *command*. Threatened and projected intent become the tickets to ride into the *Either/Or Zone*, where focus or polarization rests on a moment of decision. If the *Dimension of Greatness* is chosen, command of the situation includes attention to the greater good, the most fitting response, and making actions count. They offer guidance and support, which are provided in a way that honors and invites the responsibility of others.

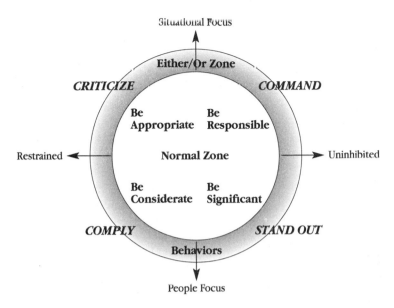

Figure 3-1

But when threatened intent leads to the *Danger Zone*, the person with the need to *command* will try harder, speak louder, overwhelming or eliminating anything that might get in the way. When projection leads to the *Danger Zone*, it becomes an accusatory and self-defeating proclamation: "You are irresponsible." As if the end justifies the means, such a relative has no inhibition about being coercive and tyrannical.

Be Appropriate

When people want to *be appropriate* and potential mistakes in judgment threaten to create turmoil, their conditioned reaction is to become critical. This brings them into the *Either/Or Zone* and a critical choice. If the *Dimension of Greatness* is chosen, they will define their standards and then make adjustments and corrections in their own behavior. If projected, their communication will be constructive, so it will be easier to hear and act on. Where others would apply emotion, they will apply logic and reason, and will encourage thoughtfulness instead of rash action.

But when threatened intent leads to the *Danger Zone,* they will fixate on their own errors in judgment, nit-pick, find fault, highlight shortcomings, and amplify the flaws in themselves that don't fit neatly into how they think things "should be." Projected onto others, their fear takes the form of destructive complaints that can only undermine confidence and guarantee failure. Not polite enough. Not dressed correctly. Not interesting enough. Not smart enough. Too polite. Too loud. Too fat. Too bad.

Be Considerate

When people with the intent to *be considerate* feel threatened or project their fear, their conditioned reaction is to *comply*. Concerns about caring and considerate behavior bring them into the *Either/Or Zone*, where care or carelessness lead to greatness or despair. If the choice is for *greatness*, a way will be found to find a balance between their own needs and interests, and the needs and interests of others. They will offer only the help they can afford to give, and build bridges of cooperation within the family. Projections will turn into tolerance, encouragement, patience, and loving kindness.

But if the threatened intent carries them into the *Danger Zone,* they will *comply* with the directives and demands of others, and struggle with their feelings afterward. Projected outward, they will fear the inconsiderate and uncaring opinions and behaviors of others, ignore their own better judgment, and keep their true feelings to themselves.

Be Significant

When people want to *be significant*, and their intent is threatened, the conditioned response is to *stand out*. This places them in the *Either/Or Zone*, where they must choose between meaning and misery. If they choose *greatness*, they will find ways to contribute positively to those whose opinions matter, will be attentive to unmet needs, and will volunteer their help when possible. They will apply their comparisons only to themselves, seeking to outdo their past achievements or rise to new heights with greater commitment and determination.

But if they choose fear instead and enter the *Danger Zone*, their need to *stand out* will make them impossible to ignore, and their projections will cause them to put others down as they puff themselves up.

And so it begins. These four changes are only the beginning of the metamorphosis that our relatives undergo. The *Either/Or Zone* is a choice point between being a great relative, or one who is difficult to deal with. And all too often, people choose the *Danger Zone* over the *Dimension of Greatness*, and behavior goes from bad to worse.

The Danger Zone

While almost everyone has the potential for greatness, the remainder of this chapter deals only with the "Eight by Fate" difficult behaviors that occur in the *Danger Zone.*

The General

Once the intent to *be responsible* transforms into a need to *command*, it manifests itself as what we'll describe as the GENERAL (Figure 3-2).

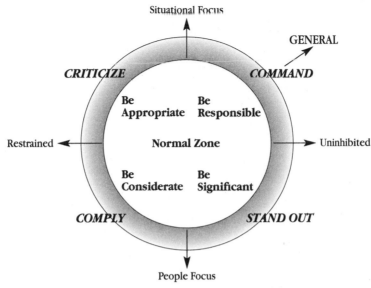

Figure 3-2

The General knows what must be done. As for those who don't, the *Danger Zone* General views them as dependent, powerless, and unable to act responsibly. The General attempts to take and keep command with a withering stare, threats, and intimidation. Opposition is eliminated and martial law is declared. Seemingly crazed behavior is meant to get others to back off, stand down, and shut up, until the territory is secured. And while some relatives may get away to cultivate their opposition, most learn to comply because it is easier than life on a battlefield.

The Judge

When the intent to *be appropriate* transforms into a need to *criticize*, it manifests as the JUDGE (see Figure 3-3).

A disgruntled perfectionist in an imperfect world, the Judge may tell you what is on his or her mind. Or the Judge may give up and step back, arms folded, mind enfolded in cynicism and hopelessness. Deciding that nothing ever really measures up or works out, the Judge wastes no time hoping for it and less time doing anything about it. Instead, the Judge passes sentence and assigns punishment. After all, the situation is out of order, and so are you.

The Pleaser

When the intent to *be considerate* turns into the need to *comply*, a person is likely to become a PLEASER (Figure 3-4).

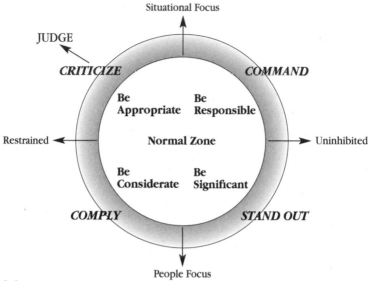

Figure 3-3

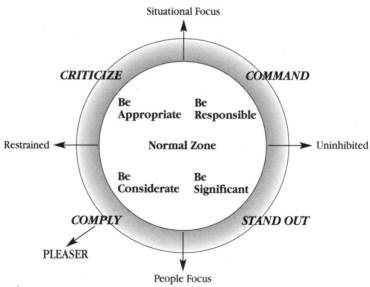

Figure 3-4

A soft touch for those in need, the Pleaser gives all but asks for little. The Pleaser forgets to take care of him or herself, but takes care of everyone else. When there is nothing left to give, the Pleaser borrows from the future to give some more. All the while, the Pleaser wonders why the good he or she has done unto others isn't being recompensed in return. Resentment leads to subtle and unconscious acts of sabotage, and the Pleaser's life becomes a mess. Then the Pleaser brings his or her problems to the family, and the family reacts.

The VIP

When the intent to *be significant* goes unfulfilled and becomes the need to *stand out*, you're dealing with the VIP (Figure 3-5).

This "very important person" is a legend in his or her own mind. Quite possibly, this is also a "very insecure person" deep down inside. The VIP may cut others down in order to seem taller or may play a game of one-upmanship, all for the sake of attention. The VIP may claim to have special knowledge not available to others or may simply act like a snob. And should a conversation turn to something the VIP knows nothing about, the VIP will twist it, turn it, and rearrange it until he or she is back in the center of it. VIPs live in the shadow of their own inadequacy, or pull in so much light that everyone else is left in their shadow.

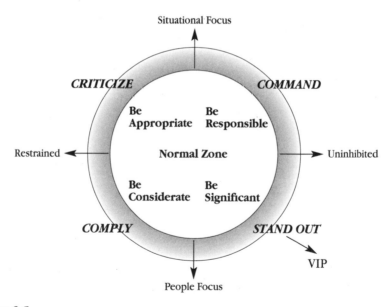

Figure 3-5

The Lens with a Twist: When Worlds Collide

Some intents overlap and combine, creating even more difficult behavior in your family.

The Meddler

When the intent to *be responsible* and the intent to *be appropriate* unite around a perceived threat, the combined need to *command* and *criticize* gives birth to the MEDDLER (Figure 3-6).

Meddlers put their nose in places they don't belong. They ask inappropriate questions, invasive and personal in nature. They comment on your relationship and give unsolicited advice. They show up where they're not invited. The Meddler doesn't seem to know what meddling is. Combining the critical eye of the Judge with the bias for action of the General, the Meddler tries to micromanage your life, to make your life conform to expectations. Meddlers insist on doing things for you that you do not want them to do, because they're certain they are right.

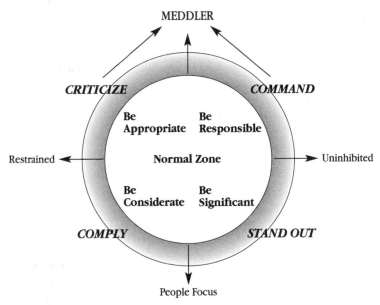

Figure 3-6

The Mystery

When the intent to *be appropriate* combines with the intent to *be considerate*, the conflicting needs to *criticize* and *comply* make for a great MYSTERY (Figure 3-7).

Their critical self has judgments about the family, or fears the family's judgments. Their compliant self has nothing nice to say, so they say nothing at all. The Mystery knows what is wrong that cannot be set right. But two wrongs don't make it right. So they don't call. They don't write. And at their worst, they disappear from your sight. They wear their isolation like a cloak, keeping a low profile around the family, or withdrawing from it altogether. The tactical withdrawal along a planned escape route keeps the Mystery alive, in the pervasive concern that's left behind.

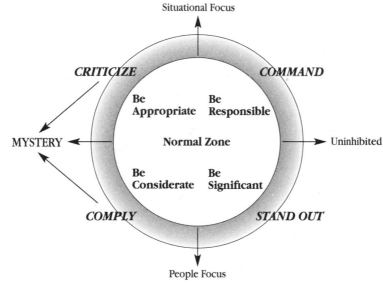

Figure 3-7

The Martyr

The need to *comply* with what you want combines with the need to *stand out* for doing it, making a MARTYR, who does unto others with a lot of strings attached (Figure 3-8).

The Martyr is a needy giver, and none of the gifts are free. Since a lot of what Martyrs give is unsolicited, they don't get the appreciation they crave. Their efforts become their burden, weighing them down and making more work of their efforts. They resent having to carry that weight, and that's when they come to you. They take you on a guilt trip, hooking you in with all they've done. "How could you do this to me?" they'll ask. "What haven't I done for you!" they'll declare.

The Rebel

When the intent to *be significant* and *be responsible* becomes the need to *stand out* and *command*, the result is the REBEL (Figure 3-9).

The Rebel challenges authority and refuses to cooperate. Rebel methods include running away, building opposition, throwing a tantrum, and undermining your support. If they can't have their way, neither will you. If they

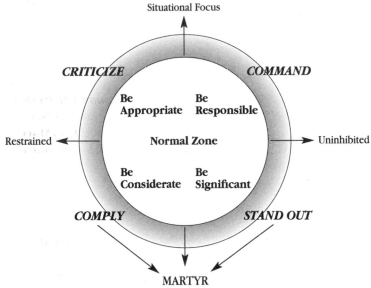

Figure 3-8

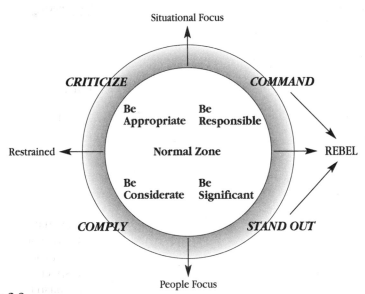

Figure 3-9

can't get away, they blow up. Family members may fear the Rebel and walk on egg shells around him or her. Some will be judgmental about the Rebel's bad behavior, only to find that they have provided an incentive for more such behavior.

To Summarize:

◆ Be *Responsible/Command/***General**
◆ Be *Appropriate/Criticize/***Judge**
◆ Be *Considerate/Comply /***Pleaser**
◆ Be *Significant/Stand Out/***VIP**
◆ Be *Responsible and Be Appropriate/Command and Criticize/***Meddler**
◆ Be *Appropriate and Be Considerate/Criticize and Comply/***Mystery**
◆ Be *Considerate and Be Significant/Comply yet Stand Out/***Martyr**
◆ Be *Significant and Be Responsible/Stand Out and Command/***Rebel**
◆ *See also Figure 3-10.*

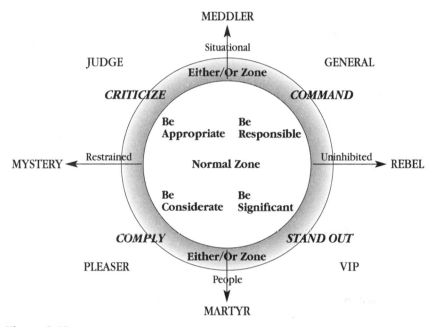

Figure 3-10

As you were reading these eight descriptions, you may have glimpsed some of your own behavior. That means you could be the reason someone else is reading this book. That's lucky for us, but not so good for you. Don't take it too hard, though. Who hasn't needed a little respect, agreement, approval, and recognition on at least a few occasions? Who hasn't been hurt, angry, resentful, or ridiculous once in a while? Just like you, your difficult relatives react to what they think is going on as it relates to what they are trying to fulfill. Their behavior is observable and your behavior is changeable. What you do about this is up to you. But you'll need some basic skills if you want to make the most of your situation. In the next section of the book, we'll explore these basic skills.

Part II

Family Camp:
A Learning Environment for Essential Communication Skills

Chapter 4

Getting to
Common Ground

If you're like most people, there are at least some people in your family with whom you can communicate, and only a few with whom you cannot. But even if you have trouble with *all* your relatives, there are at least a few people in your life with whom you can communicate just fine. Our purpose in this and the following chapters is to emphasize what you already know about successful communication and show you how to use it intentionally to get to common ground with difficult family members. Once you know what to do that works, you can begin to do it on purpose whenever you need to make your communications count.

Blending, the First Basic Skill

Blending is the basis of every positive relationship you have. (If you have only problem relationships, then you're about to find out what the problem *really* is!) Aren't you amazed at how easy it is to relate to some people, and how difficult it is to relate to others? The difference is the amount of common ground. Everybody gets along better with family members with whom they share likes and dislikes. You can identify with relatives who share your values and whose values you too share. Ideally, families create and share a lot of common ground. Sometimes you have to do it on purpose or it will not happen at all. Intentional blending makes it possible to meet people where they are or to arrive together at common ground.

You blend all the time in loving relationships. If your small child tries to get your attention and you bend down to meet him or her at eye level, you are blending by reducing differences in height. If you act silly and childlike when you play with your child, you're blending with the child.

When you go out for a meal with family and, after a look at the menu, everyone asks each other what they're having, that's a form of blending. It has little to do with hunger and thirst. But it does show interest and caring for each other, and the shared experience builds rapport.

Whether it is reminiscing about the time you threw water balloons out a window onto people below or got milk to come out of the nose of a sibling whose mouth was full, the closeness of shared memories is the experience of blending. As each of you add details and depth to it, you reduce the differences between you, with the result that you feel closer.

You blend with family when you share traditions and celebrations. You blend visually with your facial expression, degree of animation, and body posture. You blend verbally with the volume and speed of your voice when it alters to match your relatives. And you blend conceptually with your words.

Blending isn't only about having positive experiences and behaviors in common. Have you ever commiserated with someone in your family about another relative who has been driving you both crazy? When you find yourself on the same side of a problem, that's the experience of blending.

It is important to note that blending builds trust over time. And as natural as it is to blend with the relatives that you like, it is equally natural *not* to blend with relatives you find difficult. The failure to blend has serious consequences because it allows the differences between you to become a foundation of difficulty. In your immediate family, there are likely to be any number of issues that have served as points of agreement or points of disagreement over time. Even when you don't see one of these family members on a regular basis, those issues will be there waiting for you when you do get back together, and the amount of blending in the past will affect your relationship in the present. This is at least one of the reasons why some of your family members are easier to relate to than others.

Blending sends important signals to people, most of which you're not aware of, but which are influential nonetheless. People want to know that you're with them. In relationships, nobody cooperates with anyone who seems to be against them. There is no value in lukewarm. You're either "with" someone or you might as well be against them. Blending sends the "I'm with you" signals that every person, in every moment of every relationship, is looking and listening for. It's these signals that determine their willingness to move to common ground. Even your most challenging relatives want to know, "Are you with me or not?" It is a mistake to assume that just because someone is your relative, they know that you care about them, love them, and value them. As in all relationships, you're either on common ground or you're worlds apart.

Redirecting, the Second Basic Skill

Redirection should be relatively easy, if you've actively blended with your family members. So allow us to redirect your attention to the many ways in which you can blend with others.

Many Ways to Blend

Body Blending

Blending happens on many levels—mental, emotional, and physical, as well as visually and auditorally. These last two constitute your first line of access, so we will begin with them.

You can blend nonverbally with people by doing something called "mirroring." This is a natural behavior, easily observed whenever people are enjoying each other's company. You'll notice that people tend to mirror each other's body postures, facial expressions, and animation levels when they're getting along. Signals are sent through small similarities. When people you're talking with cross their legs, after a time you may cross your legs in a similar manner. They uncross their legs and lean forward, and within moments you respond in kind. If they're smiling, you smile back. It's a game of Simon Says that happens outside of awareness yet has an influence all the same. Through blending, people create an atmosphere of commonality. Fail to blend and that atmosphere is easily poisoned.

If you're having trouble with a family member, use your new awareness of blending to reduce differences in posture, facial expression, and animation. Whether they notice or not, you will be sending signals that you are not the enemy and that you're interested in improving the relationship.

Verbal Blending

Your voice also sends signals, with both volume and speed, that tell others if you're "with them" or not. If someone yells, "That was incredible," you'll either whoop back or shout, "It was?" If they whisper, "You should have been there," you whisper back, "I should have?" Some people talk faster than others, while others talk really slow. When you blend, you tend to match a person's speed of speech or voice volume. And when you don't care or don't like someone else, you'll either talk rings around the slow ones or create drag for the fast ones. If they talk too slow, you may just grow impatient and finish their sentence for them.

Tone of voice is another aspect of audible blending. But its significance and meaning run deeper than either speed or volume. A person's voice tone reflects their emotional state. That's why, at the tone, people take things personally, even if it isn't about them. Even with the best of intentions, strong emotions tend to leak through in your tone. While you're busy carefully choosing your words and suppressing your feelings, with your tone of voice you could be telling the person something quite different than what you intended. As a result, the other person might actually ignore your words, reacting instead to your tone. "Don't you take that tone with me, mister!" You can use your voice tone to blend intentionally, but first you must access positive feelings about some aspect of the person.

Emotional Blending

Misery loves company. If you're miserable and so is the person you're talking with, then you can both be happy about being miserable together. While two people in the same emotional state experience some deep blending, it is not necessary for you to be in the same emotional state as a person you're having problems with. Instead, an "appropriate" emotional state can make the difference. For example, if you burst out laughing when someone is really upset about something you said, it won't send the signal "I'm with you." But if you were to express concern about the unexpected consequence and say, "I apologize for how that sounded! I don't want you to feel that way," you would blend with their upset state and increase the feeling of closeness.

Conceptual Blending

People blend in the realm of concepts too. Words are nothing more than symbols for experiences, yet you choose them as carefully as you can and you care about their meaning. So if someone tells you something and you can grasp the concept of it, you give them the cherished experience of being heard and understood. For example, one of your relatives comes over for dinner. It's getting late, and you let the relative know that it's time to get going because you have to work in the morning. The relative replies, "I feel like you're kicking me out!" and you say, "I am!" The relative says, "I don't like being kicked out," to which you reply, "Of course you don't! What's there to like about it?" In that exchange, there is a meeting of minds around the concept of being kicked out. As a result, they understand that you understand, and they'll leave on friendlier terms than if you had said, "You've got to go," and they said, "I feel like I'm being kicked out," and you said, "Too bad, I've got work in the morning."

Blend with Listening Styles

In some families, conversation can be a virtual free-for-all. People interrupt each other, talk over each other, even insult each other, yet everyone feels listened to and has a great time. In such a family, listening is a contact sport, and you've got to learn to play if you want to stay in their good graces. Other families define conversation as sound coming in but nothing going out, passively receiving information with no more than a grunt. If you get a grunt, you know you've been heard. Perhaps you've experienced the inevitable difficulties when people from different families with different listening styles find themselves together in a social situation. The person who prefers quiet listening will likely perceive the interactive and interrupting kind of listening as just plain rude. The person who prefers conversation to be dynamic will decide that the passive person must not care enough to listen.

Consider Marylin's dynamic family, which has a different verbal and listening style than her husband:

> My family is huge! Our family gatherings can have anywhere from 50 to 80 people. And for the guys, arguing is part of the family culture. I remember many a time when two of my uncles got into arguments. Some arguments turned into shouting matches, and a couple of times they took it outside to settle things physically. Then they'd come back in, laughing and smacking each other on the back and shoulders, best buddies again. I still remember the shocked look on my husband's face after his first time at one of these gatherings. His family is totally different. They are more reserved, they do not interrupt when they listen, and they certainly would sidestep talking about differences of opinion. They never argue! To my family, the willingness to argue is a sign of caring. My husband used to be the odd man out. My relatives thought he was blah and uninteresting because he was so "polite." Eventually, though, he learned to "get into" it. Though he draws the line at getting into a physical scuffle, he is willing to bring up controversy to get people going and he takes a position on issues. And now everyone loves him!

To Summarize

Let's review. Blending and redirecting are normal behaviors that occur all the time in relationships. People blend in many ways, from body language, voice tone, tempo, and volume, to concepts and family styles. The consequences of blending or not blending add up through time to determine the amount of common ground in your relationships with your family members.

Intentional blending forces you to pay close attention, to notice things about the other person and respond in kind, to move toward rather than away. And that's what it takes to redirect a relationship toward a better tomorrow.

Chapter 5

Listen with Intention

When people talk, they want someone to listen. And sometimes what isn't said is even more important than what is said, and what is said has as many implied meanings as explicit ones. Not surprisingly, listening to relatives often proves to be a tremendous challenge. Yet listening well is essential for gathering useful information, revealing mixed messages, and resolving difficulties. A person talking to you wants feedback that they've been heard and understood. This even applies to people who don't know what they're talking about, or those who don't know what they're trying to say, or even those who won't know what they're saying until they hear it themselves.

Most listening problems boil down to a simple dynamic. When two or more people have something to say, and each person is more interested in talking than listening, misunderstanding and conflict are inevitable. It is imperative that you *make it your goal to listen first, understand second,* and save what you have to say until the person talking to you feels heard. This is no small task, because more often than not, you also want to be heard and understood. In fact an argument is nothing more than two people who want to be heard and understood at the same time, and neither person is willing to hear and understand the other person.

With family, the years of history behind a communication complicate it further. Suppose there is a long running argument between relatives, and it has gone on for years and years without resolution. Someone foolishly brings up the sore subject, and there it goes again! Siblings are the classic case. "Mom always liked you best." And the other sibling responds, "She did not, you're crazy."

Listening first is a key strategy for bringing out the best in your family relationships. This gives you the opportunity to create a clear channel into which you can add your voice, instead of competing for attention. Listening first offers you other potential benefits as well. You may learn facts of which you were unaware. You may gain information that indicates a better course of action. You may uncover difficulties before they become intransigent problems. Or you may find that there's nothing you really need to say. When your difficult relative has the experience of being heard and understood, the relative's preoccupation with his or her own thoughts and feelings gets resolved, which increases the likelihood that the relative will be able or willing to hear what you have to say.

Hearing is one thing, but understanding is something else entirely. There are two ways that your relatives experience understanding. The first is emotional, where your relatives get the feeling of being understood. The second is intellectual, where they form the opinion that they've been understood. Our approach to achieving an actual and factual understanding of what you hear requires that you listen actively instead of passively. That is, you must actively engage in gathering information rather than waiting for information to be provided to you.

The Listening Process

To give someone the emotional experience of being heard and understood, here is a listening strategy:

Step 1. Blend. When your relatives vent their emotions, blow off steam, try to meddle, martyr themselves, bark orders or putdowns at you, act like they're more important than you, talk on and on about nothing of consequence, pick at you, find fault with you, or hang their head and mutter, your task is to give visual and auditory evidence that what they're saying makes sense to you (even if it doesn't!).

Rather than distracting your relatives with puzzled looks, interruptions, statements and/or looks of disagreement, help them to completely express themselves. Nod your head in agreement, and every once in a while, give the appearance of understanding by grunting 'Uh-huh," "Yes," "Oh," and "Hmmm." Repeat back what they say to you so they know they've been heard. Make sure that all of your communication signals are giving them the idea that you understand completely whatever it is that they've said to you. At the point where your problem relatives begin repeating themselves, consider that as feedback that they need some feedback from you!

Step 2. Backtracking. Tell your relatives what you heard. Use their own words, rather than interpreting what you've heard. This works much better than saying, "So, what you're really trying to say is..." and making something up. A more assertive person might correct you, "No, what I'm trying to say is what I actually did say right before that thing you said I said that I didn't say!" A more passive person might just think such thoughts and give up trying to communicate with you. In either case, you would have created more distance between you and increased the difficulty of building a bridge. Words are symbols for experience, and the words that a person uses to express an experience are meaningful. By sticking to the actual language they use, you avoid the problem of them believing you haven't understood. At the same time you are letting them know that you value what they are saying enough to want to hear it accurately. If you refuse to hallucinate freely about the meaning of their words, and simply repeat some of them back, you give yourself a second chance to review their communication, to notice what they haven't said, and to consider other possible meanings. And it puts you in a position to ask intelligent questions to find out what it is they were really trying to say.

Backtracking is particularly important when you're talking on the phone, since the only visual information they have about you is what they extrapolate *from* the sound of your voice and the words that you use.

Step 3. Clarify.   Clarification questions are open-ended questions that require more than a grunt in response. They begin with words like *what*, *who*, *where*, *when*, and *how*. "Who are you talking about? What are you referring to? Where did it happen? When did it happen? How did it happen?" The benefit of clarifying is not limited to discovering additional information. It has a profound effect on the person who is trying to tell you something. It shows that you care enough to try and understand the person, which blends with that person's desire to be understood.

Beware of situations where you think you already understand. Once you think you know something, you stop trying to find anything out! Even if you do understand what you haven't been told (because of intuition or prior knowledge), you deny your relative the opportunity to feel understood. Parents often run into this problem. Having been children themselves, they may have a "been there, done that, bought the T-shirt" mentality when their children have something to say. But children don't just take it on faith that their parents understand. They require evidence! When parents try to bypass the listening process and start giving advice, children may resist or ignore that advice because their own attention is still on what they want to convey. Parents will gain more ground faster by backtracking and clarifying, even when they don't really need the information being offered. The experience of being understood doesn't generally happen in a single conversation. Instead, it builds up over time. If the belief has already been established that "you don't understand me," parents have to work harder to overcome it, and listen well in enough conversations to build up a new generalization that "you really do understand me!" This makes it easier to share appropriate past experiences of their own or offer some direction.

Asking the right questions often turns out to be worth more than having all the right answers. But so does holding off on the questions. Emotions have such experiential intensity that they block a person's reasoning ability. And an upset person may not even know what it is they're upset about! Asking for facts from someone overwhelmed with feelings could work against you, unless you first listen well and backtrack what you've heard. While it is virtually impossible to reason with a highly emotional person, it is possible to look and sound like you understand, to backtrack what you've heard, and then to become curious enough to ask questions. More information on the benefits of asking clarification questions can be found in our book, *Dealing with People You Can't Stand.*

Remember, asking a specific question doesn't automatically get you a specific answer. Some problem people speak in sweeping generalizations. (There's more on this below, under "The Perils of Generalization.")

Step 4. Summarize What You've Heard. If you've missed something, your summary will bring it to their attention, so that they can fill in the details they still want you to have. "So then, if I understand you correctly, this is the problem, this is who it involved, and this is when it happened, where it happened, and how it happened?"

Step 5. Confirm. Having listened carefully, you've now arrived at a crucial juncture. Rather than assuming that the interaction is complete, be certain that your relative is satisfied that the problem has been heard and understood. Ask, "Do you feel understood? Is there anything else?"

When enough sincere listening, caring, and questioning are brought together, understanding is achieved and your relative will become less difficult and more cooperative.

The Perils of Generalization

Once you've understood and practiced this first level of listening, take your listening skills to the next level. Remember that language is twice removed from experience. Studies on memory reveal that memories are flawed representations of actual experiences, filtered through prior experience, mood, intensity, and a host of other variables. So whenever people communicate about their experiences, you can be certain that they are *generalizing* about everything that happened.

You know how this works. If you are driving somewhere in a car and you get two or three red lights in a row, what do you say? "All the lights are red!" If you meet two or three people in a row who are in a bad mood, what do you say about the mood of people in general? "Everyone is in a bad mood today." Once you've formed a generalization about an experience, your radar for relevance kicks in. If you are getting married, it may seem like the whole world has decided to get married too! When you're pregnant, it may seem like a baby boom is happening. And when you're interested in a certain kind of automobile, you'll start noticing that automobile all around you. The more relevant something is to your life, the more you start noticing it. The more you notice it, the more relevance it gains. And in this way, your generalizations get stronger and stronger over time.

Family members take this ability to generalize to a higher level of reinforcement. We attribute this phenomenon to the long histories that develop between family members, and the shared stories in families that are repeated and embellished with every recollection and retelling. When family members talk about each other, they make extensive use of all-encompassing statements or phrases like:

> You always . . .
> Everyone knows . . .
> It never happens . . .
> No one ever . . .
> All the time . . .

Left unquestioned, generalized statements can produce all kinds of unintended side effects, as family members make up meanings, take offense, and then get tough, get even, give in, or give up. If the generalizations are about you, you are likely to notice what has been left out. When a person says that "someone said" without identifying the source, words may take on a ring of truth without any supporting evidence. When a person says that "good people don't do such things," they are stating rules that have apparently lost their source. By probing these gaps for details, you can connect what is said on the surface with the deeper structure that produced it. In this way, you can help your relatives go from vague to specific, and gain valuable information, while putting cracks in and even dissolving generalizations that have been the root cause of conflict in difficult family relationships.

Hidden Meanings Behind Generalizations

How can you understand the meaning behind generalizations? Let us count the ways. To help you learn how to listen at a deeper level, we will divide information into eight categories.

Missing "W"s

The missing "W" refers to detail about who, what, where, and when. The first information to ask for when cracking open a generalization is the missing W. If someone tells you, "I'm scared," your response might be "Scared of what?" If someone tells you, "Meet me!" Your reponse might be to say, "Meet you where and when?" And if your relative complains that "People don't care," you may want to ask, "Who specifically doesn't care?" It is safe to assume that any generalization they give you is based on the actions of one or more people, or something that has happened two or more times. It only takes two or three experiences to form a generalization, and a few good questions to get back to the details.

Vague Verbs

After you know the W's, it's time to clarify the verbs. Verbs are action words, and every verb is vague until you specify its meaning. If someone says, "She fools me every time!" you can ask for the specifics about how this happens. "How does she fool you?" If someone says, "He treats me like a fool!" you can ask for specifics as to how this happens: "When he treats you like a fool, how does he treat you?" or "How does he treat you like a fool?" Since you have no real idea what these action words are referring to until you've been specifically told, asking for the detail frees you up from making sense, getting hooked, and having a reaction to something that you don't really understand.

Freezers

When someone turns a verb (an action word) into a noun, we call that a "freezer." If someone tells you about their "frustration," they have taken the verb, *to be frustrated*, and turned it into a noun, *frustration*. The problem with freezers is that while actions come and go, things stay. You can be frustrated one moment, then sad, then happy, then something else. But when a person says, "my frustration," they have made it into a static thing rather than a changeable process. It is as if they are saying, "My frustration is with me wherever I go. I keep it in my pocket. I can set it on the table between us if you'd like to see it!" Here are some other freezers commonly encountered in the generalizations offered to you by your relatives—"my sadness . . ." "my misery . . ." "my depression . . ." "my resentment . . ."

Freezing an experience isn't inherently a bad thing. Some experiences are worth freezing! If people say "my confidence . . ." "my happiness . . ." "my joy . . ." they can carry positive experience around in their pocket, take it out, and enjoy it whenever they like. But if your relative freezes a negative process into a static thing that gets in the way of a change for the better, it would be wise to melt it. You do that by turning the frozen "thing" back into an action.

They say, "My frustration . . .," and you can ask, "What frustrates you?"

They say, "My sadness . . .," and you can ask, "What are you sad about?"

They say, "My depression . . .," and you can ask, "So what are you depressed about?"

They say, "I have so much anger . . ., "and you can ask, "What are you angry about specifically?"

Turning the noun back into a verb in your question gives your relative the opportunity to deal with the process of it again, and go from a stuck place about it to the possibility of movement and change.

Coulda-Woulda-Shoulda's

Whenever someone tells you what they couldn't do, wouldn't do, or mustn't do, they are telling you about a barrier in their thinking based on a fear or concern about a possible consequence. You can explore it by asking about the consequence. So, for example, if someone says, "I *have* to go to that event," you can ask, "What would happen if you didn't go?" If they reply, "Mom will kill me if I don't go," you can then add detail by asking for it. "How do you know she'll kill you?" The result is that they will give you the detail about the time or times in the past that they are now projecting into the future.

If someone says, "I just can't go," you can ask, "What would happen if you did go?" and they'll tell you the consequence that they are seeking to avoid. If they reply, "They'll be obnoxious to me!" you can get the details by asking, "How do you know they'll be obnoxious to you if you go?" The result is that they will probably tell you the past events on which they've built their generalization.

Please note: We're not saying that feared consequences are unrealistic or imagined. Everything may happen exactly as your relative says it will. But left unexplored, there is a very good chance that both you and your relative will never know what the possibilities are.

Another way of responding to coulda-woulda-shoulda's is to ask what the person can do or will do. To the person who says, "I just can't," you can reply, "What can you do?" To the person who says, "I have to go," you can reply, "What do you want to do?" To the person who says, "I won't do it," you can reply, "What will you do?"

Universals

A universal is an all-ecompassing generalization that includes the entire universe. Words like *never, always, nobody, everybody,* may sound real when left unquestioned. Once examined, it is often possible to turn a universal into a specific example that is open to change. You can do this by exaggerating the universal with your tone of voice. Then ask for a counterexample (an example where the universal is not true). So for example, if someone tells you that "They're *all* against me!" you can reply, "All? They're ALL against you? There isn't even one person who is not against you?" to bring a counterexample to the surface. Or, you could ask for the specific example the generalization refers to: "Who specifically is against you?" If your relative says "I *never* get what I want," you might reply "You NEVER get what you want? Not even one time? There wasn't a single time where you got what you wanted EVER?" in order to bring the counterexample to the surface. Or, you could ask for the specific example the generalization refers to: "When specifically don't you get what you want?"

Cause-Effect Statements

A cause-effect statement implies that when one thing happens, another must happen as well. The form of it goes like this: When X, then Y. So when someone tells you, "Her attitude really irks me," the implication is that your relative has no choice but to be irked. You can explore this by asking, "How does her attitude irk you?" or "What does she do specifically that irks you?" If someone tells you, "My brother really makes me mad!" you can reply, "How does he make you mad?" or "What does he do that makes you mad?" By asking for the connection, your relative may discover that they themselves are the missing link. "He ignores me!" Then backtrack it. "So when he ignores you, you feel mad?" If your relative says, "Her stubborness drives me crazy," you can reply, "How does her stubborness drive you crazy?" or '"How does she act stubborn?"—to which the reply might be "She won't listen to what I say!" That's your opportunity to ask, "What is it you say that she won't listen to?" Your relative may reply, "I try to tell her how she can improve her life!" You can then summarize it, including them as the cause of their own reaction. "So when you try to tell her how to improve her life, it makes you crazy?" And so on. Follow this through far enough, and it becomes obvious to both you and your relative that, rather than "her" stubborn behavior, it is what your relative says, or the way your relative says it that gets in the way or is the actual crazy-making experience your relative is having. This opens up a world of options, such as changing the way, or the words, or even the need to tell "her" how to improve her life, as a way of no longer having to feel crazy.

Parents often give their children cause-effect statements. "If you really loved me, then you would do what I tell you to do." Children sometimes reply in kind. "If you really loved me, you wouldn't tell me what to do!" If you are ever on the receiving end of such a cause-effect statement, ask for a counterexample. "Have you ever loved somebody and not done what they told you to do?" Or "Have you ever not loved somebody and done what they told you to do?" You can also provide the counterexample yourself. "When I told you to come help me with the dishes, and you said you were busy, even though you didn't do what I told you to do, did you still love me?" If the answer comes back 'Yes," then the point has been made and more options become available.

Mind Reading

This is one of the most common patterns in family relationships, and for good reason. The more you think you know about someone, the more you'll be tempted to think you know about them, regardless of how much you actually do know about them! A mind-reading statement implies that one person knows the inner workings of another person's mind, without having to ask first. If your relative says, "They really hate me, I just know it," you may want to ask, "How do you know that they hate you?" This puts your relative in a position to tell you the evidence they are using to support their claim. If your relative tells you, "They have no appreciation for how hard I work," you can ask, "How do you know they don't appreciate your hard work?" and they will tell you the evidence they use to justify their mind reading. "They never say thank you." Then you can ask, "If they ever said 'thank you,' would that tell you that they appreciate your hard work?" Or you could ask for a counterexample, an example with the reverse meaning. "Was there ever a time when you appreciated someone's hard work but didn't thank them for it?" If you know of a time, you could even offer them the counterexample. "Last year, after the reunion, when I put away all the chairs and tables and swept out the garage, you did not actually thank me. Did that mean you didn't appreciate my hard work?" By answering these kinds of questions, your relative may come to realize that there is more than one way to interpret an event, and that their interpretation is not the only possible one.

Life Rules

It isn't uncommon for family members to apply the rules they use to govern their own behavior to others in the family. A *Life Rule* is stated as a fact, with no author or authority given as reference. "Nice people smile back." "Good girls don't do that." One way to respond to this is to ask, "Nice people smile back, according to whom?" or "Good girls don't do that, according to whom?" This places ownership of the rule back where it belongs, with the person who lives by it rather than on the persons who live by other rules. Once this step is taken, your relative may be more amenable to exploring options, other interpretations, and so on.

You Can Do It

Listening as we've described it is both fun and helpful in understanding and improving relationships with relatives. However, be warned. Without adequate blending, asking these kinds of questions can be equivalent to giving someone the third degree. Just relax, be curious, and have a genuine desire to understand how this relative of yours organizes his or her perceptions of reality. Don't worry about convincing your relative of anything or changing your relative's point of view. Often, when you listen to understand, and listen for deeper meaning, the person you are questioning finds a way to the conclusion you are hoping for. And because your relative got there aided only by the agency of your helpful questions, the relative is more receptive to noticing and acting on self-discovered insights rather than ideas directly provided by you.

One of the best ways to practice asking these questions is to try them out on yourself. Take out a sheet of paper, write down one of your most troubling opinions about one of your problem relatives, and question the words you use to describe the problem. Find the cracks in your own generalizations and let a little light shine through, and you will find it much easier to do the same with others. Then, practice asking these questions with friends or close family members, before presenting them to your problem relatives. As you begin to recognize these eight patterns of generalization and the questions most appropriate to them, your ability to gain a deeper understanding with problem relatives will increase dramatically.

Chapter 6

Get to the Heart of the Matter

So far we've discussed listening as a meaningful method for building relationships. Yet sometimes, listening is not enough, because the most meaningful information is hidden—not only from you as the listener, but from the speaker as well. When you identify the hidden elements of a communication, you gain valuable influence over the direction and quality of the relationship. In this chapter we will explore these hidden aspects of communication.

Find the Good

You should never depend on someone else to communicate clearly. Have you ever been in a conversation where you found yourself wondering why the other person was telling you what they were telling you? That was an indicator that you didn't understand the purpose behind their communication.

Intent is the overall purpose or reason for a communication or action. Most people do not tell people *why* they're telling them whatever they're discussing and make the false assumption that the person they're addressing will "just know." And it is not uncommon for people to talk before they have any clear idea as to why they're speaking. So for the sake of your effectiveness with your relatives, we are going to suggest a useful (if not necessarily true) assumption. Assume that behind all communications and actions, there is a purpose. It may be near the surface or it may be deeply buried. Regardless, if you assume it's there, you may find it. The failure to recognize and appreciate purpose is a frequently missed opportunity that can have lasting consequences.

Finding the good is a powerful key to bringing out the best in your relatives. Sometimes the simplest and most compelling gift we give one another is the benefit of the doubt. But even when you can't find it, we believe it can be useful to deal with them "as if" it were there. This gives your relative a good push toward the *Dimension of Greatness.*

Whenever you listen and talk *as if* your relative has a good purpose, you are "projecting positive intent." And given the opportunity, most people will accept the positive intent you project on them. If you say, "I know you care about our relationship, and that you wouldn't want to do anything to hurt me," he or she is unlikely to respond by saying, "No, you're wrong, I am here to give you your daily adult dose of abuse." By accepting the positive intent you project on them, they take a step in the desired direction.

You can use the power of positive projection to shape the thoughts and reactions of your relatives in another way. When they engage in behaviors that you would prefer not to deal with, you can break their connection to it and reshape their perception of their own motives by simply saying something like, "That's not like you." Then tell them how you want them to be, as if they already are. Most people will gladly self-identify with a better idea of themselves, if you're willing to provide it. "You're the kind of person that . . ." If you tell your relative, "It isn't like you to just dump on me!" they are not going to say, "Yes it is. Dumping on you is the highlight of my day." It's far more likely that they will stop in their tracks,and pause in confusion for a moment. You can seize that moment to redirect your interaction with them, by giving them an excuse for their behavior: "You must have something going on that's really bothering you." The next thing you know, they'll be making a confession, telling you about a deeper problem or apologizing for their bad behavior. When you project positive intent, the most likely result is that your relative will take a step in the direction you set for them, faltering though it may be.

Since your relative may be unaware of the positive reasons behind their own difficult behavior, and since you're not certain what those positive reasons are either, you can always just make something up. Even if the intent you try to blend with isn't true, you will still get a better response and create some rapport between you than if you assume only the worst.

All statements carry some implication. That implication can be positive or negative. Consider the positive implications in these statements:

"That's not like you."
"Certainly, you care about your appearance!"
"I know you don't want people thinking badly of you!"

"You're as capable of taking care of your things as anyone."
"I know your heart, and you are a loving and careful person."
"You can do anything you put your mind to!"

Now consider the different implications in these statements:

"You're lazy."
"You're sloppy."
"You'll never amount to anything."
"You're so irresponsible."
"You just don't care."
"You're just a stubborn child."
"You would lose your head if it wasn't attached!"

We realize how tempting it is, when someone is behaving badly, to say, "That's what's wrong with you!" or "You always do that!" or "I can never count on you." The problem with these kinds of lowered expectation statements is that they shape the self-concept of the person to whom you say them.

Far better, then, to tell them how you want them to be, and better still, as if they already are that way. When your problem relative starts an argument, instead of saying, "All you want to do is argue," say, "That isn't like you! You're a reasonable person and we can talk about this in a reasonable way."

Positive Projections for the Eight by Fate

What are the potential positive intentions behind the eight Danger Zone behaviors that you can project in order to alter the trajectory of your dealings with relatives behaving badly? While the specifics of your situation and relationships are best determined by you, here are a few general ideas to stimulate your thinking:

- Appreciate the General's willingness to demonstrate responsibility.
- Appreciate the Judge's high standards, values, and principled views.
- Appreciate the Pleaser's concern for others.
- Appreciate the VIP for the difference he or she makes and for showing enthusiasm and excitement.
- Appreciate the Mystery for not saying anything hurtful.
- Appreciate the Rebel's independent views and advocacy for change.
- Appreciate the Martyr's willingness to make sacrifices for the benefit of others.
- Appreciate the Meddler for taking an interest in how your life is working out.

When you appreciate people on the level of intent, you do not have to deal with the content of their communication. Acknowledge positive intent and then move on, change the subject, end the call, go from the living room to the kitchen, or do whatever fits the logistics of the situation you are in.

Reinforce Wanted Behaviors

Another way to project positive intent is to encourage existing behaviors that you want more of. Tell them what they did, tell them that you liked it, and tell them that it is one of the things you value about them. In this way, you can reinforce what you want more of, and counter what you want less of in an effective manner.

> Sarah had just turned 18. She got her driver's license, and then promptly got into an accident. She was worried about what her mother Miriam would say. But Miriam surprised her, saying, "Thank God you're alive and no one got hurt! Cars can be fixed, but life is precious. I'm sure you're shaken by this experience, and I will understand completely if you're not ready to talk about it. If you need me, if you want to talk, just know that I'm here for you. "And that was it. No lecture. No advice. No problem!
>
> A week later Miriam told her mom she would like to talk. She said, "Mom, you did something very special last week for which I'm very grateful, and I want you to know about it." (*Tell them what they did.*) "When you talked to me right after the accident, you seemed to know how embarrassed I was, and you were totally sensitive to my needs. You didn't ask me a lot of questions or give me a lot of advice, but you left the door open for me if I needed to talk to you." (*Reinforce what you want more of.*) "I loved it. I felt so supported, so safe, after feeling so terrified in that car. I needed to just sit with it for a few days until I could get my mind around what happened, but I totally felt your love and support. I knew I could come to you if I needed to cry, or to ask for your experience and wisdom if I had questions." (*Tell them what you value about them.*) "I really value your sensitivity to my needs and the way you communicate with me with such respect. You're the greatest!"
>
> They hugged, and cried, and talked. And ever since, when Miriam wants to talk to Sarah, she almost always begins with, "Is this a good time for you?"

Dealing with Criticism

Speaking to positive intent can also be a useful way of dealing with criticism. Have you ever been criticized by a family member? We'll make this really simple. You have four choices when you are being criticized:

1. Feel bad and withdraw.
2. Feel bad and defend yourself.
3. Appreciate the criticism.
4. Appreciate and learn more about the criticism.

You do not have to engage with people over the content of their criticism. Instead, you can thank them for their good intent and then move on. You might respond:

> *"Thanks for caring about my appearence."*
> *"I am glad you care about me finding love and getting married."*
> *"I really appreciate that you don't want me to starve to death."*

Of course, there is always the possibility that you might learn something useful from a criticism. You may discover something about yourself that you otherwise might never know, or something you need to know, or something about them that will prove useful in another place and time. Or, just maybe, they will feel so much better for having vented it without any interference that they'll be done with the need to say it to you from that point on. And if they're criticizing you just to get a rise out of you, your appreciation and curiosity about the criticsm will actually take the fun out of it for them.

When in doubt, we suggest that you just say, "Thank you for being honest with me about this," and let it go at that.

We know a young man who, after moving out of his mother's home, didn't speak to her for almost a year. He was furious with her for her bossy attitude and know-it-all behavior, and he likened the sound of her voice to a chain saw that started up anytime he failed to meet her expectations. But there came a time when he was traveling and came down with a respiratory infection while staying in a hotel. Surrounded by strangers, almost delirious with a cough and fever, he found himself thinking of his mother and the excellent care she had provided him whenever he got sick in his childhood. Oh, how he longed for her chicken soup! Without thinking it through, he picked up the phone at his bedside. He dialed her phone number, and she answered the phone.

"Hello?"

After a moment's hesitation, he said, "Mom?" (cough, cough)

"Son, is that you?"

"Yeah, it is. Mom, I miss you." (cough, cough)

She started up the chain saw. "You do not! If you really missed me, you would have called, or written, or something, instead of leaving me to worry about . . ."And on she went, pouring out her anguish and despair.

But in his fevered condition, he had no energy to argue with her. All he could do was lay there, coughing and listening. And as he listened, a strange thing happened. For the first time in his life, he could hear what was fueling that chain saw. He could hear that she was willing to drive herself crazy for his sake. All those years of lectures, sermons, and tirades, he realized, were the result of her efforts to be a good mother, and she had done the best she could with what she knew. Love had been her sole motivating force, and he'd never even thanked her for it.

She stopped, as if running out of things to say. In that moment of quiet, he weakly told her, "Mom . . . " (cough, cough, sniffle) ". . . thanks for loving me. You really do love me, don't you?"

"Why of course I do! Honey, are you okay?"

And for the next 25 minutes all they had to say to each other was "I love you," and they said it a thousand different ways. Instead of arguing over differences of opinion, defending their points of view, or any of the other futile and frustrating behaviors that had marred their relationship over the years, all that really wanted to be said was "I love you."

Practice asking yourself what positive intent might be behind your relative's behavior and communication. What else could it mean? What good might they knowingly, or unknowingly, be trying to accomplish?

The next time a relative says something to you in a meddling manner, rather than defend against it, blend with the good by saying, "I appreciate that you care about me and want what's best for me. I want what's best for me too." There's a real possibility that they will stop what they're doing and reconsider how they're doing it, and real communication will ensue. The next time a relative says something to you in an attacking manner, rather than defend against it, blend with the good in it by saying, "I appreciate your desire to do the right thing here. I also want to do the right thing." There is a good chance that they will stop, calm down, and consider what you have to say.

Follow these suggestions and you'll discover that your ability to project the best onto others gives you the power to shape their actions and behavior.

Chapter 7

Reach a Deeper Understanding

There are two more elements of communication that are often hidden behind words: *behavioral definitions* and *criteria.* You can use these communication elements preventively with your relatives to avoid getting into problems with them. You can also use them to get out of problem situations once it is too late to avoid them. Both of these elements can help you to reach a deeper level of understanding.

Doing unto Others: Behavioral Definitions

It is a well-established fact that people using the same words can ascribe different meanings to them. Just as experience is unique to each individual, the way a person defines a word or a concept is deeply personal. A *behavioral definition* is an internal representation of needed evidence. It tells a person whether they are or are not getting what they want through the behavioral efforts of others. And it can tell you how to give someone else what they want through your behavior. Because of your own *behavioral definitions,* you know when you are being listened to, cared about, supported and encouraged, and when you are not. You may think you are being ignored, dismissed, abandoned, or discouraged, when someone is actually trying to do the opposite.

John and Mary have a lot in common. For one thing, they are married to each other. And they both feel unsupported by the other whenever they get upset. Oh, and they both really do their best to support each other when one or the other is upset. How can this be? The answer is in their different *behavioral definitions*. When John is upset, Mary could let him know she cares by leaving him alone for a while. That would give him time to think things through and come to some resolution, without having to be embarrassed about his feelings with her as a witness. When Mary is upset, John could let her know that he cares by jumping in, asking her questions, and helping her work her way through her feelings. Unfortunately, John and Mary don't know each other's behavioral definitions for *caring*. As a result, he applies his definition to her, and she applies her definition to him. So when Mary is upset, John leaves her alone and Mary feels abandoned. And when John is upset, Mary harasses him with invasive questions and the bright light of her attention. They do unto each other what they would like done unto themselves, and as a result, they both feel unsupported. It is a strange irony of life that, in your most personal relationships, unless you know how someone defines what they want, it can be incredibly difficult to give it to them!

Clarifying Behavioral Definitions

Obviously, well-intentioned people can have different *behavioral definitions* for the same concepts. You can save yourself a lot of trouble by learning the *behavioral definitions* of your relatives. And if you know your own, you can ask more specifically for what you need from others. Here are some *behavioral definitions* worth clarifying with family members.

What does it mean to be:

Cared for?
Supported?
Listened to?
Loved?
Appreciated?
Understood?
Acknowledged?
Admired?
Encouraged?
Helped?
Treated with respect?

You can add even more detail than a person can tell you, if you look at them through the Lens of Understanding, because those four primary intentions affect behavioral definitions in sometimes dramatic ways.

Support is likely to look and sound differently to someone whose primary intent is to *be considerate* instead of *be appropriate*. Someone wanting to *be considerate* offers support to Jackie in her new job. "I am sure you will do well and everybody will love you!" Someone wanting to *be appropriate* offers support in a different way. "Make sure you wear the blue suit. It makes you look more powerful and authoritative." If Jackie is looking and listening for *be considerate* support, she is likely to view the *be appropriate* support as a form of meddling, and is unlikely to find it very supportive.

Relatives commonly make the mistake of applying their own *behavioral definitions* to the behavior and words of others. It's the old "Do unto others as you would have them do unto you." Unfortunately, it doesn't seem to work a good part of the time. A more accurate saying would be "Find out what others would have you do unto them, and do that unto them instead!"

So how do you find out what people's behavioral definitions are? It's easy! Just ask.

Any time a relative says to you: *"You don't (support me, care about me, respect me, etc.),"* you can reply, *"I would like to (support you, treat you with care, respect, etc.). How would you know if I were doing that?"* And then get their *behavioral definition* for the thing they say they want that you haven't been doing. They will tell you what they need to see or hear that would indicate they were getting what they want.

But you don't have to stop there! Sometimes, the problem isn't what you are *not* doing. Sometimes, it is what you *are* doing that is sending the wrong message. It is in your interest, whenever possible, to find out your relative's behavioral definitions for what they don't want as well. *"How do you know when you are NOT being (supported, cared about, listened to, respected, etc.)?"* If you fail to find out these negative *behavioral definitions*, you may inadvertently engage in a behavior driven by your positive intent that has the opposite effect on your relative! Good intentions are not enough. To deliver on them, you have to know your behavioral definitions and your relative's behavioral definitions too, or your good intentions will produce frustration, disappointment, and anger instead.

Come Together with Clarity: Criteria

Another level of understanding is reached when you clarify *criteria. Criteria* are the personal standards by which you measure ideas. They are particularly important when differing ideas or points of view are being discussed by family members. *Criteria* can help you develop options that lead to fulfillment of intentions.

A family was trying to decide the best location for a vacation. Mom suggested a tropical location. Dad reacted negatively to that, and then little Johnny suggested an amusement park. Sally pushed for a resort at the ocean. As sides were taken and lines were drawn, the tug of war began. When this family came in for counseling, they used this as an example of how hard it is to do anything together as a family.

We innocently inquired of the mom, "Why do you want to go to the tropics?" She replied, "Because of the current exchange rate, we can save a lot of money and still have a great vacation." Economic was high on the list of her criteria for a great vacation.

Then we asked the father what the problem was in going to the tropics. His reply was that the water wasn't safe to drink, and he didn't want anyone to get sick. Health was an important criterion of a great vacation. Johnny wanted to go to an amusement park, because it would be fun, with lots to do! Fun, not boredom, was Johnny's most important criterion for a great vacation. Sally wanted to go to the coast, because a resort would have lots of activities that they could do together. Togetherness was high on her list of criteria for a vacation.

Apparently, these family members were not talking just about the vacation. They were also talking about *economic, healthy, fun,* and *togetherness.* Once these criteria were revealed, the next step was prioritizing them. Everyone agreed that fun was primary, and that there was enough money for a hotel but not for a resort. Then they brainstormed out loud on all the things they could do together in each vacation environment. They finally came up with the idea of going to the coast, staying in a nice hotel, bringing with them a list of interesting things to do nearby (including a trip to an amusement park!) with time together for beachcombing, swimming, and lots of movies. By sharing their criteria, the family was able to satisfy everyone's interests and have an interesting vacation at the same time.

Once you've asked for someone's criteria (What is important to you about this?) and you are reasonably certain that you know what the criteria are, summarize what you've learned. "So then, if I understand you correctly, what is important to you in this is . . ." and then name their criteria. Once again, you will have demonstrated that you listened, cared, and remembered, which blends with every person's desire to be understood. Make sure your relative is satisfied that their expectations have been fully voiced, by asking: "Do you feel understood? Is there anything else?"

If you are ever sitting at a table having a discussion with a number of family members, and the conversation begins to degenerate into conflict, you might note that the problem isn't different points of view, but rather conflicting criteria! A person who is against an idea one minute may be able to embrace that same idea the next, if it speaks to their criteria. This is true whether the conversation is about solutions to domestic and international problems, politics, social issues, or family issues. Make it your interest to discover the criteria of family members when different opinions and points of view threaten to destroy a family gathering. Then, with this information out in the open, you, or anyone else, may be able to creatively offer some resolution that is respectful of differences while blending with criteria and turning them into common ground.

Chapter 8

Telling
Your Truth

Here's an important truth: Whenever a person tells the truth, they are really telling their own version of it. When you tell *your truth,* you must recognize that it is based on your perceptions, assumptions, and opinions. Your truth may seem like *the* truth to you, but truth to tell, it is uniquely your own. Owning the truth you have to tell frees up other people to hear it and consider it. That's important, because telling your truth serves two important functions in family relationships:

1. It allows you to keep the relationship open instead of blocked. Unspoken truths (thoughts and feelings) have a tendency to turn into barriers to authentic relationship and are the splinters around which relationships become infected with dishonesty, disloyalty, and "dis-ease." Left unspoken, your truth (thoughts and feelings) becomes the main thing you pay attention to in the presence of their object.
2. Telling your truth can give another person an honest reflection of themselves, in which they can realize the negative consequences of their own attitudes and behaviors and find the motivation to change.

In either case, successful truth telling requires that you find the right time and the right place to tell it. There's a time and a place for everything, but it isn't all the time and everyplace. Successful truth telling also requires that you observe two principles:

1. Know the value of your truth.
2. Know what you will say before you say it.

Know the Value of Your Truth

Ask yourself, "What is my truth worth?" Your answer has to include the cost of keeping it to yourself! If you're holding on to something, it is bound to affect the way you behave. From awkwardness to anxiety to the absolute inability to enjoy someone's company, you must count the cost.

> Liz and Richard were married for 31 years, many of which were happy ones. Then they drifted apart, and soon they each had a relationship on the side. Each found themselves living two lives, and living a lie about at least one of them. Their conversations were awkward and strained. Their children knew what was going on, but said nothing beause they did not know what to say. One day, their oldest child told each of them to come clean with the other. Each parent seized the opportunity to admit to the other that their love had changed. The common ground on which they now found themselves consisted only of agreement that while they cared deeply for one another, their marriage was no more. It hurt to say it, and it hurt to hear it, but as the barrier of their dishonesty and disloyalty fell away, what remained was their ability to enjoy each other's company again. After a friendly divorce, Richard and Liz have remained good friends to this day, talking on the phone and visiting each other at least once a year. The children got to have two loving parents instead of two lying ones. Truth to be told, telling the truth turned out to be a better thing for their whole family than the lie they were living.

Some truths waiting to be told have nothing to do with lies, but with information about destructive behavior. When you witness someone you care about engaging in self-defeating and counterproductive behavior, the fear of incurring their wrath may cause you to bottle up information that could truly make a difference if it were known. For example, you might notice that your relative's constant criticism causes others to withdraw from him or her. You see them all alone and see the connection between their behavior and their isolation, and you know that information could be helpful. Or you might have a relative who is undermining the self-esteem of your cousin, or a sibling, and you just know that the information you have could stop those consequences from happening. Before you provide this information, you must weigh the cost of standing by and saying nothing and the benefit of successfully sharing what you have observed in the hope that they will change their behavior.

Still another reason for telling the truth might be because a relative engages in a behavior that is directed at you in a way that you simply cannot tolerate any longer. Either something has to change or you'll have to avoid them completely. Once you're at this point, the truth is, you really have very little to lose. Your acceptance of the certain demise of the relationship may give you sufficient motivation to make a last-ditch effort to save it.

Know What You'll Say Before You Say It

If you're going to tell your truth so that someone can hear it, then you must prepare to tell it in a strategic manner. You have to have the right pieces, and in the correct order. Equally important to your success is the tone you take. Both mental and physical preparation are involved if you intend to get this right. So use paper and pen or a computer, and map out what you're going to say when you tell your truth, using the following elements.

1. Positive Intent

Framing your information to make it as palatable as possible is primary. Your relative needs to know where you are coming from right up front, so there's no doubt in his or her mind that your information is offered in service to the relationship rather than in opposition to it. If your relative interprets your feedback as part of a daily dose of abuse, whatever you say will inevitably be taken the wrong way. If communication really is like dialing a phone number (and honestly, we think it is!), then stating your positive intent is like dialing the area code. It works best in the beginning, because it gets you ito the vicinity of the person you're trying to reach. First, you must speak to the person's positive intent, and then you must state your own intent.

Let's say you want to give some feedback to your relative about undesirable behavior. If you begin by saying, "I would like to give you some feedback," it may sound like you're saying, Let me tell you what you're doing wrong." Even if your relative lets you speak, this will be an attempt to listen for how it isn't true. Your relative may even become defensive as soon as you try to talk, interrupting with, "Who are you to be giving me feedback? You're not the boss of me!"

Instead, speak to your relative's interest in order to gain his or her interest. Using the Lens of Understanding, you could speak to the positive intent to act responsibly, appropriately, considerately, or significantly. Do this more specifically, and you're more likely to hit closer to home. "I know that your intention is to act responsibly in this situation." As we discussed in Chapter 6, given the opportunity, people will self-identify with a positive purpose that you assign to them.

Your projection of positive intent will move your relative in that direction. For example:

I know that you want Timmy to grow up to be somebody who will make you proud.

Or you might say:

I know you want only the best for Sharon, and that you would like to see her get herself together and have more self-respect so she can be happy.

Once you've engaged their attention (a precedent to gaining their intention), tell them where you're coming from. Tell them why you're about to tell them whatever it is that you are about to say. In our first example, it could sound like this:

I know you want Timmy to grow up as a responsible person who will make you proud. So I would like to talk with you about something that I think will help make that happen.

or like this:

I know you want only the best for Sharon and that you would like to see her get herself together and have more self-respect so she can be happy. There's something I'd like to discuss with you that I believe will really contribute to that.

If doing this makes you uncomfortable, now is the time to let your relative know about it. Your discomfort means you either care about the relative and don't want to hurt his or her feelings, or you care and are afraid of being taken the wrong way, or you think your relative might not be interested in what you have to say and may not care about you. By giving voice to your discomfort, you grease the wheels, as it were, on your ability to tell the bigger bit of truth yet to be told. At the same time, you make sense out of any mixed message you might be sending through your tone due to your discomfort, before your relative can start reacting to it. You may even win a bit of sympathy for your honesty in the presence of your discomfort.

And it is really uncomfortable for me to talk with you about this, because I worry you might take it the wrong way, or get mad at me, but I think you are worth it, so I am pushing through my discomfort and talking to you about this.

Keep it interesting by making it interesting to them.

And I know you wouldn't want me to keep it to myself if it was information that might be of benefit to you.

At this point your relative is probably wondering just what it is you have to say, and is more curious than defensive. But even if he or she feels defensive, it will be with the knowledge that this isn't an attack, that you care, and that you want to say something potentially valuable.

2. Be Specific

Now it's time for you to tell it like it is. To succeed, you must be specific. Provide at least one or, better still, two or three examples of the behavior you want to bring to your relative's attention. If you speak too generally, you leave a space large enough for misunderstanding to get through. And you will need to be specific for your relative to know what to do differently.

You may be observing behaviors that contradict your definition of those concepts, yet those behaviors may be your relative's way of fulfilling them. So when speaking specifically about the behaviors in which your relative is engaging, be sensitive to the fact that these behaviors may have been done with good intent.

For example, you notice a behavior coming from your parents toward your brother or sister. Your sibling defines this behavior as "being critical," or "being put down." Your parents define the behavior as simply "making an observation," or say they're "trying to help."

If you were to tell your parents, "You need to be more supportive of (sibling's name)," your generalization won't make sense. From their point of view, they're being supportive. By being specific, you can guide them to some recognition of what the behavior actually is, and provide a different reflection of how it's being received. You might say:

> At Thanksgiving, when (sibling's name) was having a second piece of pie, I saw you reach over to her and ask her, "Don't you care at all about your appearance?" And when someone complimented her on her dress, I remember you saying, "It's probably the only thing that still fits."

This is a crucial moment. Take too long with some people, and you lose them. Go too fast with others, and you lose them. With some of your relatives, you'll need to be concise and to the point, just like they are, and get the whole result with the least number of words. Match the length of your communication to the way they communicate, plus or minus a minute or two. For this reason, we recommend writing this out first, then editing it again and again, until it is just right and you know what it is you want to say. You don't have to memorize it, and probably shouldn't, and you don't want to give a speech either. But if you're familiar with the concepts you want to convey and the details of your examples, you're more likely to know what to say and to have the words to say it when the crucial moment arrives. Some people might call this being thoughtful. We call it being prepared.

3. Reveal the Deeper Meaning

If you're just clearing the air, you can skip this step and go on to the next one. But if you're after a specific change in your relative's behavior, you have to find his or her motivation. That motivation to change comes from either the realization that something valuable is to be gained by changing a particular behavior or something valuable will be lost by persisting in current behavior. You have to fan the flame of motivation if you want someone to make the change. For example:

> Well, I don't think you know this, because she doesn't say anything to you about it and she stays all sweetness and smiles, but while (sibling's name) seems to accept what you're saying on the outside, it hurts her, and she cries on the inside. I know this because she called me after she got home, and she was feeling crushed and hopeless, like she would never be acceptable to you. And I know you don't intend for her to feel like that. The result of this is that she grows more distant, and you have less influence. Have you noticed that she doesn't call as much as she used to, and she hasn't been visiting you as much either? Have you noticed that she doesn't talk to you about her personal life, doesn't confide in you like she used to? I'm sad about this, because I think that's not a good relationship for a mother and daughter to have. How can you influence someone who avoids you? How can you help someone who doesn't want to listen to you?

Please note: If someone starts getting defensive, repeat your positive intent. Restate your reason for telling them. Keep their perspective on the greater good of having this conversation!

If you want your relatives to listen to reason, remind them occasionally of their reason to listen. The *Lens of Understanding* is useful here:

> I know when you say these things to (sibling's name) it is because you care about her and you want her to look good and feel good, and you have some ideas about the best way for her to do that. And perhaps you do, but when you talk to her in the way I described, she can't hear where you're coming from. It just sounds like you disapprove of her, and she feels bad about herself.

In a different scenario, after giving specific examples of her problem behavior of "lashing out at her mother," a father might say to his adult daughter:

When you get annoyed at your mother and lash out at her in the way I described, it doesn't just hurt her. I can see that it hurts you too! I know you feel bad afterward. I know you feel regret, because you've told me so in the past. And I can't help but think, what if this was the last time you would ever see her again? What if your last communication with her was one in which you were annoyed? How would you feel if it was too late to say you're sorry? So you see, this isn't just about her. It is about you, and what you get to live with because of your behavior with your mother. And I am only telling you this because I love you and I love your mother and I don't want to see either of you hurting, or living with regret when the other is gone. It is very difficult for me to say this to you, because I don't want to hurt you or have you be mad at me, but I am willing to that risk on the chance that this will help, because I care about you that much.

Take your time so that the deeper meaning makes an impact. Leave a few meaningful pauses between your sentences. Allow powerful concepts to sink in. Like watering a house plant, if you add too much water too fast, it will overflow the pot. Wait a moment to let the meaning be absorbed, and then add some more.

4. Suggest Something

At this point your relative may be feeling some internal motivation to make a change. But motivation, sadly, is rarely enough. People not only need to want to change, but they need to know what change to make. If you can't offer a suggestion, you can always ask them for one. But if you want a change, now's the time to suggest or ask for it!

In our first example:

Next time you see (sibling's name) or talk to her, you could try looking or listening for something that you can appreciate about her, or about something she's doing. Just letting her know you're glad to hear from her and telling her you love her would really mean a lot to her. She might take what you say into account if she feels that you're taking her feelings into account.

In our other example:

Maybe the next time your mother does those things that annoy you, it might help if you just remember, that's Mom. That's how she is. She doesn't mean any harm by it, and she probably wouldn't do those things if she could help it. And you won't always have her around, you won't always have time with her, but at least you have this time right now. And just because she keeps doing those behaviors doesn't mean that you have to keep doing yours.

If you were just telling your truth to clear the air, and you're not really asking for any change, but were simply getting it out so it wasn't a barrier between you and your relative, then at this point you need only offer some appreciation for your relative's willingness to hear you:

> **Thanks for hearing me out. I really needed to talk to you about this, and you've been great!**

Then open your mind and heart and be willing to hear what your relative has to say in response to your truth. Don't interrupt. Demonstrate the same openess to hearing what your relative has to say as you asked for. If you offer no resistance to their views of the situation, what you've shared will have a deeper impact. And that is what they will take with them when the conversation ends and they go on their way.

5. Reinforce Behavioral Change

This step happens after you've told your truth. You get what you reward in relationships. And acknowledgment of change is a reward unto itself. People turn to appreciation like leaves turn to the sun. So when you see or hear your relative engaging in a different behavior, make sure you acknowledge it. And if your relative falls back into the old behaviors over time, take the time to offer a gentle reminder of who they are and what they're capable of, based on the better behavior you have observed. An occasional "Remember, it means a lot to Sharon when you find things to approve of in her," and "That's Mom," can remind people of the internal commitments they made to themselves. Though habits can be difficult to break, with time they disassemble and new habits do take their place.

Truth Telling Using the Lens

Within the Dimension of Greatness, you can find the perfect blend of the four intents.

Be Considerate

Considerate truth telling builds a person up rather than tearing them down. Inside every one of your relatives is the desire to be cared about. When relatives are acting out with relatives, it's usually a sign that they didn't, don't, or are afraid they will not feel cared about in some moment of time. Put someone down and they put up a defense. There's no point talking honestly with someone who isn't listening. So remember to differentiate the person from the problem, and build up the person before dealing with the problem.

Be Responsible

Responsible truth telling requires that you own your views and opinions. That ought not to be difficult, since your views and opinions truly are your own. You can use the softening phrases of *I* language to tell someone what the problem is. Phrases like "From my point of view" and "The way I see it" and "The way I remember it" take the fight out of your words, and tell your relative that what you're expressing is *your* truth, instead of oppressing your relative with *the* truth.

Be Appropriate

Appropriate truth telling is reasonable rather than emotional, proactive rather than reactive. Since shame and embarrassment are emotional reactions, you can avoid them by keeping your truthful interaction private. Find a way to keep away the prying eyes and eager ears of others. In this way, you can avoid a whole host of negative reactions to the otherwise compelling process of telling the truth.

Be Significant

Significant truth telling makes a difference, so it requires courage and commitment. If telling the truth is possible, then you do no one a favor by withholding information that could change someone's life for the better. Truth telling is no mere inconvenience because someone won't behave the way you wish. View the time you invest in the process as time that matters, because it is an extraordinary opportunity to change things for the better, and the side effects of such changes are potentially limitless.

Robin gave us this example of the power of telling the truth:

> I love my son. I've tried to set a good example for him, and other than a few typical problems over the years, I thought he was turning out fine. When Angel graduated from high school, he told us about a program overseas that would give him college credit, and asked if he could use his college fund to pay for it. He talked us into it, with the understanding that he would complete the course and get the credits. My wife and I knew he could do it. But he didn't do it. We found that out, about a month and a half after he returned home, when we got a call from the program director telling us that Angel hadn't earned the credit because he hadn't turned in the required course work. Needless to say, we were stunned, since only a day before he had talked about his interest in getting into a college.
>
> We told him that we knew what had happened but didn't know why he hadn't kept his word to complete the program. With about as casual an attitude as you can imagine, he said, "I didn't feel like it." And I said, "Son,

I've always believed in you, and trusted you to do the right thing. Even when we've been at odds, I never worried too much, because I know who you are. But now we have a problem, and the problem is not college credits. The problem is trust. I trusted you with that money because you gave me your word, and then you squandered the money and broke your word, because you didn't feel like keeping it. I don't want the rest of your college fund to go to waste. That money was put aside to support your future, not to pay for your negligence. It breaks my heart to say this, but I can't trust you at this time because of what has happened here. And the only way out of this dilemma that I can think of is for you to win back our trust. I don't have any idea how you can do that, so I'm hoping that you can come up with a plan by which you can re-earn my trust. Otherwise, that money is not available to you at all.

Then I just sat there, really quiet, and watched him come to terms with this consequence of his action. His eyes teared up and he started to try and convince me I was wrong, that he was trustworthy, that it was just "that" program. But he knew I was right, and quickly stopped trying to convince me of something he knew wasn't true. Some more time passed, and I reiterated, "Maybe you can come up with a way to regain my trust. I don't have any idea how you could do that, but if you can think of something, I'm willing to consider it." After another few minutes, he looked up and said, "What if I pay for my first four years of college? Then will you help me with graduate school?" I considered it for a moment, and asked, "And how will you pay for college?" He replied, "I don't know. But I'll find a way. I'll look into it tomorrow, and I will tell you what I find out tomorrow night." I told him that sounded like a good start, but that we had a ways to go.

Well, son of a gun, he did it, and I have to give him credit for it. He found a program through which he could earn money for college. He completed the program, got the money, and when he went to college, he excelled. When he had a lazy teacher, he would raise his hand in class and say, "Do you have any idea how much your class is costing me? I would like to get something for my money!" And we are so proud of him! Do you know what brought about this incredible change in him? Honesty. Telling him the truth about the larger meaning of what he did, what it meant to us, how I felt about it, and what had to happen to turn things around. Really, he did everything else.

To Summarize

When there is a problem with a family member behaving badly, more often than not honesty is the best policy. It's amazing what lengths people go to to deal with each other without first attempting to talk things out. An honest dialogue with problem relatives is a powerful approach to bringing out the best in relatives who would otherwise be at their worst.

Again, here's how to go about affecting change through truth telling:

Preparing Your Truth

Find the right time and place
Know the value of your truth
Know what you'll say before you say it

Telling Your truth

Positive intent
Be specific
Reveal the deeper meaning
Suggest something
Reinforce behavior change

Chapter 9

The Art of
the Apology

An apology begins in forgiveness, because otherwise the apology is an insincere mixed message with little hope of success. It ends in forgiveness, because if properly given, it can be received. An apology signals your willingness to let the past be past. And it creates the space for the endearing gift of a new beginning in the present.

But why apologize? Why forgive someone who has misunderstood you, blamed you for something you didn't mean to do, refused to talk to you, or treated you badly in front of others? Why not keep the distance between you and count your blessings that you don't have to deal with them anymore?

In our interviews, we discovered that strong fears interfere with the ability to forgive and seek forgiveness in return. Some of our interviewees were afraid that forgiving their relatives would be viewed as a sign of weakness, or of a lack of will. Some viewed forgiveness of their relatives as meaning that they had lost and their relatives had won and they themselves had been somehow defeated. Some were convinced that their relatives had committed an unforgivable act, and to forgive them would be a denial of justice, because their anger was the only penalty they could impose in the situation. They wanted to make their relatives pay for what they'd done, but it was obvious in talking about it that they were actually punishing themselves instead.

Marilyn refused to talk to her adult daughter Jennifer despite Jennifer's several attempts to apologize. The problem began during a phone call

when Marilyn expressed to her daughter how unappreciated she felt, and Jennifer, who was stressed out due to work, deadlines, and lack of sleep, blurted out, "Oh Mom, please, I hate it when you do this martyr trip." In so doing she stepped into a minefield of buried emotions, hidden resentments, and hurt, most of which dated back to Marilyn's divorce from Jennifer's father twenty years before.

Marilyn had long suspected her daughter of being in her ex-husband's "camp," and viewed her as something of a daddy's girl. Now she was sure of it. As Marilyn dug around in her memory, she found evidence to support this point of view, including the certain belief that the last time Jennifer had returned to her hometown for a visit, she seemed to find time to visit every brother and friend and even her ex-husband before getting around to a visit with her mother. Already feeling unappreciated, Marilyn told herself that she was last on Jennifer's list. And she was tired of being last, tired of being taken for granted. The conversation ended coldly. And nothing Jennifer could say would change it. Over the next six months Jennifer tried to apologize five times, but none of her apologies were accepted. She kept trying to explain to her mother that she was tired, burned out, under stress, worried about her child, and overwhelmed with deadlines, but nothing seemed to change how her mother felt and Jennifer began to resign herself to never speaking to her mother again.

The Nature of Forgiveness

If forgiveness is all Greek to you, perhaps we ought to start with a Greek word for forgiveness, APHESIS. The meaning of this word certainly seems to apply here. It means "to let go." And it explains why holding a grudge and letting go of one are very different things.

When you let go of carrying anger and hurt, you are letting go of holding on to the past, and freeing yourself up to be in the present and create a better future. So in a way, forgiveness of another is something you do for yourself. Rather than holding on to a point of view that makes you right and your relative wrong, forgiveness happens when you let go of the need to be right, and look at the situation from a point of view that holds your relative blameless for their behavior and your reaction to it. When you can do this, you can take the first step toward an apology that gains forgiveness for you and resolution of the shared difficulty.

This is often easier said than done. But for those able to make the decision to forgive, it is a way to snatch a victory from the jaws of defeat. Through forgiveness, you empower yourself to find new meaning for old injuries, to stop hurting yourself with a past event, and to get clear of the clouded judgment of anger so you can determine for yourself the right thing to do. It does not stop you from taking necessary action to prevent bad things from happening again. It does not deny you your right of self-defense. But you cannot change what has already occurred, and to stop perpetuating it requires accepting it so that you can consider the future unencumbered by it. Forgiveness is a way to stop the escalation of family conflict.

Several people told us that forgiveness was a personal exit from their family's dysfunction. It wasn't until they had forgiven their parents that the terrible childhood experiences that had tormented them and narrowly defined them lost their power to rule their lives.

It isn't easy to forgive, because it is most needed when a person is locked into a painful sense of loss, and confusion. Wanting everything to have been different than it was does not change anything. If you are holding on to a grievance or grudge toward someone in your family, you know exactly what he or she did or said that hurt you, that didn't meet your expectation, or disappointed you in a personally significant way. Each time you revisit the grudge, the burden of it grows heavier and more burdensome, and assumes an even greater quality of reality. As time passes, more of the present gets associated with the past and becomes the filter through which you participate in the relationship. If you allow this to continue long enough, the grudge consumes your love, runs your life, and interferes with any effort to improve the relationship. In a very real sense, then, your grudge becomes the wall behind which your love is trapped, and you pay the price for building it. You get to live what you cannot forgive.

But wait! What if your relative really was in the wrong, really did disappoint you, or really did hurt you with words and actions? The fact is that these are all positions taken exclusively from your own point of view. As long as you are committed to holding onto them, you will be unable to see the situation from the point of view of the person needing your apology. When you look at the same experience from the other person's point of view, it becomes obvious that there is more than one way to view the experience, and that other points of view may contain elements of truth.

What do you lose when you let go of a grudge or grievance? You lose an attachment to the past and its ability to negatively influence your present and future. What do you gain? The ability to learn something about yourself. The ability to discover something interesting about the other person. The ability to shape the future so that tomorrow is different from yesterday. And the ability to move into that future unencumbered by the past.

The idea that the other person does not deserve forgiveness is a common stumbling block to making an authentic apology. But in truth, forgiveness is not about whether the other person deserves it, but whether you are willing to have something other than pain and heartache in your relationship. Ultimately, it comes down to a decision you make about whether you want to decide how your life and relationship turns out, or you want to default on that decision and turn it over to your relative. That's why the act of forgiveness can be such a liberating experience! It is an acknowledgement of your ability to determine for yourself how your life turns out, rather than turning that power over to the object of your anger and claiming that it is the source of your hurt. No one can make you forgive another, so in a way it is a profound act of personal empowerment.

The Power of Forgiveness

Forgiveness is an incredibly powerful transformational force, and perhaps that is why it is so difficult to do. It often seems easier to blame relatives for what you experienced, because they were older than you, had more power than you, or their behavior was inexcusable by any standard of reasonable and decent behavior. It seems so real and so obvious that they are to blame that it is hard to see it any other way. And anger is the wind that blows out the lamp of the mind and makes it impossible to think clearly. Nevertheless, it was your choice to react the way you did, to interpret events the way you did, to hold on to what they did.

At some point, though, you realize that it feels awful to be angry. It can affect your emotional stability with others, and it can have damaging impact on your health. To end the damage, you've got to do one of two things: Either look at the situation from the other person's point of view, or seek to gain some advantage in understanding yourself as a result of it. You may discover how it hurts when people don't forgive you. Why inflict such hurt on someone else? Or you might realize that people do the best they can with the limited resources they have on board, and that their best may not have been what you wanted it to be, but it was their best nonetheless. It wasn't about you, it was about them anyway. Everyone makes mistakes. Everyone gets confused, and everyone inadvertently offends someone by what they did or didn't do or say. It isn't personal. Or you might realize that you are missing out on the majesty and wonder of the present moment by carrying around the past. Or you might recognize that self-interest is a primary motivation for all human beings, and that your problem with your relative has to do with self-interest being his or her highest priority and your own self-interest being your highest priority, and that this is an ordinary and unsurprising aspect of life, love, and relationships. So really, why be upset about something so ordinary? Why not do something extraordinary, move into the *Dimension of Greatness*, and just let it go?

The amount of time you allow yourself to waste on something that cannot be changed in the past is up to you.

Melina told us:

> I just don't want to waste any more time thinking the worst about other people. Life is too short. As the surfers say in Hawaii, "Acknowledge. Move on."

Give Peace a Chance

Forgiveness may be all that is necessary for you to get on with your life. But if you want the relationship to have another chance, and you need a way to get things back to where they once belonged, an apology is the restorative act that makes this possible. Where forgiveness is the end point of a past event's influence on you, an apology is the beginning of the future of the relationship. And asking for forgiveness is at the heart of an apology.

An apology is not an admission of guilt. Many of the things that people apologize for are innocent actions and statements that have been misunderstood by someone else. An apology offers some consolation for the misunderstanding, without having to agree with someone else's interpretation of the event. It is a way to acknowledge to the other person that your words or actions had the unintended consequence of causing harm.

Many of those we interviewed had difficulty understanding how something so right could turn out so wrong. How was it possible for the well-intended apology to fail so miserably? We heard numerous stories of apologies offered and rejected, and in each case, further examination revealed a common pattern. We have a name for that pattern, in the form of a made-up word: *dextification*. Here is how it might look in a dictionary:

dex·ti·fy (v.)

1. To defend, explain, or justify while claiming to apologize.
2. To hold oneself as blameless for a variety of reasons.
3. To have a good excuse for actions that produce mental or emotional distress in others.

It seems that failed apologies are almost always the result of defending, explaining and justifying one's own behavior and intentions. And that is typically what happens when an apology fails to set things right. While the intentions behind dextification are good ones, they fail to take into account the impact of the behavior, and focus instead on the reasons for it. The relative receiving the apology will feel excluded from the apology, since the apology is more about the person who is apologizing, about the apologizer's "reasons and excuses," rather than about the feelings of the person for whom it was intended.

This is hard for the receiver to hear, because he or she is feeling some pain or distress. The receiver's response to this dextification is almost always a reiteration of his or her own pain and injury. Of course that means the apologizer will try again and give another round of dextification, which then leads to more from the receiver about the pain caused, and so on. This can go on for days, weeks, months, and even years!

In the case of Jennifer and her mom, for example, Jennifer tried to apologize a number of times. Yet she failed each time. Why? Because of her dextification. She tried to explain away her own behavior, and at the same time, unintentionally, made the case that her mother was wrong to be offended. Jennifer's well-intended apologies all had a tendency to sound like "I'm sorry, but…I was tired." and "'I didn't mean to hurt you, but…I was burned out, stressed out." Every time that Marilyn heard the "but…" she stopped listening while Jennifer kept talking! Jennifer had so much to say, and none of it was heard. She defended what she did. She explained what she did. She justified what she did. And she could, too. After all, she had been at her wit's end that day. She wasn't thinking clearly. She didn't mean any harm. She was sleepy. Cranky. And so on. Marilyn met all of this with the cold shoulder and then complained to her other daughter that Jennifer didn't love her, didn't have time for her, and didn't appreciate her at all.

If you want to apologize to a relative successfully, in order to end the conflict and return the relationship to either a positive or neutral condition, you've got to fight your urge to dextify. Instead, put yourself in your relative's shoes. See the event through your relative's eyes. Listen to what you said through the other's ears. You don't have to take your relative's side, or accept the blame, but you do have to empathize with it, and be sincerely sorry for doing something or saying something, that was taken in a way that caused distress. "I am really sorry you felt I wasn't being understanding."

Before offering your apology, it may help you to conduct a few mental rehearsals first. That way, you will have a stronger sense of the gist of it, of what you want to say and why you're going to say it.

With all of this in mind, here is a recipe for a successful apology:

1. Let your relative know that you care about them and that you care about the relationship. Place the value of the relationship above any particulars of it.
2. Apologize without dextification. Let your apology be about your relative instead of about you.
3. Wait for your relative to respond, and listen closely to the response when it comes. Whatever your relative has to say, hearing and understanding it must take precedence over your reactions to it
4. Set a new direction for the relationship that makes a fresh start on a foundation of mutual positive intent.

Jennifer was ready to give up on her mom and never see her again. And though on the surface she said her mother "was crazy," inside she felt deeply hurt because she had tried so hard, only to be rebuffed and rejected. Meanwhile, her father and sister offered their encouragement and urged her to keep trying. They gave her all kinds of advice, like, "It's more important to have love than to be right," and that not talking with her mother over some little thing was too great a shame, even though she might feel her mom was keeping it going.

One day, Jennifer was doing her laundry, packing for a business trip that would take her to the city in which her mother lived. She had no plans to call her mother while in town, though it saddened her deeply that their relationship had come to this. Then, in a flash, it hit her: What if something happened to either of them, and she never had the opportunity to speak to her mother ever again? Jennifer loved her mother, faults, foibles, and all, and the thought of losing her before this got resolved was too much! She felt a great urgency to do something. But what she had been doing wasn't working. What else could she do?

The answer swept through her in an instant: She had yet to try looking at this from her mom's point of view, stubbornly clinging to her own instead. What was it her mom was talking about that day, anyway? What was it that she needed? What was it that she had wanted to hear? And suddenly she understood what she had to do, and that it needed to be done as quickly as possible.

Hours later, when Jennifer arrived in her hometown, the first thing she did was call her mother. She said, "Mom, I just landed at the airport, and you're the first person I've called. I'm here on business, but the most important business is making sure you know how much I love you." She told her how much she had missed talking with her these last six months. She said she was sorry for everything that had happened, and that she would love to get together if her mother had time for her, and start over, start afresh. She told her that her weekend was wide open, and asked her when would be the best time to come over? And her mom's anger melted away.

Chapter 10

Changing Your Reactions

Your reactions to relatives, other people, and situations are a group of triggers we call *associations*. It comes as no surprise that the word "association" is related to the word "relatives." What may come as a surprise is how powerful associations are in determining your relationship to your relatives, and how much leverage they give you to change your world! That's because your world is constructed from your associations, and your associations determine how you relate to the world.

You know firsthand how this works. You associate certain songs with certain years, months, or even days in your life. If you hear those songs, you are instantly transported back in time. You associate certain foods with comfort, or home, or love. Catch a whiff or taste of them and you are reminded of some other place. A car, a bike, a wagon, a name, a face, or a stupid jingle from a commercial can all work their magic on your perceptions, feelings, and thoughts. Your associations serve as triggers for memories, attitudes, and opinions, and these triggers generally exist outside of your awareness, attached to your senses of seeing, hearing, feeling, smelling, tasting, or combinations of these sensory experiences. And this is no static event. Your mind is constantly making new associations and reinforcing old ones.

You probably didn't decide to attach a particular song to a certain time of your life, but your mind did that for you. You can use this process of making associations on purpose, and you already do! There you are, in your kitchen, with your hand on the refrigerator handle, when you suddenly remember that your keys are in your bedroom. You close the refrigerator door, release the handle, walk to your bedroom, and then find yourself having a memory lapse. "What am I doing in here? What did I come in here for?" So what do you do? You go back to the refrigerator and put your hand on the handle, and that helps you to remember, "My keys!" Sound familiar? Do you wonder why this works? Is it a magic refrigerator handle? No, but you were holding the handle when you thought about your keys, and that formed the short-term association between the two objects.

You won't always think of your keys whenever you touch the refrigerator handle because you touch it too many times, while thinking too many different things, so it all just collapses together. Some associations come together quickly and then fall apart when no longer useful. But other associations last for years, even a lifetime, whether they are useful or not. What makes an association stick? Repetition and intensity are the processes that lock associations into your nervous system. Repetition, like the song that plays over and over and over until you can't get it out of your mind. Intensity makes an experience memorable, like getting terribly sick after eating a certain food, and then not wanting that food for a long time afterward.

People can trigger memories, attitudes, emotions, and opinions, and there is no better example of this than in a family. Because our contact with certain family members is repeated countless times over time, just seeing or talking with them can bring out the best or the worst in you. If you ever had a repeatedly negative interaction with someone, or a particularly intense one, then you know how just the thought of that person can trigger powerful emotions and responses in you. You have associations piled up on top of each other, some going back to infancy, a time when they may have made a formidable impression on your psyche.

You form associations because of the roles you play in your family's dynamics. Perhaps Father had the role of the lord and master. "Just wait till your father gets home…" Perhaps Mother played the role of the caretaker. "Eat, eat, what can I get you?" Perhaps a sibling played the role of boss in the lives of the younger siblings or served as a surrogate mother, caring for or advising during the absence of a parent. Then there is the role of the child who is dependent on parents, and therefore yields to their demands. And there is the role of the rebel, polarizing in reaction to the controlling behaviors of parents.

As you grow up, you learn to associate certain roles with certain people and certain roles with yourself, and in this way, your associations become a part of your personality and behavior toward yourself and others. As you matured and left the nest, you probably took on new roles, but you may not have left the old ones behind. If they are still active, they will activate in the presence of the relatives with whom you learned them, through repetition and/or intensity, sometimes on a daily basis over the course of many years. How else do you explain the 60-year-old mother who is not just asking but telling her 30-something child what to do regarding dental hygiene? Can you imagine her telling such things to members of her bridge club? Probably not. And so, because of the associations formed regarding the roles that were played in your family, the fact that you are a mature, secure, independent person can dissolve in the blink of an eye during an interaction with your family.

Amalya told us:

> My husband pointed this out to me. He told me, "When we are there at your family gatherings, I don't even recognize you. You are really protective, really scared, very shut down, and you hardly say anything. It's like you become the opposite of your usual self."

And in that sudden transformation from who you are to what you were, all the skills you've learned, the attitudes you've developed, and the ways of being that you cultivated, the ones that seemed so natural and automatic to you, disappear in the onslaught of family associations.

Baina told us:

> I think I've developed some effective communication skills as an adult. With the man in my life, I have no problem asking for what I want, or stating my intention clearly and directly. I'll say, "I'd like to tell you about something and what you can do to help me is to listen and reflect back, but first let me rant for a while." And he gets it immediately. But when I am with relatives, all that learning and development somehow goes away and the six-year-old in me comes out once again. I mean, I am 48 years old! And I can't believe how fast I can immature!

While associations may be powerful, they are subject to change. But changing them requires that you identify the triggers for them. If you know what those triggers are, you can defuse them ahead of time, or ameliorate their effect with strategies that have taken them into account. What follows are some strategies that you can use to change your associations and create new ones with your family.

Strategy 1: Create Neutral Turf

Frederick told us:

> I woke up one day and realized my parents aren't going to be around forever. They don't have any children or grandchildren that live near them. They can't reach out and grab someone to love once a week. So Marie and I made a commitment that we will spend one week a year with her parents and at least one week a year with my parents. But to do it in a way that allows us to develop new and more loving relationships, our strategy is to go on vacation with them on neutral turf, somewhere outside of their nor-

mal day-to-day lives. After all, the main reason we get together with them is to have some quality time with them, because we know there will be a day when there won't be quality time.

The problem with visiting them in their homes is that it creates a lot of confusion about roles and pecking order. Their house isn't your house, and the rules are different. In my home, I don't usually make the bed in the morning. But if I don't make the bed at my parents' home, my mother will do it for me. That's a pattern we developed when I was a boy. In my home, breakfast is no big deal. But in my parents' home, it is a very big deal. My mom was the traditional, stay-at-home, take–care-of-everyone mom. So when we visit their home, she asks us what we want and then makes our breakfast dreams come true.

But from my wife's point of view, around my mom and my dad, I become their son in many ways, and they become the responsible parents. It disturbs my wife, who starts viewing my behavior as lazy, or thinks of me, and us, as taking advantage of a 77-year-old lady. It's ironic that while my mom and I can comfortably fall back into the old roles, the old patterns, it creates problems for me in my more immediate family relationship with my wife. But what can I do when I'm in their home? If I stepped into the kitchen and tried to get a pan to make myself breakfast, my mom would be elbowing me out of there like we were hockey players

I see the same thing when we go to the home of my wife's parents, although it doesn't bother me the way it bothers her. Obviously her parents love her dearly, and if her mother wants to bake her favorite German chocolate cake, then I say God bless her for that! From my point of view, it makes her mom happy to make that cake, though I recognize that it is a lot of work for her.

Frederick and Marie were in a real dilemma. By allowing their mothers to fulfill the roles they associate with their children, they came to feel uncomfortable about taking advantage of them. And for the moms, while they may enjoy their role as provider of breakfast and baker of yummy treats, doing so probably was a lot more work now than it was in their younger years. Yet their associated roles seemed to obligate them to behave in this predictable way. Both Frederick and Marie have told their moms not to go to "all that trouble," but it doesn't do any good. They do it anyway. The associations to family and home are too strong for them to resist.

That's where neutral ground proves to be solid ground for an evolving relationship, because it eliminates the sense of obligation.

Frederick continues:

At my in-laws' home, you would think they had an international sports channel broadcasting out of their living room. My father-in-law has a large screen TV, with that picture-in-picture feature. Then, he has another TV on top of that TV, and it also has the picture-in-picture feature. Then there's a third TV to the side. Really, it looks like the control room at CNN! He has a board with remotes velcroed to it, so they can watch and control all the TVs simultaneously. If I sit down and watch for five minutes, my head starts spinning and I think I am on some kind of hallucinogenic sports drug! I don't know what sounds match what picture, or even what it is that we're watching. My mother-in-law has learned to live with and schedule around the sports center, but she is less tolerant about life revolving around the televisions when company is present in the form of visiting relatives. That can lead to conflict between her and my father-in-law.

When we meet on neutral turf, a lot of that stuff disappears. People aren't obligated to clean up the house before, during, or even after the visit, because we're not in a house, we're in a hotel, or a resort, or on a ship, and these things are taken care of. They don't have to even get into those roles. The normal agendas are disrupted, because there's no bridge club, nothing that needs to be picked up, no need to compete for attention or to get distracted, no hockey game calling out for attention. On neutral turf, my mother-in-law doesn't have to be critical of the sports center when company is present. It's not an issue.

It is interesting to note that not only do they have roles, but the roles reinforce other roles in a sort of role chain reaction. While Mom might be able to tolerate the sports center when it's just her and her husband, once family arrives, she takes on a critical role with her husband, to which he reacts with his "I'm in control here" role, which then changes how everyone else in the house feels and reacts.

Frederick continues:

Every few years, or when some big life cycle event comes along, we surprise them and put the airfare and hotel in a card as a present. We usually meet up outside the U.S. That's because Marie and I work for large companies, and we are always hooked to cell phones and pagers. When we leave the country, those things don't work so well, which helps us break free of our work roles so we can enjoy our families.

There are so many advantages to all of us in meeting somewhere outside our normal lives. At this point, we all have agreed to never go back to the same place twice, just to avoid our vacations becoming too much of a routine. We have now developed vacation roles, but they're not so hard to live with because they are constructive and based on the present instead of the past. We have softer expectations of each other. For example, when we're meeting my parents, I always arrange the land transportation. My dad loves foreign languages, so he works on learning the important phrases ahead of time. He is proud of his ability to do this, and we compliment him on his outgoingness and willingness to talk to strangers, which makes him feel great. My mom is in charge of deciding the tour we're going to do. These travel roles have evolved informally. For example, we used to get into the Yes behavior you describe in your book, *Dealing With People You Can't Stand*. You know those patterns, like "What do you want to eat?" "I don't know, what do you want to eat?" "I don't know, are you hungry?" "I don't know, are you? Whatever you want is fine with me." My parents are extremely polite and always want someone else to make the decision about where to eat. They would say, "I don't care, I don't care, I don't care." And the truth is they really didn't care, until afterward, when it turned out they wanted something else. Now we go to all-inclusive resorts, or on cruises, and the restaurant part of it comes with the package. We make a schedule: Monday here, Tuesday there, and now that indecision is taken away. We have been doing this for going on ten years. We tag the first week of January for her parents and Thanksgiving week for mine. We have only been in the U.S. for one Thanksgiving or Christmas in 17 years. Her parents prefer to spend Thanksgiving with the other sisters anyway, so that's why we sorted it out that way.

Notice that when the location changes, the roles tend to change too. And you don't have to leave the country to apply the power of Neutral Turf. The key here is to leave normal surroundings behind that might lure people into old patterns and deprive them of the joys of this moment in time. Many of the people we talked with shared examples like Frederick and Marie's, where their parents or siblings seemed like different people, flexible, happy, resourceful people, once they got together in new surroundings.

Strategy 2: Create a New Dynamic

Just as each person has family roles, so family dynamics change according to which family members are present. How you are with your mother may be different from how you are when you are with your mother and father together.

Kira told us:

My overriding goal when I am with my parents is to remember who I am in my life now. I got tired of going home and reverting to the stupid and uncomfortable teenager I once was. I now spend time with each of my parents separately, rather than with everybody together. It is so much easier to develop a positive relationship with them one on one, because when they are together, it's like gravity pulls them into their parenting roles. I schedule time with each of them, and they like it so much that they've returned the favor. Now sometimes they visit me the same way, just one at a time, for some quality time together.

I find that this has really helped me to see them as people instead of the larger category of "parents." It feels like we have so much more common ground. I did this to survive, you know. I used to find that time with my family was like walking through a minefield. Now I'm able to avoid the mines.

Andy says:

Strategically, I prefer to visit my family when it's just me. By keeping the number of people down, I have more space. No sisters! Both my sisters are boisterous, and they put me to shame when it comes to talking. That makes it hard to have any private time with my parents. Likewise, I prefer to visit my sisters when my parents aren't around. It sounds odd, but we're all much closer now.

In these examples, one-on-one time proved to be a new dynamic. But sometimes you can change the dynamic by adding more people!

Roger says:

My wife and I both have a positive relationship with my mother. We used to call her separately, but noticed how much more fun it was when we talked to her together, with one of us on the extension. The group dynamic of the three of us is more lively, more entertaining, and leads to less annoyance and irritability than when it was just me and her or my wife and her talking. In the past, I found that I got irritated at having to repeat things I had already told her a few times. Having the three of us on the phone keeps me from getting frustrated, because my wife can find a way to repeat what I said in a way that my mom hears it. Our group conversations are more like a party line. Nowadays, we might spend 30 to 45 minutes all hanging out on the phone together in a single conversation. That never happened when we took turns.

Strategy 3: Find a New Environment

As we said earlier, places (such as the house you grew up in) are triggers for associated memories, attitudes, behaviors, and opinions. In fact, the power of these associations is so strong that some people find it necessary to leave town in order to get some geographic distance from the pain or heartache of the past. The home you grew up in or the city in which you lived as a child will almost certainly contain some powerful associations, whether positive, negative, or both. If you stay in your old bedroom when visiting your parents, that is bound to stimulate old associations. A 37- year-old man told us how uncomfortable it was for him to go to his grade school daughter's PTA meeting because of the negative associations he had with being in a school.

It wasn't that he had been ostracized or had any major traumatic experiences in the school environment. But he associated the feelings of being trapped and bored with being in a classroom, and simply sitting in one of those small chairs in his daughter's classroom was enough to bring it all back.

Kira says:

> When I visit my parents and spend time alone with my dad, we like to go to the Japanese gardens because it supports us in being a bit more calm, centered, and having perspective. It was in the Japanese gardens that he was once honest with me about a problem he observed in my relationship with Mom. He told me how I sometimes got short and irritated with her, and then hypercritical, after which I'd feel angry at myself. If he would have told me this while were in their house, I suspect I would have had a hard time hearing it. But the gardens were such a calming environment that I was able to hear his feedback rationally instead of reactively. Something about the calm of that place allowed me to really hear it from him.

Strategy 4: Gain A New Perspective

Perspective is a matter of looking at details in the context of the big picture, and seeing the larger significance of a person or situation. You will find exceptional power, for example, in seeing your own parents in the context of their own childhood. As their behaviors take on a more innocent quality, it becomes apparent that much of what they did that bothered you in your childhood was actually something they learned in their childhood to cope with their own circumstances.

Lilia told us:

> In the big picture of life, I have discovered that this moment will pass all too quickly. So when I am with my parents, I am acutely aware that this is the one moment we have for sure, and there are no guarantees that there will be another one after this. Lucky for me, I got this new perspective without having to go through a traumatic loss. But a dear friend of mine wasn't so lucky. She lost her parents in an accident, and when she told me that her last conversation with them was an argument, it really got my attention. I thought, "Do I want my last conversation with my parents to be one about anger and frustration?" And the answer was a resounding "No!"

Elle told us:

> I was extremely critical of my mother for years, and I finally figured out why. You see, I used to identify closely with her when I was growing up, probably because of all the comparisons everyone else in the family made, especially when I was little. My aunts and uncles all said, "You look just

like your mother!" and "You sound just like your mother!" When they said the same things to her about me, she seemed flattered, but as I got older, I started noticing some of our similarities and got really concerned. At least a few times in my life, I remember I actually felt doomed to become just like her. When I was 30, I would open my mouth and hear my mother coming out, like telling my own children, "Here is how you should eat that soup," and "You should take a jacket." It made me mad, and I acted out my anger.

But the behaviors I used to be so critical of in my mother are less threatening to me now than when I was younger. That's probably because I am learning to accept her as she is, and I'm also learning to accept myself. The less harsh I am with myself, the more tolerant I am with her. I can trace this back to a big realization I had a few years ago. It dawned on me that just as there are a few similarities between us, there are lots of differences, and I am not the same as her. I started looking for the differences, and then I started enjoying them. Now I just want to know her for who she is, instead of who I thought she was when I was afraid of whom I was becoming.

Now when I open my mouth and hear my mother, I am more likely to react with laughter. It is my choice to be frustrated or laugh at it. I can let it bother me and everyone gets to have a bad time or I can laugh it off.

Li Mei told us:

I recognize now that my parents are just people who, like me, have needs and insecurities. Our parents are someone else's children too, and knowing this means I don't always have to think of myself as the child when I'm around them. They want to be loved and accepted, they need reinforcement when they do nice things, and I can do these things for them instead of always wanting them to do these things for me. This perspective is a powerful one. A parent can look at his or her adult child and see how independent the child is. And a child can look at a parent and see the child inside. By changing the age reference point, people can realize that their parents and children have their own lives to lead, mistakes to make, and lessons to learn, instead of taking everything about each other personally.

Ben told us:

When I go to a family gathering, I consciously say to myself, "Just visiting." If something weird happens, I smile to my wife and say, "JV". This immediately puts it in perspective for me. Whatever is going on is not going to go on forever. In fact in the scheme of things, the visits are always short, so no matter how weird things get, I know that it will be over soon.

Strategy 5: Reverse the Roles

Another way to break associations in roles is to actually switch roles. Dov told us:

Now that I have income of my own, I can send my parents gifts. That has been a fun role reversal for all of us.

Joe told us:

My dad, who is in his eighties, used to pick me up at the airport whenever I came to town on business. It was great to see him, but his driving was a little spacey. Usually, I would be all wound up from a cross-country flight, and so it was easy to get irritable with him. Not to mention adjusting to the 3-hour time difference, which was a matter of concern because it meant getting up really early for my business meetings, and here was Dad driving slow, people honking, and me giving him a hard time, which only added to his distractions from driving. What should have been a nice visit would start off this way every time, with me getting irritable, then feeling bad about getting irritable, then feeling frustrated about feeling bad, and so on like that.

The turning point was the day I decided to come in a day early so I could have some time to adjust to the time difference. Knowing that I wouldn't have to get up early the next day did a world of good for my mood, and I noticed that I wasn't all stressed out about Dad's driving. So the next time I came home, I again arrived a day earlier, and asked Dad if I could drive, telling him it would be "fun" to drive in my hometown again. And that's when he told me a real shockeroo…He hated driving at night, because he couldn't see that well, and I was welcome to drive. In fact, he said he would prefer it! And it turned out that he had always assumed he was supposed to drive, because, well, he was Dad, and Dad always drives! My driving was a real role-reversal, and we were both more relaxed and had a really good time in the car and all the next day. We had very different conversations too, because it seemed like we had met on a new level. Now, I not only do the driving when I visit, but I also do my fair share of picking up the tab when we go out to dinner.

Simon told us:

I like to call my son for advice. He is very adept on the computer. I remember the first time I asked him for advice; it was a magical moment for both of us. It was a complete reversal of our normal roles. At first it was strange and tentative, but then he got to talking. We ended up staying on the phone much longer than we normally do, and it wasn't just the computer talk because we were finished with that in the first half of the conversation. We just kept going, talking about all kinds of things. Switching roles like that allowed us to get out of the traditional father-son roles and just meet as two adults with some common interests.

Strategy 6: Find the Right Time

Have you ever been in a hurry, too busy to talk, with deadlines to meet, and a relative called to talk? Your reactions to people can be related to where you are on the blood sugar curve, your hormones, the length of your to-do list, your overall energy level, and whatever you have going on at the moment. That's why it is important to find the right time for dealing with relatives.

Pierre told us:

I try to control the circumstances when I talk to them. I am a call screener, and I make no apologies for that! I learned that if I am focused on something else and talking to my parents at the same time, there's a very good chance that I'll say something that gets me in trouble with them. If it isn't a good time for me, I could become short-tempered or impatient, and that could push their buttons. So even if I hear my mother's voice on the machine, if I can't give her my full attention, I don't touch the phone. I don't want to spend precious minutes, days, or even months apologizing for my behavior anymore. Now that I decide when to talk, the good energy between us has had a chance to grow.

Of course, nobody's perfect, and sometimes, even when I think it's the right time, it turns out it was a bad time for her. So I also make sure to apologize as quickly as possible for any misunderstanding, even when it isn't my fault.

Tyrell told us:

One technique we use when we're expecting a call from a friend is "the signal ring." We tell them we're screening calls, but that if they need to reach us, just let it ring once, hang up and call right back. Lately, we just don't answer the phone unless we know who is calling. We do check the voice mail, though. This has virtually eliminated all the marketing calls, the wrong numbers, and helped us contain the time we spend talking to our sometimes too-friendly relatives. I have 35 people related to me all living within a ten-mile radius of my home. If they need me, they can always come over to get me. I have an aunt and uncle who always want to invite us over for dinner, to discuss certain topics. But my wife and I are not really interested in those topics, nor do we enjoy dinner with them. Since they don't know the signal ring, their calls automatically go to voice mail, and that gives us enough time to strategize how we're going to weasel out of their invitations. Even my mother doesn't know the signal ring, so please make sure to change my name in your book. The reason I don't tell her how to get through is because I only want to talk with her when I have nothing else going on. Otherwise, it's too easy for her to push my buttons. All in all, there are only 20 people who know the signal ring. You are number 21. But if you tell anyone else, I'll have to kill you.

Strategy 7: Change Your Mode of Communication

As we pointed out in our book *Dealing With People You Can't Stand*, there are meaningful differences between face-to-face, phone, and written communication. Each has its own advantages and disadvantages.

Alice told us:

> In the past I haven't been very open with my sister. But I find that, thanks to e-mail, she and I can share all kinds of things in writing that we never would have shared in person. We talk now about ourselves, our relationships, our ideas, our sex lives, all kinds of things. Even though we're far apart geographically, I think we're closer now than ever. I think it works like this because it breaks us out of old patterns by nature of it being relatively new in our lives. In person, we seem to fall back on old roles from our childhood. In writing, it is easier to relate to each other as the people we are now!

In this example, when the sisters are face to face, they trigger associations that affect their behavior. When they put it in writing, they are free to hear the words in any way they want, and to interpret them in any way they want. And because the give and take is punctuated by the time it takes to read and respond, no one interrupts anyone, and no one makes faces that the other can see and then must feel compelled to respond to.

Alice continued:

> As she and I have been more revealing about our own insecurities and jealousies, it has allowed us to speak in the same tone of voice with each other as we do with friends. E-mail has given us an avenue to get to know each other in a new way, and as a result, I've never felt closer to my sister.

Joe told us:

> I was amazed the first time I got an e-mail from my daughter, who is away at college. Everything she said sounded so mature, so clever, and so wise. Even though I knew it was from her, the difference in the "tone" of it stunned me. And when I replied, I think my communications were more thoughtful, respectful, and less controlling than I tend to be with her in person. It's like we were meeting as two adults instead of our normal father

and daughter roles. I had mentioned that to her and she said she noticed the same thing. I sounded completely different to her, like a "person."

Our favorite example came from Jane, who told us:

My doctor told me I needed to reduce my stress level because of my high blood pressure. So I had to think of a way to deal with my daughter. She is divorced, and the mother of 19-year-old twin boys. She used to call me all the time to vent her anger and frustration, but she would never let me give her any advice on how she might turn things around.

I devised a plan to stop this without having to resort to angry words of my own. We have caller I.D., so I called her one day when I knew she was not at home, and I left her a message to call me. When her call came, the message on our answering machine told her: "This is your mother. If you are calling to ask for help or advice, press 1. If you are calling to vent your anger or frustration, press 2 or stay on the line while I connect you with your father. If you are calling to tell me you love me, or to ask how I feel, press 3. If you are calling to chat, or have any other conversation, press 4. Remember, your mother does not like curse words or a loud voice."

Well, guess what? It worked! If she starts to tell me something angry now, I say, "It's time to press 2," and she laughs and stops immediately. Or else she says, "I'll call Dad later!"

Strategy 8: Change from the Inside Out

When you want to change your inner condition around problem relatives, your life is a reservoir of resources just waiting to be tapped. All you need is a model. Modeling the behavior and attitudes of others is a natural way to learn. When a child enters the world of pretend, it isn't just to have a good time. It is a safe way to model conditions and behaviors and try them on for size. If you ever swore to yourself that you would never to do or say what your parents did or said, and then noticed yourself saying and doing those things, that was your natural tendency to model at work. Since you can do it without even trying, imagine what is possible when you do it intentionally.

Start within to work this out, by following these three steps.

1. Find an Example

What is the inner condition you want to have around your relatives? How do you want to feel when they push the button? Confident? Calm? Assertive? Amused? Give it a name, and then find it, either in yourself, or in your idea of someone else. If there is an area of your life where you have that condition, you can model it and use it wherever you like. If you can think of someone who knows how to be the way you want to be, that's enough for you to model. In fact, your model doesn't have to be patterned after a real person, or even after someone that you know. If you believe that Indiana Jones or Oprah Winfrey have the inner abilities needed to handle your relatives, then you have enough information for successful modeling.

◆ *Find it in yourself.*
Maria wanted to be more objective about her mother's bad behavior. When she asked herself, "Where in my life do I have the ability to be objective?" the answer was obvious: Counseling others! Recently, she had graduated from a master's program in counseling. Her specialty was working with children. She found it easy to be objective with children. Their dysfunctional behaviors made sense, as the best choices they could make in their circumstances. Her objectivity gave her perspective and made her flexible in her communications. "Wouldn't it be great," she thought, "to have that kind of objectivity with my mother!"

◆ *Find it in someone else.*
Fred wanted to make his wife happy by learning to be more sociable at family gatherings. When visiting her family, her ongoing complaint was that he just sat there and didn't interact with anyone. It wasn't that he was antisocial. He just didn't have anything to say. When he asked himself, "Who do I know that knows how to be social?" he immediately thought of his friend Gary. That was someone who could be social with anyone at any time. He could walk into a room, start a conversation with a stranger, get everyone talking with everyone else, and make a party fun—all without having to be the center of attention. He knew how to draw people out, even quiet ones like Fred. Gary was an ideal model for the behavior that Fred wanted to have.

Once you've identified the needed condition, you want to make it real. This requires some focused concentration. Find yourself some place where you won't be disturbed and spend some time doing this really well. Because the more intense the experience of it, the more useful it becomes.

2. Explore the Example

Remember a time and place when you or your role model had the condition or ability that you want to model. The more details you can notice about it, the better this will work, because intensity and focus builds stronger associations than vague generalizations.

Maria closed her eyes and imagined herself when she's a counselor with children. She noticed her posture, her mental state, her breathing when in that situation. She noticed that her arms and shoulders were relaxed, and that her inner dialog told her that what she was doing was important.

Fred imagined what it would be like to be his friend Gary. "He seems so relaxed, comfortable with himself, and interested in others. His hands are open. His breathing is slow and easy." What kinds of things did Fred think Gary says to himself in a social situation? Things like, "Hmmm, that's interesting!" and "I wonder who that is?" and "I've got to see this for myself!" In Fred's mind, Gary seemed to lead with his heart, his hands, and a friendly smile. "He seems so at ease. Hey, maybe that's why everybody else feels so at ease with him!"

To add depth and definition to your example, spend a little time exploring the differences between how you want to be (as yourself, or as your role model), and how you've been in the past. Go back and forth between an example of each until the differences are obvious to you.

3. Move It and Use It

Now that you know what you want, and how it works, it's time to put it in the context where you need it. Where do you want this change to occur? When, specifically, do you want this inner condition to occur? If you can identify the exact kind of thing that set you off in the past, you can associate your new condition with it. Is it something your relative says? Something your relative does? Is it the look on your relative's face? If you think you know what it is, make the association. Close your eyes and imagine your relative doing or saying whatever it is that pushed your button in the past, only use your model to play out the fantasy. The more times you repeat this, the stronger the new association will become. Practice makes perfect!

Quick Summary

1. Create Neutral Turf
2. Create a New Dynamic
3. Find a New Environment
4. Gain a New Perspective
5. Reverse the Roles
6. Find the Right Time
7. Change Your Mode of Communication
8. Change from the Inside Out
   a. Find an Example
   b. Explore the Example
   c. Move It and Use It

Part III

Family Gatherings, Get-Togethers, Show-Ups, and Showdowns at the Not-OK Corral

Chapter 11

Know Your Magic Numbers

There are three "magic numbers" to know when it comes to dealing with your relatives: Geography, Frequency, and Time. These numbers can mean the difference between having a good time that strengthens your family relationships and having an awful time that damages relationships to the detriment of family. The purpose of knowing your numbers is to keep you as close to the Dimension of Greatness as possible, while keeping everyone you deal with out of the Danger Zone. These numbers are relative, of course, to the relatives you are dealing with. But ignoring them can be hazardous to your relationships.

Geography

Perhaps you've heard the song "How Can I Miss You When You Won't Go Away"? It refers to the value of distance in relationships. Do you live close to your relatives, or far away? How close? How far? What do you think about the distance between you? From the information we've gathered, keeping some geographic distance is the number one coping strategy people use to deal with relatives who are difficult to deal with. (It also happens to be a consequence of living in a highly mobile world full of opportunities. So if your relatives live far away from you, that doesn't necessarily mean they can't stand you!) Keeping your distance is easier to do in some countries than in others. In a large country, families have room to spread out. In smaller countries, keeping your distance is sometimes easier said than done, though some family members will try to get "as far away as possible." And because the borders of nations don't necessarily define one's possibilities or interests, some people view the world as their country and can put even more distance between themselves and their sometimes difficult relatives.

How near or far away a person lives from their family is bound to have an impact on how often that family can get together and how formal (planning required) or informal (spontaneous) such get-togethers will be. If you live nearby, visits tend to be more informal. If you live far away, visits are usually more formal. If you live in the same town, even if you're across town, then dropping by or spontaneously getting together becomes more of an option. If you live across the country, more planning is usually required. The farther away you live, the more time you will need to get together. The closer you live, the less time is required in a given visit.

Frequency

You've heard it said that absence makes the heart grow fonder, and familiarity breeds contempt. How often do you see your relatives?

Geography is just one of the variables that influences frequency of family contact time. The greater the distance, the less the frequency is possible. The less the distance, the more frequent the possible contact time. But regardless of geography, and thanks to the technology of telecommunications and e-mail, you still have to know your magic number on frequency. In every relationship there is an optimum number of times, whether in a week, a month, or a year, where you and your relative can both enjoy the relationship. And there is probably a number that represents too much contact, too often.

This number is likely to be different for you and your relatives. If you live in the same town, for example, you may find that getting together twice a month is perfect for you. Two contacts a month and you feel close to them, love hearing what's going on in their life, and enjoy their company. Your relatives, on the other hand, may want to get together more often. If they don't at least hear from you every few days, they feel abandoned or think that you don't care about them. In this case, you must weigh the relative value of holding the line with the frequency that works for you versus making concessions to their frequency needs. If two get-togethers a month is just right for you, but you notice that twice a month seems to make them act more needy with you, or worse, they pass into Danger Zone behavior, you might want to experiment with the frequency to find the magic number that works better for both of you. If getting together with them three or four times a month keeps them satisfied and out of that Danger Zone behavior, then a small adjustment can put your relationship on a better trajectory. Of course, the opposite could also be true. Suppose you notice that when you see them four times a month they get a little too involved in the everyday things going on in your life. They not only want to know what's going on, but they also want to give you unsolicited advice and opinions. In that case, you may decide that twice a month is the maximum frequency you can stand.

Jeff told us:

> We live about a mile away from my wife's parents, and I just dread the calls. We wonder what excuse they'll come up with today for getting together with us. Frankly, we get together with my wife's parents more than we do with our friends. We will be at dinner with them, and they'll tell us they want to come over for breakfast. I'm thinking, Hey, one meal with them a week is all the frequency I can handle. This counts! This is the meal! It is actually easier to make up an excuse, or even tell a lie, in order to have a little space in our lives. Lately I've tried using humor to get out of seeing them so often. I tell them I have so much to do tomorrow, I'm having my navel pierced! I laugh, they laugh, and hopefully that's the end of it.

Time

Time flies when you're having fun, and the opposite is also true. Too much time with relatives and some people start getting a little crazy. Not enough time together, and some people start making stuff up to account for those missing. How much time do you spend with your relatives when you get together with them? When you meet for a casual dinner, or plan a formal family event, what is the magic number of days, hours, and minutes that you can successfully enjoy the relationship before it moves into the Danger Zone? Though this magic number is important for everyone to know, it is particularly important when there are great geographic distances involved. A kind of "time distortion" occurs when relatives have to travel great distances to get together. Because of the expense and logistics involved, there may be a tendency to spend more time together than is optimal for anyone. To make matters more difficult, when you're the one who is visiting relatives, you may not have much private space in which to spend some of your time. And when you're around, your relatives may find it hard to get away too! The result is often that feeling of being "stuck" with the relatives instead of enjoying the family.

There is probably an optimum amount of time for you to enjoy a family visit. Once you cross that magic number of Time, it only takes one of you to drag both of you into the Danger Zone. That's why knowing your magic number can help you enjoy the relationship and contribute to the future of it by keeping your associations positive.

Sonja told us:

> The value of time? I have seen it plenty of times, both with my daughter and my mother. They love each other, and most of the time they get along great. Well, for about three days, anyway. At that point they start butting

heads. When we first arrive, my mother accepts my daughter as she is. But it never fails, after three days, she starts trying to control my daughter, which of course she cannot possibly do because of the fact that my only-child daughter is incredibly strong-willed. Tensions mount. They both feel bad about their reactions to each other, but both of them fall into the trap time after time. I have noticed, however, that if we limit our visit to three days and leave on the fourth day, neither of them crosses the line, they don't fall into the pattern, and we all leave wanting more, feeling great, and looking forward to the next visit.

Darrie told us:

I know that I have about a three-hour threshold with my family on any occasion. This makes the Christmas holiday a challenging situation, and I've had to come up with a way to make it work. Christmas for my family has traditionally revolved around two events, each of which consumes three hours or more. First, there's Christmas Eve at my uncle's house. It is a tradition that we eat beef stew, ceremoniously light real candles on their tree after dinner, and then settle in for a condensed reading of Charles Dickens's *A Christmas Carol*. I think my family has done some version of this forever. Then it's the Christmas dinner at the home of my parents.

My husband and I live about two hours away by car. We used to dread the holidays because it consumed so much time and energy. But for the past few years we have chosen to attend only one of the two events. This allows us some private time at home during the holidays, which we enjoy and yet still gets us together with family. We also choose to stay in hotels, despite my parents' attempts to get us to stay with them. This gives my partner and I some time for the two of us to be together and to open the presents we give each other privately. Though our parents at first found it hard to understand, my husband and I want to enjoy our personal relationship during this holiday too. If we stayed with my parents, there would be no respite except going to sleep and the feeling that we were "holed up" in the guest room. Without limiting the time we spend with them, an activity that otherwise ranges from barely tolerable to somewhat enjoyable would without a doubt become intolerable to us both. Neither of us wants to be miserable with the other during the holidays. We're just not willing to make that sacrifice. Limiting the amount of time we spend with my family has made the limited time we spend more enjoyable too, for us and for them. And we mix it up every year, so it doesn't feel like an obligation. This year we're going to spend Christmas Eve in the hotel and then go to my parents' home for breakfast on Christmas morning. After that, we'll open presents with them. Then we'll drive home and cook our own Christmas dinner and celebrate with friends. Since we change the pattern of family events each year, my parents now know that the holiday is sort of "up for grabs" as to what we'll do and when we'll do it. The result is that they don't take our visit for granted. They don't assume we will join them and then get mad if we don't.

Knowing your magic numbers of Geography, Frequency, and Time, and then setting limits around them, is crucial to making the most out of visits with relatives. Go over your limit, and you pay the price. But know your numbers, know your limits, and you're on your way to relative enjoyment.

Magic Number Worksheet

Pick a relative _____.

Geography

How far away do you live from this relative? _____.

How far away would you like to live from this relative? _____.

If your answer is that you live closer than you want to, evaluate if it is worth it to you to move. If moving is not an option, reduce the frequency of visits or time spent on any particular visit. If your answer is that you live too far away, evaluate the value of moving closer. If that isn't possible, you can increase the frequency of visits or time spent during visits.

Frequency

How often do you see this relative? _____.

Would you like to see them more or less than you currently do? _____.

What is the optimum number of times you would like to see this relative in a year? _____. In a month? _____.

What is your preferred method of getting together? _____ ___.

For example, you might find that seeing them once a month is good, but keeping in touch in-between with a weekly phone call or e-mail is just right.

What is the frequency of the different kinds of "getting together" that keeps the relationship positive and out of the Danger Zone? _____.

Time

How many days do your visits average? _____.

How many hours of contact do you spend with them on a visit? _____.

What is the optimum amount of time you and your relative can spend together comfortably? _____.

What is the amount of time you can tolerate before the relationship collapses into the Danger Zone? _____.

Chapter 12

Do an Obligation Evaluation

The feeling of obligation runs strong in most families, but stronger in some than in others. Parents who sacrifice everything for their children may develop a sense of entitlement, and children tend to be born with the attitude toward their parents that "This was your idea, you owe *me*!" Some family obligations are incurred by specific promises made ("I promise I'll call!") or not refuted ("I expect to hear from you when you arrive"), debts real and imagined ("The least you can do is show a little respect for my wishes"), and gratitude ("There is nothing I wouldn't do for you!"). The feeling of obligation can be the call of conscience ("I know how lonely they must be, I can't just ignore them"), or the demands of duty ("There's no one else who will take care of them, they're my parents, I will do what I must"). Some relatives attend to their own needs by intentionally cultivating a sense of obligation in others. And some relatives prefer to love with no strings attached, and to trust that what goes around will come around again. Whether internally or externally imposed, every person must eventually deal with their own sense of obligation to family.

Sometimes the feeling of obligation is your own creation. The dictates of duty and conscience can be powerful motivators that serve as the kick in the pants that gets you to do what is right when nothing else will do. But some obligations are conferred by others and act as an oppressive energy that breeds resentment. Because of this, some relatives take care not to impose a sense of obligation on others. Perhaps they feel an obligation to themselves to allow their relationships to be defined by love and freedom rather than by duty and guilt. Maybe they just prefer to let others make their own decisions and commitments. Other relatives confer obligation on to others as a way to get their way when they think there's no other way. When someone tells you that you "have to do it," they imply that you have no choice.

In fact, when it comes to family events, the feeling of obligation to attend is often accompanied by the belief that you have no other choice. As a result, many people think of family events as occasions when they're torn between "I have to" and "I don't want to." But on closer examination, these competing ideas offer important clues that you can use to resolve the feeling that you have no choice. To help you go from "have to" to "don't have to" to "don't want to" or "really want to!" we offer you a pre-obligation checklist. While you don't have to use it, you may want to give it a try.

Pre-Obligation Checklist

In order to bring conflicts to the surface and clarify your options, answer the following questions as honestly and openly as possible.

State the Nature of the Relative Emergency

What is the event to which you feel obligated to attend?
Where and when does this event take place?
What else do you have going on at that time?
Who is sponsoring it?
Who else is likely to attend?
What is involved in attending the event? Time? Money? Energy?
  How much?
What is the nature of your obligation to attend? Is it duty, conscience, a
  promise or commitment? Guilt? Fear?

Acknowledge Your Feelings

How do you feel about attending the event?
How do you feel about feeling that way?
How would you like to feel regarding the event?
Do you feel any pressure to participate? Where is it coming from?

Worst Case Scenario

Is the timing of this event in conflict with the timing of some other event?
Is the expense of attending this event in conflict with some other expense?
What is the worst possible outcome if you don't fulfill this obligation?
What is the worst possible outcome if you do fulfill this obligation?

Best Case Scenario

What is the best possible outcome of attending this event?
What is the best possible outcome of not attending this event?

What might you gain by attending the event?
What might you gain by not attending it?
What other options do you have regarding this event?

Count the Cost

Remember, whenever you say "Yes" to doing something, you're saying "No" to doing something else.

What do you lose by fulfilling the obligation?
What would you not get to do that is more important to you?
What do you lose by not fulfilling the obligation?
What would you not get to do that is more important to you?

Make Your Best Choice

There's no such thing as a *perfect* decision, but there is such a thing as your *best* decision.

Which of your options will cost you the least or gain you the most?
What do you choose to do?

If you choose to attend the event, then we invite you to use the strategies in the following chapters to make sure you've made the best choice.

Chapter 13

Know Your
Support Strategies

There will be times when your stressed-out loved ones could use your support but you are planning to visit other stressed-out loved ones and not-so-loved ones. And there will be times when you need to know how to get support from your loved ones so you don't have to be one of the relatives who is stressed out!

These times are related to the three stages of family events: before, during, and after. Giving and getting meaningful support can be an important aspect of each of them.

The Before Stage

Lighten the Load

Stress has a nasty habit of multiplying itself, building up over time until a single straw breaks the proverbial camel's back. Attending a family gathering preloaded with stress is a certain recipe for trouble. If your spouse (or child) is preloading, don't just stand there! When the stressful load falls, it could land on you! So when a family event is pending, you may find it a good idea to pick up some of your loved one's stress burden and lighten their load.

Diego told us:

> When a weekend is approaching that includes a visit with my wife's family, I pay attention to her anxiety levels. Going to see her family is often

stressful enough when we get there, so we do what we can to make sure we don't get there carrying a load of stress. For example, I take responsibility for anything in her workload that I can. Taking care of things like planning, packing, and all the details of getting the kids out the door have become my way of supporting her so we can arrive in a reasonable condition. I make sure the kids are totally handled, that they have the stuff they need for the trip and for the time we're at her family's home. Such a simple thing as being helpful in this way leaves her with the energy she needs to focus on preparing herself mentally, emotionally, and physically. This has so changed the way that she is with her family that I've noticed a change in all of them. They don't seem as reactive to her, and she isn't as reactive to them. At this rate, going to visit them could one day turn out to be fun!

Command Performance

Does your spouse's family have events everyone is expected to attend? In some households one person in a marriage draws a defensive boundary between themselves and their in-laws, hoping to keep them out or at least keep them away where they can't do them any harm. They resent the seeming need to show up at something that is of no interest to them, and tell their spouse that "It's your family, you go!" Nothing adds to stress like the message "You're on your own!"

It's good to know your limits, but it isn't good to draw a boundary that essentially abandons someone you love to the people that drive them crazy. And consider this: If your spouse's family is hard for you to deal with, chances are that they're even harder for your spouse to deal with! Just as many hands make light work, partnering on a mission of endurance makes for less to endure. Misery loves company, but you don't have to be miserable to have company in this endeavor. Do the command performances together, from a place of mutual support.

Bella writes:

Both of us have families that expect us to show up at family get-togethers. We both have a harder time with our own family. But we've made a pact to support each other rather than abandon each other in a time of need. We show up together for the command performances. We support each other in being polite with our difficult relatives, and we endure the difficulties together. We remind each other that this too will pass, and we pump ourselves up and tough it out, because we know that in a very short time we'll be able to return to our normal lives. What makes it bearable is doing it together. It's great not to have to deal with them alone.

Good Excuses

If someone in your immediate family really doesn't want to do something with the rest of your family that you particularly enjoy, chances are you'll have more fun going it alone than you would dragging them along. But there's no reason to cause any strain between the different members of your family—close, extended, or otherwise. In such a case, the best way to say "Excuse me!" without creating problems is to come up with a good excuse.

Marianne told us:

> Every summer my family goes on a fishing trip and they want us to come along. I enjoy it because my family is a lot of fun. But my husband doesn't like the whole outdoors camping thing, or catching and eating fish either. This year when the invitation came, I saw his face turn cloudy and I knew that he wasn't really wanting to get on board. So together we came up with a reason that he couldn't come, one my family would accept without creating bad blood between him and them. I'm glad we did it too. For me, the fishing trip was one of the best ever, because he wasn't there wanting to be somewhere else, and I wasn't distracted worrying about his feelings. We fished, we camped, and we ate fresh fish every night, right off the fire. And my husband . . . he enjoyed the time home alone! He said he turned up the stereo full volume and had it running nonstop while I was away!

The During Stage

Support Your Energy

When you feel burned out and irritable, you're more likely to say the wrong thing. You're also likely to realize the right thing to say at the wrong time. To keep wrong things and wrong times from wearing you down, you need to know how to keep your energy up!

Renee told us:

> I make sure to allow time during visits with my family to do the things that are important to me because they work for me. One thing that really works for me is working out. Not only do I feel better when I do it, but it keeps me in a better head space. I used to leave out the workouts during family visits, and it was hard for me to get through them as a result. Now it's a whole different thing. I have all the time I spend working out to myself, and that keeps my attitude and energy in just the right place.

Randy told us:

> When visiting family, the first thing I do is go out for an espresso, just like I would when I'm in my own home. This gives me a morning cushion before

dealing with everyone's stuff, and I can mentally prepare myself for the new day and its activities. When evening comes, I know what's coming next morning, so I have something to look forward to as we sit around at night.

Marta told us:

My mom loves to make cookies and cakes, and I love to eat them. Problem is, all that sugar gives me headaches and makes me cranky. And when I'm cranky, Mom and I have problems. So I've told her that the only time I'm going to eat the fun food is at night, so I can be fun for her to be with all day long.

Juanita told us:

I take naps in the afternoon, usually when my dad turns on the TV to watch sports. I used to sit around all day hating the sound of the TV and wishing I could be somewhere else, but not anymore! I tell my parents that taking naps is part of my health regime, and they not only accepted the idea, but my mom liked it so much that she does the same during my visits. Dad gets to watch sports in peace, and both Mom and I feel refreshed when dinner time rolls around. It's been great for everyone.

Steer the Conversation

Some conversations are like runaway trains. They start downhill, the brakes give out, and before you know it there's a messy crash, emotions are all over the place, and you just know that the clean-up is going to take a long time. Families are predictable, so you probably know by now that if certain subjects come up, the energy is going to go down. Such conversations rarely end up anywhere useful or leave anyone in a positive place. So it's in your interest to recognize the topics and talkers ahead of time, and have a plan for rerouting the train before it derails!

Dana told us:

Doug is my father-in-law. Sometimes when he's not around, my wife and my mother-in-law get into a Doug-bashing session. I used to let them go on. I guess I thought maybe it would lead to something useful. But nothing good has ever come from it. It is now obvious to me that such conversations only mean trouble. The gals get themselves so worked up over some little thing he's done or said that when he returns, a fight or argument is inevitable. The longer they go on, the harder it is to stop them. So I get involved now as soon as I notice that they're into it. Since my mother-in-law loves our kids, and my wife loves to brag about them, I just bring up their names, knowing they'll take it from there.

Remove Some Stress

If you can relieve a relative of just a little of their stress, your good deed will come back to you as an grateful family member who is easier for you to deal with.

Darren told us:

> My mother gets stressed when things don't seem to be getting done or she's worried about something. This has gotten worse over the years as she has aged, because she can't do as much cleaning as she used to. So we do things for her, and turn clean-up time into a family activity. We might say, "Come on kids, let's go outside and rake some leaves!" If she expresses worries about finances, I get on the Internet and do some research for information on refinancing. Anything she expresses worry or concern about is an opportunity for me to lower her stress load. The result is that instead of a stressed-out and worried mother when we visit, I get to enjoy her company.

Fred writes:

> My dad-in-law is kind of a dud, and being a dud around company drives my mother-in-law crazy. So I try to engage him in things, take him out for a game of golf, invite him to come with me for a run to the store, anything that gets him away from her and gives her a break. She's a lot happier when we visit now.

Get Some Space

The default choice for many people is to stay with the family members they visit. If you enjoy staying with them, then by all means continue to do so. But our interviews reveal that staying with relatives can be at the root of much of the difficulty that people experience on family visits. Do you really need to stay with your relatives when you visit? Is it wise to do so? You may find that it's worth it to you to make the extra effort and add the expense of maintaining some space of your own. Many of the people we interviewed who have happy family relationships say that getting a room somewhere (bed and breakfast, hotel, friends in the same town) gives them a feeling of security, just from knowing that they have a place to which they can retreat when the need for space arises.

Jane told us:

> We could stay in their house but then the stress goes to bed with us. After a couple of days, it takes a real toll. I like knowing I have a space of my own. A hotel room, for me, is like a light at the end of the tunnel. My husband

and I say we're tired, then we go back to the hotel, have a drink at the hotel bar, de-stress and get some perspective on the events of the day. Tomorrow then becomes a new day instead of just "another day." We've made a game out of finding a new out-of-the-way place to stay on every visit. I tell my parents that we learned to do this in marriage counseling and that it keeps our marriage alive. They don't want to mess that up, so they now support us in staying elsewhere!

MaryAnn says:

For a long time we were the ones making the effort and using our vacation money and time to get together as family at my parent's home. A few years ago we thought we should change that. Now we invite everyone to our town for the holidays. And sure enough, the whole family comes here now. We only have room for two people, so we do a drawing to determine who gets the spare room. It's sort of a holiday contest, and everyone likes the suspense and game of it. But what I like best is that I feel more in control in my own home, because I can bail out and go to my own room, or take the dogs for a walk, instead of feeling like I need a place to hide because it's someone else's home.

Adjust Your Attitude

There are all kinds of ways to give yourself an attitude adjustment that keeps your energy up during family visits. You can change your point of view so that family time is learning time.

Don told us:

I go to a family gathering looking for the value in it for me. I just assume there is some lesson in it and that if I learn something about myself from my time with them, it will make any pain I experience worthwhile. As a result, I've discovered how I came by many of my worst habits and attitude. I modeled them after my parents or developed them defensively to deal with my siblings. Just seeing where it all came from has made it easier, and more motivating, for me to change them.

You can lighten yourself up. Garth tells us:

I used to get really angry about my brother-in-law Pete, because I think he's an awful and unscrupulous person. But I've found a way to laugh instead of taking him personally. Now, I mentally attach the words "mental patient" at the end of whatever he says or what anyone else says about him. So if someone says his name, "Pete," I mentally attach the words "mental patient" right afterward. It really lightens me up and puts this lowlife in perspective. I actually learned this technique from my son. During a couple of his teen years he had a certain tone in his voice whenever he replied to any-thing I said to him. It sounded like he was adding "You jerk" even though he didn't say it out loud. It made me laugh, and that's how I remembered to try it on Pete, the "mental patient." I'm just like that. I like to laugh. When something, anything, rubs me the wrong way, I find that it is easier to let go of if I laugh at it. You ever hear someone say, "Someday I'll look back and laugh?" I say, why wait?

Or you can go with the flow. Jared told us:

When I get around relatives, I try to just decompress and let things happen however they want to. I don't mean shut down and be nonparticipatory. But really, family isn't like work, where I'm responsible for a lot of people working on projects, or where things need to be delivered. So if they're arguing about politics or religion or anything else that makes their blood boil and they ask me my opinion, I say that I'm just having a cup of coffee, or enjoying the furniture, or that life is too short to get hung up on this, that, or the other.

Suzi told us:

I used to have some pretty strong ideals about how things should be in my family. I always wanted more than it was possible to get, and I always came away disappointed. But then, thankfully, I finally realized that just because people are born of the same parents and raised in the same house doesn't mean that everybody is always going to be close or get along. Now that I accept the relationships for what they are, I find that they all have their moments. I'm no longer measuring each moment by my fantasies of how it "ought" to be. Instead, I'm choosing to enjoy them for what they are, exactly as they are, and take my happiness where I find it.

Or you can go on a treasure hunt. Here's how Faith describes this:

Attitude is so important, you have to look for the good. My dad used to play a game with me. We would go out for long walks, and in order to get me to walk another few minutes with him, he'd say pick a number between 50 and 200. Then we would walk that many steps, stop and look for treasure. And the neat thing was, when we looked, we always found something to treasure. Whether it was a pretty rock, a bug, or a leaf, branch, or flower, there was always something to appreciate as special.

So now when I go to a family gathering, I look for something to treas-ure, and sure enough, I always find something. It could be a three-minute conversation with an uncle or with a cousin I haven't talked to before. One time I was chatting with the 24-year-old son of my cousin and his girlfriend, people I didn't really know at all. They were fascinating people who were cool natural-food types and did interesting things in their lives. We had fun talking for an hour. And the only reason this conversation happened was that I had decided ahead of time to look for a treasure. I saw people I didn't know, and I sat down with them to see what treasure was there.

And you can listen from the inside instead of from the outside.
Dawn told us:

To really listen, to really hear what people are saying, I try and park myself in their shoes. I try to imagine being them and having the experiences they describe. And because I do this, I feel like I know my family much better than most people, and they seem more interested in me, too!

The After Stage

Though it is always nice when your baggage arrives after you've taken a long trip, some baggage is better left behind. When the family event is over, that's the time to debrief and de-stress the whole event in a supportive environment.

Surface the Stuff

Anything you stuffed at the family event may become stuff you're better off without. You may be able to wait until you get home, or you may need to bring it up on the way home and let it out sooner. But don't stuff the stuff any longer than you have to!
    Clarence told us:

On the drive home, the kids are usually asleep in the backseat. That's the time I know I can do a lot of listening. I know that if we wait until we get home, everything is more likely to get stuffed and shuffled off into the background of our normal day-to-day routines. So I usually bring up discussing our visit on purpose, because I know it will be good for her and ultimately us. I will ask her how she did, what she learned, what she would have done differently, questions like that. And when she does cope well, I always compliment her in order to reinforce it for next time. I also try to give her encouragement when she finds a positive angle for a negative experience.

Just Listen

You know how good it feels to just be able to say what you're feeling, dump it out without interruption, and have someone listen without trying to fix you or change your mind. This is a wonderful way to get everyone breathing again.

Carrie told us:

> I like knowing that at the end of the day I can vent with my husband. Knowing I'm going to have that outlet later makes it easier to hold myself together during the holidays. Once we're alone, we just let each other talk uninterrupted about how we're feeling about our family. Sometimes we talk about baggage from the past and how it affected us, and sometimes we talk about here and now stuff. We both come from equally crazy families. We have been married 21 years and we've been together 30 years. We've essentially grown up together, we know the characters, we know the play, and we know each other's issues with family. So we don't judge, give advice, try to influence—we don't even have to ask questions to understand—we just listen and empathize.

Make Light of It

Penelope told us how to make a game out of the whole event:

> My partner and I de-stress and lighten ourselves up by playing the "Didn't It Drive You Nuts" game. We name moments or things people said, and see if we have some common ones. We make good fun of it and have a good laugh about it. If something drove one of us nuts that didn't faze the other, we make that into a guessing game. "I bet it drove you nuts when . . . " and of course we try to guess each other's number one "It drove me nuts!"

Learn Something

Any experience you can walk away from after having learned something makes the next one easier to deal with. So when you debrief, here are some questions you can ask to make sure you've harvested as much learning from the experience as possible:

> What worked, what didn't work?
> What would you do different?
> What would you not do again?
> How was the timing of it, too long, too short; what would have been optimum?
> What is one thing that would have made it better?
> What are you glad didn't happen?
> What parts were worthwhile?

By applying a bit of support before, during, and after a family event, you can can reduce or eliminate past and future stress. And you may surprise yourself with how resourceful you can be in your interactions with difficult relatives!

Quick Summary

◆ **The Before Stage**
  • Lighten the Load
  • Command Performances
  • Good Excuses

◆ **The During Stage**
  • Support Your Energy
  • Steer the Conversation
  • Remove Some Stress
  • Get Some Space
  • Adjust Your Attitude

◆ **The After Stage**
  • Surface the Stuff
  • Just Listen
  • Make Light of It
  • Learn Something

Chapter 14
Rules of
Non-Engagement

When it comes to attending family events, you always have a choice:

1. Go
2. Go and suffer
3. Don't go

You've already examined these choices in the Pre-Obligation Checklist. If you decide to go, and you choose not to suffer, then you have two more choices:

4. Go with a different attitude
5. Go with a different attitude and behavior

To avail yourself of one or both of these two choices, we offer you the Four Rules of Non-Engagement:

1. Decide in Advance

If you wait to make the decision about responding to negative or controlling comments until you've begun your visit, events may overtake you. Instead, make a conscious choice before you arrive about the kind of experience you're going to have when you get there..

Liam says:

I make a conscious choice to have a pleasant experience, no matter what. By reminding myself what I want from this experience, I have more control over my state of mind and the tone of any conversations we may have.

But it isn't enough to make the choice not to have problems with a predictably argumentative relative. You also want to make a conscious choice about what topics to steer clear of, and what you will do if those topics come up. Consider what Carissa told us:

My mother-in-law has strong opinions about everything. Her argumentative nature is so strong that if I responded to the troubling things she said, just for the sake of discussion, I was guaranteed an argument, and more likely an attack, which almost always led to a fight with my husband in the car on the way back home after visiting her! But I now realize that I actually have a say over what ultimately gets discussed, because I can avoid the problematic topics when they come up. If I don't take the bait, the topic eventually goes away, and usually sooner than later. Now, on the way to her place, before I talk with her, I do a little talking to myself. I tell myself exactly what I'm willing to talk about and what I'm not willing to talk about no matter what, and I stick to it. The only thing I sacrifice is some spontaneity, a small sacrifice compared to the misery that saying what I think used to cause me! Really, I could care less if I express my opinion to her about those subjects. If she ever changes her attitudes, okay, I'll be open to having a more honest relationship with her.

How will you know what to avoid? Luckily for you, people are predictable. The things that set them off in the past are the same things that will set them off for the foreseeable future too! If they hook you the first time, it's understandable. But if they bait the hook and you keep jumping for it, you have no one but yourself to hold accountable for the mistake.

2. Plan for Sore Subjects

Joseane told us:

My husband's former mother-in-law is a sore subject with my in-laws. My husband told me a few stories about her, and she was apparently a real piece of work. Her name was Maggie. Mention her name to either of them and they spin off in anger. My father-in-law just tightens his jaw and keeps his thoughts to himself, though you can see it aggravates him just to think of it. But my mother-in-law has held on to her bad feelings about Maggie ever since my husband's divorce, and somehow she finds a way to bring up Maggie's name in every other conversation that she and I have. It took me a while to figure out how to handle it, because it comes up out of the blue. We could be talking about food, travel, pets, children, whatever, and then for no obvious reason, she brings up the subject and starts reacting to it. Next thing I know, she's telling the same story for the gazillionth time about how inconsiderate Maggie was, how mean she was, how absolutely awful she was.

I generally find talking with my mother-in-law to be a pleasure, but when she starts down the "Maggie" road, her whole tone changes. She sounds hurt and defensive, self-righteous and mad, all at the same time. I understand. Based on what she's told me, and on what I've heard from my husband too, Maggie had some serious psychological problems. If even half of what she's told me is true—and I think it is—Maggie has got to be a pretty miserable person. But my mother-in-law was really damaged from dealing with her. There's something there that she just can't get past, and she needs to resolve it somehow. That's how I see it, anyway. For the longest time I felt really bad for her. I used to try and convince her that she should live and let live, that this former problem person in her life is now gone and she should be grateful she doesn't have to deal with her anymore and let it go, because why drag it around? But my efforts never worked. It didn't calm her down, and sometimes she got so worked up that I was worried about the effect of it on her health. I don't worry about it anymore, and I accept that she may never resolve this, and she may have to live with her bad feelings for the rest of her life. It's her right to do so. Now when she starts talking angrily about Maggie, I just nod my head, wait till she's done, and then change the subject to anything else! I am purposely vague. I just say "Uh-huh." And if she asks me, "What do you think?" I know she isn't really wanting my opinion, so I say, "Well, you know what's best for you." And the funny thing is, when I do that she tells my husband, "I'm crazy about that girl. She is so wise."

Joseane's plan is simple. She acts like she's listening, and when she's asked to take a position, she defers back to the questioner for the answer. You have other options too. You can speak to their intent instead of getting caught up in the content of what they're saying. If your relative says, "You should dress up more," you can say, "Thank you for caring about my appearance."

If your parent asks you, their adult child, whether you're brushing your teeth, you can reply, "Thanks for caring about my hygiene."

If your relative comments on your body size, as in, "Looks like you've put on some weight," you can reply, "Thanks for caring about my health." If that causes them to launch into a monologue of self-justification, as in, "Well, I do care about your health. I've read that people who are overweight are . . . "

just nod your head, grunt occasionally, and let them go on until they tire of hearing themselves talk. By refusing to get caught up in the content of what they've said, you have time to breathe, gather your wits, and create a cushion of non-engagement around yourself.

3. Keep Your Perspective

You are more resourceful with perspective than without it, and you feel better too! One way to keep your perspective is to find entertainment value in difficult behavior.

Ben told us:

> I find it incredibly amusing when people get weird. Sometimes I even play circus music in the back of my mind. It sort of animates their behavior, turns them into a caricature of themselves, and makes them look to me like a cartoon! Then my biggest challenge is not letting them see how hard I'm laughing inside.

Mina told us:

> I tell myself that it beats being in a war zone, or any other horrible thing I can imagine.

Tomas told us:

> Life is hard for lots of people, and I know that there are parts of living that they're no good at. I tell myself they're doing the best they can, and just let it go.

4. Use Reminders

Sometimes it's useful to have a reminder system for your intentions. Garth told us:

> Whenever we find ourselves obligated to attend some kind of family function, I've developed the habit of reminding myself that "all things will pass." I get a small red stick-on dot that I put on my watch to mark the time we're leaving. It's a perfect stealth reminder that helps me keep my perspective. As we are walking in the door, I look at the red dot and remind myself of the end point. If things start to heat up, I just grin and think, "All things will pass" again.

It's said that there's strength in numbers. When it comes to reminders, the weakest number is "one." Instead, partner with other family members who understand the difficulty of dealing with that special someone. Develop a signal system, exit strategy, or other method of mutual support that can get you through the worst behavior without engaging with it. If you travel together to the event, then discuss your intentions and the strategies you will use for focus and support. If you travel to the event alone, then sponsor a pre-event strategy phone call.

By considering your obligations and developing your options in advance, you can remember the rules and keep your perspective. Support yourself before, during, and after events, and transform the stress of a family event into shared success.

Quick Summary

Rules of Non-Engagement
1. Decide in Advance
2. Plan for Sore Subjects
3. Keep Your Perspective
4. Use Reminders

Part IV

Bringing Out the Best in Relatives at Their Worst

Specific Options for Dealing with the Eight by Fate

Chapter 15

The General

Fable:
Wolfie and the Major

There once was a defender of wildlife, and Wolfie was his name. Wolfie was outgoing and friendly, so soon other animals became his friends instead of his food. Even rabbits spoke fondly when they mentioned his name. The day came when Wolfie could no longer bring himself to hunt. Instead, he often defended his new friends from the rest of the pack.

This led to a falling out with his family, particularly his father, a wolf from the old school. Everyone called him "the Major" because he assumed the lead in every situation, and ran the pack with authority and power. His philosophy was simple, and everyone knew it because he repeated it often. You could hear him howling in the forest as he tried to drill it into his son. "If it moves, you kill it. When you kill it, you eat it. DO YOU HEAR ME, PUPPY? I CAN'T HEAR YOU! BARK IF YOU CAN HEAR ME!"

No one dared to challenge him. No one, that is, except Wolfie. As Wolfie grew in assertiveness, there was a constant clashing of wills with the Major, and they saw each other less and less. Then Wolfie fell in love with a real dog, a collie named Lassie, and despite the Major's disapproval, they married. Not long after, they had two rambunctious cubs nipping at their heels.

As time passed, Wolfie realized his parents wouldn't be alive forever and felt the urge to visit, so they could meet their grandcubs. Wolfie's mother was contacted, and a location was chosen. The family would reunite at a well-known deluxe forest retreat.

The journey took several days, and when at last they arrived, Wolfie and Lassie went straight to their quarters. The cubs were all wound up from traveling so far from home, and soon they were bouncing off the walls. All Lassie wanted to do was unpack and take the load off her tired paws. But only ten minutes passed before they heard the sharp rap of a single knock, and the Major's gruff voice growling, "We meet for dinner in the shared space, 6:30 p.m. sharp." It was plain enough. The Major was wasting no time in assuming command.

They got to the shared space about 14 minutes late. Wolfie noted a distinct look of displeasure on his father's muzzle. "At last. So good of you to join us," the Major said pointedly. Lassie tried to explain the reasons for the delay, but the Major brought her up short by baring his teeth and emitting a low warning growl. "Enough waiting. It's time to order." He signaled to the waiter, a rodent who appeared at his side a moment later. The Major ordered for both his wife and himself. His eyes narrowed as he stared at his son for a moment, then moved his gaze to Lassie and the cubs, who had yet to collect themselves and focus on the menu. The Major started tapping his claws on the table, louder, and then louder still. "If you can't make up your mind," he barked, "get the special."

"Thanks, but no thanks. I don't eat animals," Wolfie stated plainly.

"Are you still on that kick?" the Major snapped with disgust. But before the familiar argument could begin, they were interrupted by a fight between the cubs. "Did not!" said the older cub. "Did so!" said the youngest. "Did not!" "Did so!" The Major curled his lips back and raised his hackles. "Why can't you control your children?" he barked. Lassie cowered and looked away.

Dinner conversation was stilted, and everyone was ill at ease. Whether it was the food, the travel, or the company, Lassie now had a headache. "Let's go back to our quarters," she whispered to Wolfie.

"On to the evening's entertainment," the Major said. Then he gave his "follow me" paw signal, and began to lope away from the table.

"Listen, Dad, Lassie doesn't feel well," Wolfie said. "I don't think we're going to go on with everyone."

The Major didn't miss a beat. Straightening his tail, ears up, he said, "We didn't come all this way to be together as a family, only to be pulled apart by a sleepy dog. You will come with us now. You can go to your room after. Now . . . " and he gave the "follow me" signal again. Ears pinned back, tails tucked between their legs, the rest of the pack began to follow.

When the General feels responsible, then, like it or not, commands are issued and your compliance is expected.

Understanding the General

In our Lens of Understanding, the General's behavior originates in the Normal Zone, out of the positive intent to be responsible (Figure 15-1).

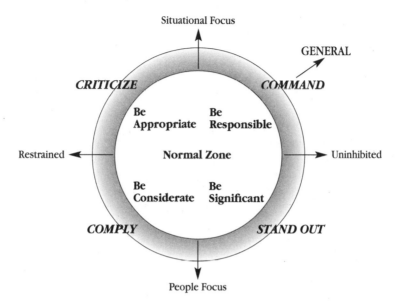

Figure 15-1

There are two ways that the intent to *be responsible* can lead to the General's difficult behavior:

1. Threatened intent: Fear of being irresponsible
2. Projected intent: Seeing others as being irresponsible

The General's difficult behavior begins when someone who wants to *be responsible* does a general survey of the field of engagement. The observation is made that the situation appears either to be out of control or needing some direction. Further, others in the family appear to be missing opportunities, wasting resources, wasting time, or worse yet, wasting their lives. It would be irresponsible to do nothing, and no one else seems ready or willing to take charge of the situation and move things in the responsible direction. That's when intention becomes the need to take Command, the General appears, and the behavior moves from the Normal Zone to the Either/Or Zone.

But the Either/Or Zone is a fork in the road, a choice point out of which comes greatness or danger.

In the Dimension of Greatness, the responsibility, and ability, of the General to take command has a tremendous upside for family members. Responding to the call for action, a General steps up, takes charge, and follows through. Not one to watch things happen or wonder what happened, the General can be counted on to make things happen. And it is not uncommon for the relatives of a benevolent General to feel grateful for the protection and leadership the General provides.

In routine matters, the General keeps the overview. At a family gathering, the General will notice the time and will make certain that dinner is done, and a kitchen detail is organized to clean up when the meal is done. The General gets everyone in the car in time to make it on time to the movie. Faced with a challenge, the General takes action. Focusing on greatness in responsibility, the other intentions are brought into a fine balance to produce the best possible outcome.

But if they take the other fork in the Either/Or Zone, by polarizing out of fear or projection, the behavior moves to the Danger Zone. There, instead of providing leadership, the General demands compliance and attacks resistance to their ideas and direction. The internal demand to Command keeps growing in intensity, until the General is perceived as a domineering and ruthless dictator with no clue of the dissension in the ranks.

Range of Difficulty: From Gruff to Ruthless

The General tends to have an all-or-nothing, take-no-prisoners approach to a perceived lack of responsibility in others. Their command strategies range from gruff General to ruthless dictator.

Yes or no, up or down, go or no go, the gruff General makes a determination about the situation and how to handle it, and then issues orders. A failure to act on those orders is likely to be viewed as a form of insubordination, and they push ever harder for action.

Or the General may escalate, finding it necessary to use more extreme measures. Like a dictator who overthrows the government and establishes a military regime, the tyrannical General does not hesitate to use any and all methods of intimidation and coercion to overwhelm the will of others when it suits his or her purpose. Over time, relatives learn quickly to comply, submit, and withdraw in fear of it getting worse.

One Bad Turn Deserves Another

The General's difficult behavior is not without consequence. Immediate family members may live in fear under the General's dictatorial regime. They may easily become Pleasers, submitting to the General's will. Other family members may not go down without a fight and may become Rebels who try to organize some resistance or undermine the General's control. Still others may opt out completely, becoming Mystery people who use geographic distance to get out of the General's sphere of influence.

Damage Done

The problem behavior causes harm to both the General and to those who must deal with him or her. When people avoid the General, important relationships become distant and superficial. Generals may never get to know their children when they become adults or to see their grandchildren, because an adult child or adult child's spouse wants nothing to do with them. Or if the General is the adult child, he or she never enjoys quality time with a parent before the parent passes on. And if a rebellion happens, this can only increase the General's stress and add to the general frustration everyone experiences in the situation.

Dealing with the General

Attitude

Is it worth it to you to establish a boundary between you and the General? Then you must prepare your mental defenses to allow no crossing of that line.

Your emotional reactions are your greatest enemy in dealing with the General. Almost any sign of emotion on your part could be perceived as a sign of your vulnerability, so "At ease!" is the order of the day.

As the final part of your attitude adjustment, consider the part you may have played in bringing on the General's overbearing stance toward you. Did you fail to establish boundaries earlier on, perhaps in the planning stage of the situation, or when the first orders were issued against your will? Did you go along at first, out of fear or discomfort, only to change your mind later? Were you distracting others from fulfilling their responsibilities? Put yourself in their boots for a moment and take a look at the situation through their eyes. This may give you useful cues and clues as to what is required of you.

Demeanor

The General tends to view situations as battles won, battles lost, and battles yet to be won. You want your behavior to send advance signals that you're focused, constructive, and nonemotional. You must come across as assertive, not aggressive. Take charge of the situation in a proactive way by knowing what you want before you speak. If you have something to say, say it.

Cautions

Don't attack. If you get angry and make your own demands, you run the risk of escalating the situation and making it harder on everyone else along with yourself. And your lack of self-control comes across as irresponsible to the General.

Don't defend. After all, the best defense is a good offense. If you try to defend yourself by offering a considerate explanation, you'll find that it changes nothing except that it further antagonizes the General.

Don't withdraw. If you do, you'll signal that you're weak. Then the General will feel an even greater responsibility to show you your place. Instead, buck up, bucko, remain in place, make strong eye contact while keeping your face neutral, and pay attention to your breathing. Allow the General's commands to move over you, then past you. Remind yourself that you are not obligated to serve in the General's army.

Options with the General

When dealing with the General, your options include (but are not limited to):

◆ Let Them Be in Charge
◆ Give Them a Choice, Let Them Decide
◆ Agree to Disagree
◆ Set Up a Secure Perimeter
◆ Give Them a Glimpse of Greatness

Let Them Be in Charge

If it doesn't make much difference to you, and it clearly seems to matter to them, you lose nothing by letting them be in charge. Your compliance in this case is strictly voluntary. Instead of feeling coerced, you can utilize their willingness to run things for your own benefit.

Give Them a Choice, Let Them Decide

If you have a desired outcome and see several ways to achieve it, you may get a positive response faster by making suggestions than by making assertions. Run your ideas by the General and ask for his or her opinion. This lets the General maintain a sense of responsibility while considering your ideas. But get to the point. If it takes too long to hear what you have to say, the General may lose interest and move on before you've finished.

If your General has positional power over you—for example, if you're still underage and your mom or dad is telling you what you have to do and it doesn't work for you—you can always ask for another option: "Is there some way that this can work for both of us?"

Michael gave us this example:

I was 14 and had a lot going on. It was Saturday morning, and I had plans to go roller-skating at the rink with some of my friends. But when I sat down at the breakfast table, my mom told me she had other plans. "Today, we're going shopping to buy you pants." I hated shopping for pants, yet I recognized it as a necessary evil. But not today! "Mom, I've got plans!" I said. "Well, you're just going to have to cancel them. You need pants. I'll not have you going to school dressed in rags." My response was, "Mom, I understand that you want to get me new pants, and that you've set time aside for this today. Since I already made a commitment to my friends this morning, is there some way we could resolve this that would work for both of us?" My mother must have been impressed at the maturity I was demonstrating, because she immediately offered an alternative. "Will you go with me tomorrow if I let you go skating today?" I told her, "I sure will!"

Problem solved, and no disrespect required!

Sometimes you have to draw a line in the sand, and establish a boundary about what is and is not acceptable to you. You must do this in a way that doesn't threaten the General's sense of responsibility. The idea is to give them control of the decision about their response. First, you assertively present them with clear choices. If they do A, then you will do X. If they choose B, then the consequence will be Y. If C is chosen, then you will do Z. The decision is the General's, but the choices come from you. This works because you are not opposing them, nor taking away their authority, and therefore this does not constitute a rebellion. Instead, you're establishing a framework for responsibility that includes both you and your relative.

It's possible that a determined General will attempt to override you. Therefore, at least one of the choices you give them must include what you'll do if they persist in doing whatever it was that prompted you to establish the boundary. For example: "If you continue to tell me what to do, then I'll turn around and walk away." Or: "If you continue to bring up this subject, I'll pack and leave within the hour."

Joe told us:

I was 30-something at the time, and I remember getting off the plane from my home in Hawaii. I walked across the tarmac and up to the gate where my parents were waiting. I had on my puka shells, I had long hair, and I wasn't even through the gate before Dad started making comments about my hair being too long and my puka shells looking weird.

I stopped walking. They turned and looked back at me in surprise. I looked my dad right in the eyes, then at my mom, and in a calm but direct tone, I said, "Mom, Dad, I came home to have a good time with you and enjoy your company. I did not come home to be criticized or told what to do. So before we walk through this metal gate together, you have a decision to make. If the criticism is important to you, I'll be happy to take the next flight back. If you want me to stay, then we're not going to talk about my hair or my shells anymore."Then I just looked at them in silence and waited for them to understand the choice before them.They made up their minds quickly too.They looked at each other, and then Dad turned to me and in a matter-of-fact tone said, "We apologize. We won't say anything more." And they didn't. At least on that trip.

A take-charge-of-your-life attitude, combined with direct communication, is an irresistible blend for the General. While such a strong stance might be considered rude in some other part of the Lens of Understanding, the General interprets determination and stability as signs of confidence, internal fortitude, and personal responsibility. When you help the General to understand that you are responsible for yourself, you eliminate the General's need to take responsibility for you.

Agree to Disagree

When an agreement does not appear within reach, sometimes the best you can hope for is an agreement to disagree. (This option is also useful with the Meddler, the Rebel, and the VIP.) By offering this option and then moving forward as if the agreement to disagree has met with the agreement of your relative, you can set aside what is disagreeable and move on.

First, state the nature of the agreement:

"It seems that the only thing we can agree on here is that we disagree on politics."
"This appears to be a hurdle that we aren't going to get over, so I say let's sidestep it."
"Since we're not going to change each other's minds or opinions, why bang our heads against each other? Who needs the headache?"
"We don't have to let this disagreement define our relationship."

Then redirect their attention to something else, which is more agreeable to you both:

"So let's just enjoy our Thanksgiving dinner instead."
"So let's talk about the kids instead."
"So let me show you my new laptop instead."

Then act as if you have their agreement. Don't wait for it, just assume you have it and move on.

Set Up a Secure Perimeter

If you haven't drawn any boundaries or established any treaties, and suddenly the General begins an assault, you can disrupt the takeover by establishing a secure perimeter. You can just say no to the General's commands. Here's how you do it:

Listen
Backtrack the command
Blend with their intent
Tell it like it is: state your boundary
Redirect with a presupposition

Listen. Do some reconnaissance and find out where your relative is coming from, what he or she is trying to accomplish, and why it matters.

Backtrack the command. This serves a twofold purpose: It lets the other person know you've been listening, and it buys you the time you need to consider your next steps. When you backtrack, remember to use the General's actual words rather than translating them into your own. Since words have personal meaning, changing them might create the impression that you didn't really understand what your relative was trying to tell you. This might cause them to escalate, or to repeat previous words with greater intensity to make sure they've been heard correctly.

The General is moving forward fast and has a short attention span because there's little time to waste. You don't have to say everything back to them, just two or three brief sentences that include the main words they just used. If your relative curses, you would be wise to avoid such words in your backtracking, as curse words are spoken for effect and are *not* the key words of the communication. Coming from you, they might be heard as fighting words and a call to arms.

Blend with your relative's intent to be responsible. You will find this intent somewhere behind the front lines of their words and actions. When you speak to it, you meet the General on this very powerful common ground.

Begin with: "I appreciate . . . " or "Thank you for . . . " or "I understand that you . . . "

Example One:

GENERAL: "Here's Bob's phone number. You call him on Monday."
YOU: "I appreciate that you want me to find a career that's fulfilling to me."

Example Two:

GENERAL: "Finish up your drink and let's get moving."
YOU: "Thanks for wanting us to get to the evening's entertainment on time."

Blending with positive intent is one of the most powerful things you can blend with. It serves as a reminder to people about where they're coming from or trying to get to, and may bring the self-defeating nature of their behavior into their awareness.

Tell it like it is: state your boundary. This is when you present your bottom line, and draw a line in the sand. What you actually say depends on your unique situation, but keep it brief, direct. and to the point.

Example One:

You: "I have no interest in Bob's business, and don't want to work for him."

Example Two:

You: "I'm enjoying the drink, and I don't think there's any reason to rush."

Redirect with a presupposition. This is a method to speak as if the way you want things to turn out is exactly how they will turn out. When you presuppose something, you speak as if what you're saying is "supposed" to be true.

For example, if someone says to you, "Will you pay cash or use credit?" the question supposes in advance that you will be paying. If you tell your relatives that, "As soon as you get a copy of the Ricks' book, *Dealing With People You Can't Stand*, I'll show you the parts that will be most helpful to you!" you are supposing in advance that they're going to get the book and that it will help them (and it will!).

With the General, you want to presuppose that the outcome you have in mind is the outcome that will take place.

Example One:

"When I've finished my own job search, I'll let you know what I've found."

This supposes in advance that you're doing your own job search.

Example Two:

"When I've finished my drink, we can get going."

This supposes in advance that you will finish your drink.

You don't have to worry about sounding too strong. This is exactly the way the General talks. A presupposition implies that you have taken responsibility ahead of time for how something turns out. So it is likely your relative will recognize this form of expression as having some authority that deserves their respect. But if it makes you feel better, or puts others at ease, you can end with a "Thanks!"

You:

"Thanks for understanding."
"Thanks for waiting."
"Thanks for your patience."

Give Them a Glimpse of Greatness

Sometimes you have to draw a bigger line and tell your problem relative the truth about how his or her behavior is self-defeating, and what you think would be better instead. The overview is the same for honesty with any of the problem behaviors. Plan it, write it, rehearse it, pick your time and place (see Chapter 8 for more details). Your goal of honesty is to give them a glimpse of greatness.

Here's what's involved:

1. Positive intent
2. Be specific
3. Reveal the deeper meaning
4. Suggest something
5. Reinforce behavioral change

However, there are two aspects of honesty among these five items that are specific to the General:

1. Positive intent.   Appreciating your relative's responsibility is a key to gaining access to their willingness to change. You can tell your relative that you appreciate:

" . . . wanting to keep this on track."
" . . . your willingness to take charge."
" . . . your wanting me to be responsible about this."
" . . . making sure we arrive on time."
" . . . making certain that everyone is safe."
" . . . wanting me to drive carefully."

3. Reveal the deeper meaning

"If you want (name of person you are talking about, i.e., Jane) to learn responsibility, then you have to allow Jane the chance to be responsible. Saying something before Jane has had a chance to speak prevents her from taking that responsibility."

or

> *"Some of your relatives keep you at a distance because they don't want to be controlled. If you want to have an influence on them, then you don't want to inadvertently drive them away."*

or

> *"How can I be responsible for myself if you keep trying to control me? If you want me to be responsible for myself, get out of my way and let me learn my lessons for myself."*

or

> *"When you backseat drive, it actually distracts me from paying attention to the road. I know you don't want to create unsafe driving conditions, so thank you and let me concentrate."*

Fable Finale: Wolfie and the Major

The Major was getting on in years. The pack was invited to a milestone birthday party for him, along with some of the Major's old military pals. Lassie didn't want to go. "I don't care to be criticized about cub-rearing," she said. "I don't care to be ordered about." Wolfie whimpered and begged her to reconsider. "He won't be around forever. We haven't gone in a long time. The cubs can play games with their cousins." One of the cubs, overhearing the conversation, yipped with glee. "Games! Push and Shove! Wrestling! Yippee!" "All right," Lassie relented. "But on one condition!" She told him in no uncertain terms that if the Major started barking orders at her, or criticizing her parenting, her cubs, or their food preferences, Wolfie would pack up the pack and they would leave immediately. "I won't stand for it, and neither should you. You have to draw the line with him!" said Lassie. The youngest cub piped in, "Yeah, Dad! You'll tell him!"

When they arrived at the party, the Major was in typical form. Everyone was running this way and that at his commands. It wouldn't be long before the party turned into a hunt. Wolfie knew he had to seize the moment or the moment would quickly pass. It was his father's birthday. Wolfie wanted to celebrate it and was determined not to let the Major drive them away. So he pulled his father aside, bared his teeth, and defined his boundary. "Dad, we came to celebrate your birthday. But we are not here to hunt anything down or make anything afraid. We're not going to kill any little animals. If that's the kind of party you want to have, that's your right. But we'll turn around and leave immediately. So you decide if you want us to stay. If you do, you'll have to be satisfied with sniffing stuff, playing games, and enjoying each other as family and friends."

The Major said nothing at first and just stared Wolfie in the eyes. Then he growled and grumbled what sounded like consent. It seemed the matter was settled.

But the respite only lasted until the second meal. That's when the Major began his tirade on what was and wasn't food, and he focused his attack on Lassie. "You know your cubs are not going to grow big if they don't eat animals. A wolf needs to kill in order to eat. Your cubs need some serious discipline too. The way you coddle them, they will have no killer instinct at all!"

Lassie, being a nice family dog, didn't say anything. But she looked over at Wolfie, and he could see that she was seething. He knew he had to say something. He interrupted the Major's lecture by barking loudly. When the Major looked over at him, Wolfie said, "Dad, I hear that you think the way we're feeding and raising our offspring is irresponsible, and that you think they need more discipline and less coddling. Both Lassie and I appreciate that you care about the health and well-being of your grandcubs." Then Wolfie stopped speaking for a moment, and the pause hung in the air. Wolfie placed his paw on his father's shoulder and continued, "But my cubs are my pack, and I am the leader of my pack. We will raise them however we please, just as you did with your pack."

All the other wolves watched in silence. Not one of them had ever stood up to the Major before. Wolfie finished what he had begun. "Though we disagree about diet and discipline, we don't have to let that get in the way of enjoying our brief time together. We can leave right now, if you prefer. But we came to celebrate with you. What do you say we put our disagreements aside and go mark our shared territory instead?"

The Major bared his teeth, not to growl, but to smile. "Agreed," was all he said. But later on the Major was overheard talking to one of his old military buddies. He pointed his paw at Wolfie, who was overseeing the games, then nodded his head and said, "That's my cub!"

The moral of this story is that a good way to stop someone from ordering you around is to make certain they know you're responsible for yourself.

Quick Summary

◆ Let Them Be in Charge
◆ Give Them a Choice, Let Them Decide
◆ Agree to Disagree
◆ Set Up a Secure Perimeter
  1. Listen
  2. Backtrack the command
  3. Blend with their intent
  4. Tell it like it is: state your boundary
  5. Redirect with a presupposition
◆ Give Them a Glimpse of Greatness

Chapter 16
The Judge

Fable: Olivia Owl and Robin Robin

"Hi there, Auntie Olivia." Robin chirped.

"Well, whoo, whoo, is this," Olivia Owl replied, "but my favorite niece Robin Robin."

Robin landed on a branch perpendicular to Aunt Olivia's so she could look into her big yellow eyes without having to turn her own head. Although Robin had known Auntie Olivia all her life, there was still something disconcerting about the way she looked at you directly, with both eyes at the same time. It was almost . . . human, and it made Robin's neck feathers tingle. But one thing was certain, Olivia Owl had a penetrating gaze that could, and usually would, look right through you.

"So, Auntie, I heard you went to a flock party. How was it?"

"Well, the food was terrible. The nuts were so hard that everyone had problems getting them open. Except, of course, that old bird Tara Toucan. Can you believe the beak on that bird? And you should see her colors! Why I never! Perhaps that's what they wear in the jungle, but she will never make it in this forest dressed like that."

"Well, Auntie Olivia, wasn't there anything you liked about the party?" Robin Robin chipperly inquired.

"How can you like a party with food like that? For one thing, everyone knows you don't serve worms at a flock party. They simply won't stay fresh. And all those seeds, seeds, seeds. Not a single field mouse. I am a

141

carnivorous bird, you know. I think they were just being cheap, cheap, cheap."

Before Robin could reply, Aunt Olivia went on, "You remember Daisy and Dahlia Duck, your distant cousins? They were there too. I know they are amphibious birds, and yes, they do have to float, but you can't tell me their backsides have to be that big! I just don't understand whooo, whooo, could let themselves go like that."

Robin fidgeted nervously on the branch. She didn't like hearing Aunt Olivia putting down any of the many members of her extended family. But Olivia didn't notice, and continued her commentary.

Suddenly Olivia Owl became very focused, gazing off into the distance. Robin didn't see anything, but Olivia said, "Don't look now and don't say anything, but here comes Betty Blue Jay."

From a distance, Robin heard Betty's unmistakable loud screech. "Hello, Olivia Owl! Hello, Robin Robin!"

"Hoo, Hoo, to you Betty, " they replied as Betty flew into view and then flew away. " My, aren't you looking nice!" Olivia called after her. As Betty disappeared from view, Olivia turned to Robin and said, "What blue trash!"

But Robin could barely hear what her auntie said, because of a deafening noise overhead. She looked up to see a flock of at least 30 crows. They circled a few times, squawking loudly, then rumbled off toward the horizon. Aunt Olivia Owl muttered, "Yech, that's all we need, a gang of crows stirring up trouble around here. There goes the forest! A bunch of avian hooligans, that's what they are. Making all that noise. Do they think our auricular areas are ornamental? Look at them. Common crows, and they think they're so tough, flying around in those black feather jackets."

Robin Robin's fidgeting intensified. She didn't want her auntie to know that she was dating the leader of the flock. Perish forbid that Olivia might turn her critical eyes on her! "Well, Auntie," she said nervously, "it was nice visiting with you, but I must fly!"

"All right, Robin. Wait, turn around and let me adjust your tail feathers. You are the symbol of spring, and have a reputation to keep up. You shouldn't fly around all ruffled, as you so often do."

And as Robin Robin flew away, she couldn't help but wonder what Olivia had to say about her when she wasn't around.

The Judge sets a standard that no one can meet, then pronounces judgment along with a running commentary of criticism.

Understanding the Judge

In our Lens of Understanding, the Judge's behavior originates in the Normal Zone, out of the positive intent to *be appropriate* (Figure 16-1).

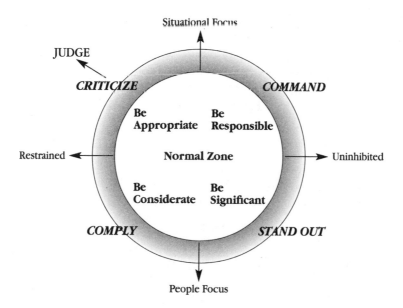

Figure 16-1

There are two ways that the intent to *be appropriate* can lead to the Judge's difficult behavior:

1. Threatened intent: fear of being inappropriate
2. Projected intent: identifying inappropriate behavior in others

The Judge's behavior begins when someone who wants to *be appropriate* rises to the bench in the courtroom of discernment to determine what is truly proper in a given situation. The observation is made that someone or something is out of place, out of step, out of accord, or has failed to conform to the Judge's high standard. That's when the intention of the Judge becomes the need to be critical. The behavior then moves from the Normal Zone to the Either/Or Zone, and the Judge appears.

But the Either/Or Zone is a fork in the road, a choice point out of which comes greatness or danger.

In the Dimension of Greatness, the desire for appropriateness and the willingness to examine things critically can provide critical advantages to the family. Wanting to do the right things for the right reasons, a great Judge is discerning and wise, tough but fair, and offers valuable insights, information, and ideas to assist others in bringing about the best possible results.

Whether in matters of appearance, decorum, business practice and ethics, the management of financial affairs, or raising healthy and confident children, a Judge in the Dimension of Greatness helps assure that critical thinking is applied and a reasoned approach is taken, and makes evident those details that might escape the attention of a casual or careless observer.

But if the Judge takes the other fork in the Either/Or Zone, by polarizing out of fear or projection, the behavior moves into the Danger Zone.

In the Danger Zone, the Judge, instead of providing guidance and clarity, becomes critical, finding fault in everything and everybody. The internal demand to criticize keeps growing in intensity. Then the Judge is perceived by the family as a disgruntled perfectionist, a hopeless cynic, or a relentless nitpicker.

Range of Difficulty: from Small Claims to Hanging Judge

In the court of the Judge's opinion, you're either innocent or guilty. There are few shades of gray to interfere with their judgment, but several ways to hold court.

There's the small claims Judge, who complains to each family member about the failings of every other family member. This Judge presents evidence, passes judgment, and then further passes the judgment along as gossip and rumor.

There is the the nit-picking Judge who fixates on details of no real consequence, like the neat-freak who keeps cleaning up after cleaning up. This Judge prefers order in the court. In an effort to build a wall against the chaos, he or she covers the carpet and furniture with plastic, and then closes off the room so it cannot be disturbed by human touch.

Then there's the cynical Judge, who only looks up to tear something down and believes that others are motivated only by selfishness.

There is also the Probation Officer, who likes to look over your shoulder because you're in the Officer's domain. The Probation Officer will tell you what not to do as you do it, what will go wrong before it happens, what doom awaits you if you take unapproved-of action, and what never was or will be right, no matter how hard you try.

Finally, there is the "hanging Judge," who throws the book at you if you disagree with anything. Hung up on one narrow point of view, the hanging Judge imposes rules and pounds the gavel to drown you out if you keep trying to argue your case. In the court of the hanging judge, the rulings of the judge are supreme.

One Bad Turn Deserves Another

The Judge's difficult behavior is not without consequence. It in turn produces difficult behavior in others. Relatives learn to fear the Judge's critical eye and keep to themselves, like the Mystery, who reveals nothing personal to avoid the personal intrusions. Others may come to judge the Judge, and

thus become a difficult Judge themselves. And some relatives turn into difficult Rebels, resenting the relentless criticisms and negativity, and acting in
opposition to the Judge's very definition of right and wrong. Others become
Pleasers, trying and failing, over and over, to measure up to the Judge's
impossible standards. The Pleasers struggle with low self-esteem and depression in their relationships with the Judge, as they internalize the criticisms
and learn to apply them to themselves.

Damage Done

The problem behavior causes harm both to the Judge and to those who
must deal with him or her. The Judge may wind up in constant pain because
the world refuses to conform to his or her standards. The Judge may wind up
with no influence whatsoever over situations that actually could be made better by a constructive approach. Over time, the Judge may develop such a
sense of helplessness and hopelessness that it becomes profound inertia and
despair. This creates an atmosphere of doom and gloom around them, an
emotional hazard for any who might get too near. This atmosphere may iso-
late the Judge completely, as family members choose the easier path of
avoidance because they can no longer tolerate the certain criticism and ever-
present negativity. As for the loved ones who have internalized the criticisms,
nit-picking, and fault finding, they come to view themselves as letdowns, and
their feelings of failure become their undeserved reward for their failed efforts
to measure up.

Dealing with the Judge

Attitude

Get defensive, and you condemn yourself. Say nothing, and you seem
guilty. But you don't have to correct the Judge, if you correct yourself instead.
If your highest priority is self-defense, and you don't want to be found in contempt in the courtroom of his or her opinion, then let go of the need to correct the Judge who is wrong about you. Instead, correct yourself. The attitudinal key to dealing with the Judge is to counter the negative rulings, whether
stated directly or implied, in the privacy of your own mind. You do this by
telling yourself the positive corollaries to the negative judgments.

THEY SAY OR IMPLY: "You are a lousy friend."
YOU SAY TO YOURSELF: "I am a good friend and that's why I'm still on the
                        phone."

THEY SAY OR IMPLY: "You totally screwed it up."
YOU SAY TO YOURSELF: "I know I did the best I could."

THEY SAY OR IMPLY: "I was waiting for you for a half hour and set down my package, so it's because of you that I forgot about it."
YOU SAY TO YOURSELF: "It was not about me, she set it down."

Doing this will help you to keep your perspective. Offering encouragement to yourself is the ray of light that keeps your thinking bright in the otherwise gloomy presence of criticism.

Demeanor

Your demeanor must indicate that you have nothing to defend, but that you do have a case to make. Be wary of making big leaps of logic. It is essential in your approach that you go slowly, step by step. A wry amusement may be useful in this regard, as it indicates that the charges don't really apply to you. Avoid saying anything sarcastic, though. When you present your case, you must build it in a way that says, "A careful examination of the evidence is all that is required of you. I'm certain that when you've considered what I have to say, you'll draw the appropriate conclusion." Be dispassionate, at least until your closing argument. A calm, methodical, logical, and consistent approach is the best way to get past the guards and get your day in court.

Cautions

Don't question the court's judgment. If you do, the Judge will likely fine you for contempt. If you tell the Judge that he or she is wrong, by inference if not by intent, you are out of order! Instead, recognize that what the Judge has said reflects only one view of the facts. You aren't there to contradict them. You are there to offer new evidence, or to interpret the facts in a new way.

Beware of the polarity response when dealing with criticism and negativity. The polarity response makes the Judge want to go the other way when you ask them to go your way. You may be familiar with this, if you have ever dealt with a two-year-old child:

YOU: "Time for bed."
CHILD: "I don't want to go to bed."
YOU: "I said it's time for bed."
CHILD: "I don't want to go to bed."
YOU: "All right, you have to stay up all night."
CHILD: "But I'm tired."

Adults do this too! In some ways, criticism is, by its nature, a polarity response to the unruliness of life. So, Judges have a well-developed polarity response, and you would do well to avoid it. Contradiction drives them into it. A logical case leads them out of it.

Options with the Judge

When dealing with the Judge, your options include (but are not limited to):

◆ Acknowledge, Move On
◆ Return to Sender
◆ Appeal the Sentence
◆ Go for the Polarity Response
◆ Give Them a Glimpse of Greatness

Acknowledge, Move On

This option works great with the small claims Judge. Sometimes you're better off acknowledging the judgment and then moving on, rather than taking the time and expending the energy to try and change your relative's mind. If you choose this option, give thanks for their good intentions, and then go your own way.

"Thanks for being honest with me about how you feel."
"Thanks for bringing that to my attention."
"Thanks for your thoughtful suggestions."

If the judgment is about someone else in your family:

"Thanks for wanting their life to work out."
"Thanks for letting me in on what you're thinking."
"Thanks for your insights."

Then change the subject, get up and move, or offer to get them something. (see *Backtracking* in Chapter 4 and *Positive Intent* in Chapter 6.)

Return to Sender

This option works well with the nit-picking, fault-finding Judge. If you're tired of hearing the Judge passing judgment on other relatives whom you care about, you can return the judgment to its owner by asking the Judge to own the judgments. It may be obvious to you that others don't want to go by the Judge's laws. However, it may not be obvious to the Judge. That's because Judges refer to an internal law-book of their own making, and mistakenly assume everyone has a copy. The best way to let them know that nobody else has the book is with a gentle backtrack and then a question regarding the authority by which they're passing judgment.

First, backtrack the judgment, so they'll know what you are specifically referring to. Use as many of their words as possible, so there's no mistake about it.

"When you say that people shouldn't be seen in public that look like that,
I'm curious to know how you decide that? According to whom?"
"When you say that the proper thing to do is keep your mouth shut and
don't talk back, how do you know that? It's the proper thing according
to whom?"

If the response you get is a generalized, "Everybody knows it," then ask for specifics. If your relative says, "Everyone," ask, "Who specifically?" If he or she says "Always" ask, "When specifically?" If your relative says, "It's just common sense!" bring it back around by asking, "Common sense to whom?" If your relative says, "Any thinking person," ask, "To whom specifically is this regarded as common sense?" Keep bringing it back around until it lands squarely in the Judge's court. You'll know it's back in the court when your relative says, "Me!"

Appeal the Sentence

Here's the situation. Suppose you're dealing with the "hanging Judge." A negative comment is made about you or about someone in your family that you care about who is having a hard time with the Judge because of all the judgments. The judgments follow the comparison format of "You're too much" or "You're too little" or "You're not enough" or "You're not even close." In any case, you can either appeal the decision of the Judge or you can take your appeal to a higher court (the court of your own opinions!).

Bringing your appeal to the hanging Judge's court only applies if you have specifics about new or unexamined evidence that directly offers a counter-example to the Judge's opinion. For example, the Judge says, "Your daughter isn't even trying to lose weight." If you know what steps she's taking to lose weight, you can introduce your new evidence. Ask a leading question, while suggesting an explanation for how the Judge was unaware of the information you're presenting. The information you offer reveals that his or her generalization isn't accurate.

I can tell this is important to you." [positive projection] "I guess you didn't know that she's cut out sugar and simple carbohydrates from her diet the last three weeks. [Leading question that introduces new information.] She's been talking with me regularly, and is very frustrated with how difficult this is for her. Yet she perseveres, and I'm proud of her because I understand how much effort this is going to take to see it through."

Then, if you have an alternate sentence to suggest, offer it, in order to shift the Judge from judgment to constructive actions. Engaging your relative in this way gives him or her a chance to revisit the Either/Or Zone and make a new choice. If your information is solid, and your references as a character witness are good, this may be enough to influence the thinking of the Judge, reducing the sentence to time served, or at least diminishing the harshness of the criticism for the moment.

If a public judgment is happening to someone else in your family and you want to help them out of the awful situation, then try making your appeal public. Say something encouraging to the person being judged, and ask the person to account for his or her success or progress. To the person being judged for appearance, you might say, "You look really nice. What have you been doing? Whatever it is, keep it up."

If, however, the judgments are directed at you, take your appeal to the higher court of your own opinion. This is the attitudinal approach we recommended earlier in the chapter. Place yourself under the influence of your own attitude by providing counterexamples to yourself. If someone criticizes you for the way you look, say something encouraging in the privacy of your own mind. "I'm making a big effort to deal with this, and I'm making progress." If someone says, "You are to blame!" say to yourself, "I'm doing the best I can. Those accusations are about them, not about me." Maybe you can't tell the Judge the truth because he or she can't handle it. But *you* can handle it, so make sure to tell it to yourself! This keeps you free of your relative's negative characterizations, strong in your knowledge of the facts, and focused in spite of his or her behavior. It's bound to influence the Judge's opinion of you in the long run, and it keeps you in charge of your own destiny.

Go for the Polarity Response

It is a common mistake to try and change the Judge's mind. Unless you've been granted an appeal, you are likely wasting your time. However, you can use the Judge's judgment intentionally to turn the prosecution into a defense.

Lucky for you, the Judge has a strong polarity response. While it's both ironic and paradoxical, the fact is that people who judge others tend to strongly dislike being judged themselves. Simply crowd them out of the role of prosecutor, by taking what they said and saying it in an even more polarizing manner, offered in the form of a question. Here are two examples:

Example 1

JUDGE: "Jeff doesn't apply himself in college. He just plays and runs around all the time, and acts like it doesn't matter. He is a disgrace to the family."

YOU: "You think Jeff is intentionally trying to disgrace the family? Do you think he's stupid?"

JUDGE: "No, I'm not saying that."

Example 2

JUDGE: "Loretta doesn't care how other people see her. She always looks like a mess, and it's embarrassing."

YOU: "You think she doesn't know how she looks? You think she likes
        looking that way? You don't think she hates looking that way?"
JUDGE: "Well, no, of course she hates it!"

Notice that, in both these cases, the Judge winds up affirming something
opposite to his or her original judgment. That's the beauty of the polarity
response. You don't have to convince anyone. You get them to convince
themselves.

Then you can provide some reinforcement for the Judge's new position.

YOU: "I'm relieved to hear that you know that."

This has the potential to put the Judge back in the Either/Or Zone.
Typically, the Judge will then express regret about feeling helpless to bring
about a change for the better. If ever there was a time to offer a suggestion,
this is it!

JUDGE: "I just wish she would listen to me."
YOU: "I've found that what works best in this kind of situation is to offer
        encouragement. When people feel bad, they don't change. When
        people feel successful, they accumulate successes."

Give Them a Glimpse of Greatness

Sometimes you have to draw a bigger line, and tell your problem relative
the truth about how judgmental behavior is self-defeating and what you think
would work better instead. The overview is the same for honesty with any of
the problem behaviors. Plan it, write it, rehearse it, pick your time and place.
(See Chapter 8 for more details.) Your goal of honesty is to give your relative
a glimpse of Greatness.

1. Positive intent
2. Be specific
3. Reveal the deeper meaning
4. Suggest something
5. Reinforce behavioral change

However, there are two aspects of honesty specific to the Judge:

1. Positive intent. Appreciating your relative's attention to right and wrong
is a key element to gaining access to his or her willingness to change.
    You can tell your relative you appreciate:

" . . . *wanting her to do the right thing.*"
" . . . *the way you care about his appearance.*"

"   *wanting this to turn out well.*"

"*. . . wanting me to have a good life.*"

"*. . . wanting me to have a fulfilling relationship.*"

3. Reveal the deeper meaning. Show your relative the benefit of change by revealing the self-defeating consequences of his or her behavior. It is likely that your relative is looking at a detail and failing to see the big picture, and a clear example may help to bring the big picture back into view

"When you did this, here's what happened."

or

"You're losing the people you care about because when you say critical things to them about others, they worry about what you'll say about them behind their back. Then they want to stay away from you."

or

"Because she tries to be nice, she doesn't say anything to you when you say these things to her. But I know she internalizes your feedback and uses it to feel bad about herself. This lowers her self-esteem even further, which makes it even less likely she'll make the right choices that are so obvious to you."

Fable Finale: Olivia Owl and Robin Robin

The day had arrived for the big migration to the south. The migratory birds had packed their nests and were saying their good-byes to the non-migratory birds.

Robin Robin had prepared for this moment for over a month. It wasn't the migration that concerned her. She had done that many times before, and could do it with her eyes closed. But today, when she said her good-bye to Aunt Olivia Owl, she planned to talk with her about her critical behavior.

Robin landed on a nearby branch and chirped, "Greetings, Auntie Olivia!"

Olivia Owl sat silently staring, her big yellow eyes focused unblinkingly on Robin Robin. Feeling intimidated, Robin's resolve briefly wavered.

Finally, Olivia Owl spoke. "Well, I'm glad someone had the decency to fly by to say good-bye. Dahlia and Daisy Duck are already gone. Of course, given how plump they are, they probably need an extra day to fly. Have you seen your brother, Ray Robin? I haven't. Maybe he flew into a glass window and knocked himself out, like he did last time. Sitting there on the ground unconscious for all that time, he could have been gobbled up by somebody's house cat. But it serves him right for zooming around so recklessly. Whooo knows! Perhaps the impact is what made him forget his manners. I heard the geese have already left too, and I haven't even heard a word from Gabby or Gertie Goose. As Canadian geese, I expected them to be a little more polite than some of the locals!"

Robin Robin knew she couldn't be a chicken. She had to talk to Aunt Olivia because she could no longer stand the constant stream of critical comments, but she loved her aunt and knew she meant well. Robin didn't want to become one of the many birds that were permanently migrating out of Aunt Olivia's life. She took a deep breath.

Olivia seemed to stare at her more intently. "Why are you fidgeting so much? Are you in hurry? If you need to fly off, go ahead."

Robin looked directly at Olivia, "No, I'm not in a hurry. It's just that I love you, and I have something to tell you that is very important for me to say and you to hear. But it is difficult to say it."

"Well, hoo, hoo, I love you too, Robin. What could be so difficult? Just say it!"

"As you wish. Auntie, I know how much you care about everyone. And because you are nocturnal and carnivorous, you have exceptionally good eyes, so you see the details that others often don't see."

Robin paused, as Olivia sat in silence with those big yellow eyes staring at her. Then she continued.

"But the things you say sound so harsh to me. You have so much wisdom to offer, but some of the things you say sound harsh, instead. So I have to ask you. Do you really think Dahlia Duck doesn't care how she looks? Do you really think she is trying to be a disgrace?"

"No! Of course not."

"I am relieved to hear that."

"I just wish she would listen to me. She really doesn't have to be that large."

"Have you influenced her at all, Auntie?"

"It doesn't seem so. I swear, she must be preparing herself to become a dish of Peking Duck at a Chinese restaurant."

Robin went on, "Well, I find that encouragement works better than criticism in these situations. Because if you only tell her what is wrong, she feels bad about herself. And when she feels bad, she heads straight to the park and starts quacking to the humans for more bread. And it isn't just her. Do you really think that all the migratory birds just forgot to say goodbye? Is it possible that some of them didn't want to? Because when you tell a bird critical things about other birds, the bird you say it to worries about what you say about them when they're not around. They may stop coming around to avoid your criticism. And if they stop coming around, you lose the opportunity to help them.

Olivia blinked her big yellow eyes and shifted her position on the branch. Robin thought to herself, Wow, Auntie is actually uncomfortable. I didn't know she was capable of discomfort! Robin knew there was no turning back now. "Auntie, I know a secret way to get people to like and listen to you. Would you like to know what it is?"

Olivia blinked again and said, "Pray tell, Robin, what is it?"

"All you have to do is say nice things about others when someone comes around. And instead of telling others what's wrong, ask them how you can best be of assistance to them! You have a lot of help to give, but you have to say it in a way that others can hear." They sat there in silence for what seemed like an eternity, until Robin said, "Well, Auntie Olivia, I am really going to have to fly. I love you! Have a nice winter." She then turned and said, "Do you want to help me fix my tail feathers? I can't go flying around all ruffled."

Olivia Owl blinked her big yellow eyes, "That's all right, Robin Robin, you look fine just as you are."

They sat for another moment, and then Olivia said, "Thank you, Robin."

Then Robin flew south for the winter, looking forward to returning in the spring more than she ever had before.

The moral of this story is that a little bit of encouragement goes a longer way than a lot of criticism.

Quick Summary

- ◆ Acknowledge, Move On
- ◆ Return to Sender
- ◆ Appeal the Sentence
- ◆ Go for the Polarity Response
- ◆ Give Them a Glimpse of Greatness

Chapter 17

The
Pleaser

Fable: Carrie Chameleon

Carrie was a caring chameleon, concerned with everyone else's feelings, always willing to go along in order to get along, ready to change her color to suit somebody else's needs. Her brother Carey was a different sort of reptile. He had a mind of his own, and you could count on him to take a stand for what he believed in. Having done a lot of personal development work, he could maintain his true color regardless of his surroundings if he had a mind to.

Carey was in the middle of a big project. He had been sitting on a brown rock in the sun for over an hour, maintaining a green color without moving at all! "Possibly a new record," he thought, and then his beeper went off. Without moving anything else, he focused a single eye down on the text message coming through. It was Carrie, and the scrolling words read, "Do you have some time for me? Can I come up there? I need to see you. Please?"

Whenever her caring had carried her too far, Carrie counted on Carey. Though she was middle-aged (about 6 years old), she would always be three years his junior, so he still thought of her as his "li'l sis." And if Carrie needed him, he would make himself available. "After all," he thought with wry amusement, "I'm not going anywhere."

As he maintained his stationary position, Carey thought about his sister. Carrie was kind of cute, and she could be amusing to watch, what with her rotating eyes, opposable toes, and long tongue. But she was a soft touch for scoundrels, and as long as Carey could remember, one reptile after another had crawled into her life. They took what she had until she had nothing left to give, and then moved on, leaving her behind like a molted skin. There was that Gila monster she had married, though everyone had tried to talk her out of it. He went away with most of her stuff. Then there was that horned toad, who left her pregnant. After that, a string of real snakes slithered through her life. Carey could only watch helplessly, as Carrie changed her color to match these lowlifes. Somehow, Carrie couldn't see beyond their oily demeanor to the slick scales that covered their worthless hides. And once they had squeezed all they could out of her, they crawled or slithered away as quickly as they had come, leaving her feeling used, brokenhearted, and empty.

And that was just the half of it. Carrie was so concerned about others, and so quick to change, that even lizards with good intentions took advantage of her. One time, her parents said they needed her to help them with their affairs. So she dropped everything and came crawling. She had to pass on a promising career, and cross a desert, because they wanted her to live close by. It wasn't like she was their only offspring. They had been hatching babies every few months for as long as he could remember. But Carrie was always eager to please, trying pleasantly to live up to their demands and expectations, and all the while hurting on the inside, personalizing their criticisms, beating herself up over their disappointments. Where others saw her as having a sunny disposition and ready smile, it seemed that only her brother Carey knew the truth about Carrie's depressing thoughts and negative self-image, because she always turned to him in times of trouble.

Suddenly Carey heard a scratching sound and looked down from his rock. It took him a moment to make out Carrie down below, looking as brown as the sand. He made a mental note, "One hour and 35 minutes without moving or changing color. Yes, definitely a new record!'

Carrie seemed to be waiting for him to respond. She looked completely defeated.

"Come on up, sis, and freeze position with me for a while."

And no sooner did she scamper up on the rock next to Carey, as he suggested, than her color began to change to match his.

The helpful and pleasant Pleaser, often smiling on the outside while hurting on the inside, attends to everyone's needs to the neglect of his or her own.

Understanding the Pleaser

In our Lens of Understanding, the Pleaser's behavior begins in the Normal Zone, with the positive intent to *be considerate* (Figure 17-1).

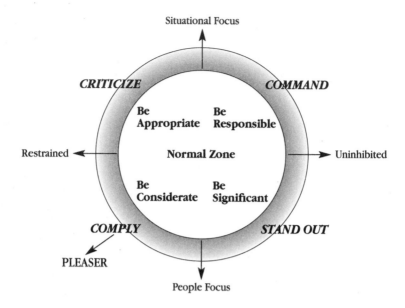

Figure 17-1

There are two ways that the intent to *be considerate* can lead to difficult behavior:

1. Threatened intent: fear of being inconsiderate.
2. Projected intent: perceiving others as inconsiderate

The Pleaser's behavior begins when relatives, who want to *be considerate*, come to believe that their own strong feelings might be hurtful to others, or believes that the feelings of others may be hurtful to themselves, if they're not careful. Defensively, wanting not to offend at any cost, they don't make insensitive remarks, get into arguments, or share unpleasant or troubling feelings.

Yet in spite of their best efforts to keep the peace, people behave badly toward one another. If bad behavior is directed at them, the intention to *be considerate* grows in intensity until it becomes an intense need to *comply*. That's when the Pleaser appears, and the behavior moves from the Normal Zone to the Either/Or Zone.

But the Either/Or Zone is a fork in the road, a choice point out of which comes greatness or danger.

In the Dimension of Greatness, having a relative who cares deeply about wanting to have harmonious relations based on mutual consideration can be a real blessing in a family. At his or her best, the Pleaser is a champion for families to stay together. A family at its best is harmonious, a sort of mutual-support group that provides a safe harbor in an often turbulent world. Maintaining that harmony requires that members be able to attend to the greater good and recognize that the needs of the many are often greater than the needs of any one person.

The Pleaser notices when someone puts time and effort into making or buying the perfect gift. Such a relative is certain to speak of appreciation and thankfulness at a family gathering, if not when people are all together, then at least one-on-one. You can always count on Pleasers to respond to a request for help, ready to lend a hand, happy to pitch in, willing to give what they have, even if they have very little. A Pleaser, coming from greatness, will recognize that nice isn't always nice, and that the greater good is sometimes best served by telling an unpleasant truth. There are times when it takes great strength to yield, to answer force with patience, to react with kindness instead of stubborn pride.

But if the relative takes the other fork in the Either/Or Zone, polarizing out of fear or projection, the behavior moves into the Danger Zone.

The Danger Zone Pleaser comes from a place of weakness rather than strength, acting nice on the surface, going out of their way to help all in need, all in the hope of being treated in kind. The internal demand to *comply* keeps growing in intensity, until the Pleaser becomes known to the rest of the family as a patsy, a washrag, a wimp, and in time, as the spineless coward to whom very little care is given.

Range of Difficulty: From Pleasant to Pushover

Pleasers want to please you. They really do. The compliance patterns of the Pleaser range from being pleasant to being a pushover.

The pleasant Pleaser is uncomfortable with conflict and will avoid it at all costs. Such people tread very carefully around you, and try to anticipate your next moves. If they don't have anything nice to say, they won't say anything at all. And if they do have something nice to say, they'll babble on with no sense of time.

The babbling Pleaser has a lot to say about nothing, and as a result, says nothing that means much of anything. Such babbling is a way to keep some distance while seeming to be close, and this constant chatter gives babbling Pleasers the comforting illusion that they are in a caring relationship. Both the pleasant Pleaser and the babbling Pleaser will do what you tell them to do, and tell you what you want to hear, but will never tell you what you need to hear, or what they need to say. Unless they feel completely safe, it is easier to go along in order to get along

There's also the pushover Pleaser, who gets used and abused by people with an agenda. Masters of denial and wishful thinking, such pushover relatives are willing to believe whatever they are told, and act as if it is true, in spite of any evidence to the contrary. Their willingness to please makes them the toxic dumping grounds for everyone else's stuff, and places them in the line of fire when relatives behave badly. Then, when they finally realize they've been taken advantage of again, they retreat into depression, resentment, and heartache because the world is not a nice place.

One Bad Turn Deserves Another

The difficult behavior of the Pleaser is not without consequences. The Pleaser waits to see which way the wind blows, whereas the General views Pleasers as unable to control their own life. The General then takes responsibility for the Pleaser, and thus gains a loyal grunt, as the Pleaser does his or her best to comply. For the Judge, the Pleaser's behavior is an invitation to criticism and scorn. The Pleaser is unlikely to contradict the Judge, but will internalize the criticism instead. The result is that the Pleaser plummets to deeper and deeper depths of low self-esteem. From the Rebel's point of view, the Pleaser's compliance is a sickening sight, making the Pleaser a frequent target of ridicule. For the Martyr and the Meddler, the Pleaser's behavior is an advantage waiting to be taken. And though the Pleaser finds the behavior of the VIP extremely distasteful, the Pleaser will not stand in the way of the VIP's attention-getting behavior.

Damage Done

While Pleasers go along on the outside, on the inside they take notice of the rude and inconsiderate behavior of others and keep score on the relationship. Eventually, as the score becomes increasingly lopsided, the Pleaser's building resentment makes going along ever more stressful, leading to strange eruptions of out-of-character snippiness and surliness that are quickly apologized for and suppressed. At the end of the family gathering, the stressed-out Pleaser wishes everyone a pleasant goodnight, goes out the door, gets in the car with his or her kids, and then in the safety of that friendly environment, unleashes the resentment. And if instead the resentment simply continues to build over time, it becomes a deep-seated loss of trust in the Pleaser's own judgment that forms an impenetrable barrier to the betterment of any relationship.

Because of this go-along behavior, the Pleaser relative often ends up bringing new problems into the family, problems that the family would rather not have. Such problems are generally the consequence of a Pleaser's failure to notice when someone is taking advantage.of them. Then family members reluctantly get involved to rescue the Pleaser from the mess. The ironic conclusion is that the Pleaser gets pushed away. Relatives always have a reason or excuse not to see the Pleaser, as a way of staying out of his or her problems. As a result, the very people the Pleaser wants most to please hold the kindest person in their family at a distance.

Dealing with the Pleaser

Attitude

You may want to try to knock some sense into Pleasers, or confront them about their consistently irresponsible decision-making. But remember, people don't change just because they feel bad about something they've done. Their shame and guilt become a private world of hurt and self-criticism from which nothing is learned, setting the stage for a repeat of the pattern at the next opportunity.

Instead, put yourself in their place, and have a bit of empathy for their unfortunate patterns and predicaments, while knowing they are not broken. They simply lack clarity and resourcefulness. These are problems that can be made clear and resolved with patience, perseverance, and gentle encouragement. Remind yourself that you can change the future by helping the Pleaser to think clearly enough to bring his or her own interests into balance with the people he or she seeks to please.

Demeanor

The Pleaser has to feel safe enough to let his or her guard down, in order to talk freely and honestly with you about problems. This requires a considerate and empathic demeanor on your part that speaks from a place of concern and possibility. Relax in the moments of your conversation, so that there is no rush, no hurry, and no need to worry about your taking any offense or placing judgment on the Pleaser's humanity. Let Pleasers know that you believe in them, even if they don't yet believe in themselves. And let them know that change is possible, once they are ready to make it, and that you'll be there cheering them on.

Cautions

Don't get intense. Too loud, too harsh, too strong, and you'll be right back where you started. The Pleaser is sensitive, and sudden changes in your demeanor could be interpreted as threatening, making it hard for the Pleaser to hear you, hard to understand you, and hard for him or her to think about what to do differently.

Don't be critical. Feedback is one thing, but criticism is something else entirely. You can help Pleasers understand the role they play in their own life by being constructive instead of critical, talking about what can be done instead of what wasn't done or has been done poorly. Fail to heed this caution and you may think you're succeeding only to discover that they were going along with you in the moment simply to avoid the appearance of conflict.

Don't offer advice. The problem with advice, no matter how good, is that if it doesn't work, it leads to disappointment. Disappointment leads to failure and depression, and change seems impossible to a person who is depressed about his or her own failures. One more thing to consider about advice: Implemented poorly, the best advice can produce wave after wave of side effects, each affecting the person's life in unpleasant and unwanted ways.

Don't expect once to be enough. Instead, consider this as a work in progress. It takes time to build trust, and confidence building takes even longer. Each mistake, each stumble along the way, when used wisely, is a learning opportunity.

Options with the Pleaser

When dealing with the Pleaser, your options include (but are not limited to) the following:

    See Your Part in It
    Create a Context for Change
    Empower Them with Skills
    Harness the Anger
    Give Them a Glimpse of Greatness

See Your Part in It

Perhaps they care very deeply about you, or they have conflicted emotions regarding you. They don't want to disappoint you, they don't want to say "no" to you, or they don't want to trigger you into a frightening reaction. For any or all of these reasons, they may go along with you just to get along with you. If you are commanding, or critical, or self-absorbed, your relationship with them is standing on very shaky ground and will sooner or later be a source of constant disappointment to both of you. If you own a part of the problem, you can do something about it! Acknowledge it to them. Tell the truth about it, apologize, and tell them what you will do differently.

    Don't let them take on things better left to others or that you ought to do yourself. If you suspect that they're going to agree to something that they should not take on, suggest that they think it about it for a day to make sure it really works for them, before having them tell you what they're going to do. Or let them know that it would please you more if they didn't do certain things to please you, and instead looked out more for themselves.

Create a Context for Change

What is a context for change? It is a framework that has several elements.

Safety. Some measure of safety is required to balance the risk involved in moving in a new direction. It is far easier to take a leap of faith or try something new when you have support and encouragement, than it is when you are on your own. So provide a relationship in which Pleasers can gain insight into themselves.

It can be the most difficult thing in the world for a considerate person to tell it like it is to someone else. And it is unlikely that they will, unless they feel comfortable with you and confident that they won't be attacked, criticized, or harassed for expressing their strong feelings. What they require for honest communication is that you be considerate of them, that you feel for them, that you care about them.

Make it safe to be honest so that you and the Pleaser together can honestly examine the mistakes that have been made and the lessons they offer. The key to safety is nonverbal blending and verbal reassurance. Let them know that their feelings are important to you. Let them know that talking things over is a great way to gain insight and influence in relationships. And if it takes them a while because they're all bottled up, be willing to be silent in order to draw them out.

Ownership. When people change their life for the better, they do so because they feel that they can. There is a sense of ownership that kicks in, that tells them that they have a say over the past, the present, and the future, and they recognize that their choices today will determine their tomorrows. A correct understanding of the ownership of the problem leads to ownership of the solution. Gently help them to connect the past with the present, and then connect the present with the future. Explore these connections with them by asking about the connections instead of talking about them. The mistake most commonly made with Pleasers is to give them advice. But Pleasers are quite capable of solving their own problems, of having great ideas, and discovering their own goals. When you patiently ask enough questions, the fog of their emotions is lifted, and the cause-effect relationship between their choices and the consequences of those choices is revealed.

However, there is no follow-through unless there is commitment. In the moments of your conversations with them, they may want to take your good advice, they may say they're going to follow through, and they may even mean it. When they try to get you to tell them what to do, when to do it, where to do it and how to do it, just say no. Say it gently, and say it kindly, but say it. A polite refusal keeps ownership where it belongs. Let them know that your involvement depends on them making progress. Let them know that as much as you care about them, your capacity to be involved is not limitless, because you have a life of your own that requires your involvement and care. Set a framework of ownership that holds them accountable for reporting on their progress, so you know that they are following through.

Questions. Address self-defeating behavior as it occurs. Difficult Pleasers make their life more difficult by believing the worst about themselves. They say, "I'm stupid," and they believe it. They say, "I'm incapable of learning this," and they believe it. If you tell them they are wrong, they'll go along with you on the outside while maintaining this self-defeating stance on the inside. So when they tell you their negative affirmations about who they are, what they do, and why their life is such a mess, the simplest and most effective response is to say it back to them, and then help them reflect on what it means to them.

PLEASER: "I'm too stupid to change."
YOU: "You're too stupid to change? In what way are you too stupid to change?"
PLEASER: "I just have bad judgment, so I keep making the same mistake."
YOU: "What is the mistake? What bad judgment leads to this mistake?"

By backtracking their self-defeating statements and then asking who, what, where, when, and how questions, Pleasers will have a chance to examine up close, and personally, the limiting assumptions and self-defeating behaviors by which they have been defining themselves.

If a Pleaser engages in mind reading, ask, "How do you know that?" and give the the Pleaser a chance to justify such projections.

PLEASER: "They don't care about me."
YOU: "How do you know they don't care about you?"
PLEASER: "I don't know. I just can tell."
YOU: "You can just tell from what?"
PLEASER: "The way they talk to me."
YOU: "So when they talk to you that way, you think they don't care?"

If you can get the Pleaser to a point where the connection is obvious, you can then offer a counter example in the form of a question, and raise some doubt in the place of certain misery. Once you have introduced the doubt, you can ask if the limiting belief is even necessary. The obvious answer at that point will be, "No."

YOU: "Is it possible that they could care about you and still talk that way?"

PLEASER: "I suppose so."

YOU: "Then, really, do you know for certain that they don't care about you?"

PLEASER: " I suppose I don't."

YOU: "Is it necessary to believe it if you don't know it for certain?"

PLEASER: "No, I suppose it isn't."

You can also ask the Pleaser for new meaning. This is called "reframing," and the idea is that there are plenty of ways to interpret anything. Instead of settling for the first meaning, ask for a second one, and even a third one, until the Pleaser finds a way to make meaning that makes sense to him or her.

YOU: "What else could it mean when they talk to you that way?"

PLEASER: "What do you mean?"

YOU: "Well, is there any other way to account for their behavior? Any other reason you can think of to explain the way they talk with you?"

PLEASER: "I suppose they could feel frustrated."

YOU: "Would they be frustrated if they didn't care?"

And there you have it! You didn't need to change the Pleaser's mind. All you have to do is question the limiting assumptions, and you give the Pleaser a much-needed chance to discover his or her own thinking, and its relationship to the choices to be made.

Honesty. When Pleasers take the risk of being honest with you, it is no small matter to them. It is a huge undertaking with the potential for unforeseen consequences. When they are willing to be honest with you, notice and acknowledge it. Telling the truth is hard for a person whose inclination is to comply. But getting reinforcement through acknowledgement and example helps the Pleaser to learn that other options are available than going along to get along.

Empower Them with Skills

If the Pleaser relative in your life has a life that is a mess, the missing piece could be something as simple as goals and plans. Invest some time in exploring where your relative wants to go with his or her life, what kind of relationship he or she is interested in having with you and with others, and then help your relative define goals and create an action plan.

By starting small and then working up to larger goals, a Pleaser can learn this skill and then learn to use it on his or her own.

Not all goals are created equal. Some goals are long-term, others are short-term. With the Pleaser, you'll do well to start with short-term goals. Some goals are external (selling the house, writing a book), while others are internal (speaking up, being confident). Work from the inside out, setting goals first for how they can deal with the problem people and situations in life, and second what they specifically want to accomplish regarding these.

When Pleasers express the desire to be more comfortable speaking up, then help them be specific about the sort of comfort they are interested in. Assume that what comfort means to you may be something very different than what it means to them, so ask questions to gather information about these meanings.

PLEASER: "I don't want to feel afraid to say how I feel around Mom."
YOU: "What do you want to feel? If not afraid, then what?"
PLEASER: "I just want to be more confident speaking up around Mom."
YOU: "More confident in what way?"
PLEASER: "I want to be honest about my needs."
YOU: "What needs do you want to be honest about?"

Goals have to be proactive, rather than reactive, heading toward something rather than away from something else. So if the Pleaser says, "I don't want to feel bad (angry, afraid, etc.)," respond with "If you don't want that, what do you want?"

Goals are best stated in the present. If the Pleaser has the goal, "I will be confident when dealing with my mother" and walks into the house and Mom starts yelling, he or she will think, "Yikes! Maybe someday I will be confident with her, but not today!" But if, instead, the Pleaser states the goal as if it is happening now, the Pleaser's mind and body will organize around it. If the Pleaser has the goal, "I am confident when dealing with my mother," and walks in the house and Mom starts yelling, he or she will be more likely to think "Wait, I am confident when dealing with my mother," and act according to the plan. Stating internal goals in the form of "I am" works better than the future-based "I will." That's because in the real world, tomorrow never comes.

Lastly, goals have to have dates attached, so they are targeted instead of general. The dates don't have to be realistic, but they give the Pleaser a place to start. "I am confident when dealing with Mother during my November visit this year." So once your Pleaser has a goal clearly in mind, help your relative to strategize and plan. By working through these kinds of questions with your assistance, the Pleaser comes to see how tomorrow really can be different from yesterday.

Harness the Anger

Sometimes, still water does indeed run deep, and a sleeping volcano contains the power to erupt. There may be a seething cauldron of bubbling hostility hidden beneath the placid face and friendly smile. Release the rage, and you release the power that comes with it.

Resolve and determination, and in particular, self-determination, can be the result of harnessing justified anger. Anger can be turned into will. So help the Pleaser to talk openly and in an unobstructed way about hurt feelings and unexpressed anger. Help your relative to feel the strength of his or her feelings, and then aim it at something worthwhile.

Give Them a Glimpse of Greatness

Sometimes you have to draw a bigger line, and tell your problem relative the truth about how his or her behavior is self-defeating, and what behavior you think would work better instead. The overview is the same for honesty with any of the problem behaviors. Plan it, write it, rehearse it, and pick your time and place. (See Chapter 8 for more details.) Your goal of honesty is to give them a glimpse of greatness.

1. Positive Intent
2. Be Specific
3. Reveal the Deeper Meaning
4. Suggest Something
5. Reinforce Behavioral Change

However, there are two aspects of honesty specific to the Pleaser:

1. Project Positive Intent

"I appreciate
. . . how much you care about the relationship"
. . . that you want everyone to be happy and get along"
. . . that you want to prevent conflict"
. . . that you want everyone to feel good"
. . . that you want to help"

2. Reveal the Deeper Meaning

Explain to Pleasers that by going along, they have a false relationship rather than a real and caring one, and that the things they hold back and don't say become a barrier to relationship. Tell them that they are so busy being what everyone else wants them to be that they never get to be themselves. The result is that people don't get to have a real relationship with them, and in that sense, they're being inconsiderate to others.

"If you just go along with this, by letting him take advantage of you, you are really letting him take advantage of all of us. We have to deal with him too."

Fable Finale: Carrie Chameleon

Carrie Chameleon was again visiting her brother Carey, who was sunning himself on a rock. She had been meeting with him weekly for some time, and found their talks to be a source of strength and support. She remembered how their talks began. He made her feel comfortable with his calm, relaxed attitude as they sat on the rock, in the same position, facing in the same direction, for almost an hour. Sitting perfectly still, they soaked up the sun. Once Carrie was totally relaxed, Carey cranked one eye around to look at her and said, "I want you to know that your feelings are important to me." He let her absorb that before continuing. "If you want to confide in me about what really hides in your heart, I'm here to hear you." He sounded as if they had all the time in the world. "Sometimes, talking to someone you trust can help you gain insight into your own relationships and behavior. Ultimately, if you learn something about yourself, you become happier, and so does everyone around you."

The happiness of others was very important to Carrie. Since Carey was so relaxed, safe, and open, Carrie couldn't help but be interested in his offer.

"Really? I can talk to you about my feelings?"

Carey reassured her, "Nothing you say could ever change how I feel about you, Sis! I think you're wonderful, and you are welcome to any support I can offer."

Carrie's fears were melting away in the warmth of his love. Soon, her feelings tumbled out in words and tears. "I must be stupid. I always make bad choices. That's why the reptiles I've dated all turn out to be snakes."

Without so much as moving an eye, her brother calmly responded, "You know Carrie, you just did something important."

"I did?"

"Yes, you said, 'I always make bad choices.' The fact that you know that YOU make choices instead of blaming others for your choices, is the first step to making better choices in the future."

"Gee, it is? I hadn't thought of that!"

Carey took his time, because he wanted Carrie to stay relaxed. The next step was to put a crack in her generalization about always making bad choices. He waited for the right moment, then said, "You know, you don't always make bad choices."

"I don't?"

"Was it a bad choice to come here today?"

"Well, no."

"Then you've just made some bad romantic choices, that's all. Instead of feeling bad, maybe you could feel good about learning to understand how you made them. And maybe you could feel good about changing the way you make choices in the future!"

"But what if I can't change?"

Now Carey turned his head, rotated his eyes, and looked right into one of his sister's eyes. "You're a chameleon! Change is always possible! What do you want out of a relationship, anyway?"

"I don't really know."

"I know. That's why you end up with such snakes."

"I see what you mean. Well, I don't want someone who is going to use me."

"Then what do you want?"

"Ah, someone who is considerate of my needs."

"Which needs?"

"I don't need to be put down. I don't need someone to be mean to me."

"Then what do you need?"

"Oh, right. Gee, it sure is easier to think about what I don't want. Is that a lizard trait to keep from getting eaten by predators?"

"Nah," her brother replied, "It's a habit of thought. Humans do it too. But I find it more useful to turn what I don't want into what I do want. I learn from the past, apply it to the future, and then change in the present. I may be a chameleon, but I can still be true to myself. You can too!"

"Gee, Carey. You are really wise. Does that come from sitting in silence on this rock every day?"

"You'd be surprised what you can learn while sitting on a rock!" he said enigmatically.

Carrie chuckled. "Well, I've learned how lucky I am to have you as my relative!"

"And I feel the same way about you, Carrie. That's why we are going to explore your history for more clues the next few times we talk, to keep you on track to a better future. Why, I bet a month from now, finding the right romantic reptile will be as easy as changing your color!"

Carrie smiled at that thought. Then they both closed their eye and soaked up the sun.

The moral of this story is that there are few things so pleasing as learning to change by learning from your own experience.

Quick Summary

◆ See Your Part in It
◆ Create a Context for Change
  • Safety
  • Ownership
  • Questions
  • Honesty
◆ Empower Them with Skills
◆ Harness the Anger
◆ Give Them a Glimpse of Greatness

Chapter 18

The
VIP

Fable: Dena and Doug Donkey

It was the middle of the afternoon, and Dena Donkey wanted to jump the fence. Ever since her divorce, she had been working like a mule to support her foals. She heard a sound at the front of the pen and hoped it was a new trainer with some new opportunity for improvement in their lives. Alas, it was only her older brother, Doug Donkey, scratching himself against the fence post. Doug was always braying about himself, going on about his accomplishments, his living standards, his travels, and his "exceptional" offspring. He's a donkey who thinks he's a thoroughbred, Dena thought. I wonder what he's come to brag about today! she wondered as she trotted, reluctantly, to the fence.

"Hey, Dena, how ya doin'?" Before she could answer, he declared, "There are important developments in the Equus business that could affect us all. It would appear that the *Equus hemonius*, or the Asian ass, may be going extinct in some parts of the world. So I'm leading a summit of *Equus asinus*, or the African ass, to consider counter strategies. Say, did you know that *Equus asinus* includes *Equus asinus asinus,* domesticated donkeys like you!"

"I know what genus and species we are." Dena snorted.

Doug went on as if he hadn't heard her. "For the month of May, I shall be in Mongolia, then Tibet, and then on to India. Then, a fortnight in Mali, West Africa, followed by a month in the Hawaiian Islands. I suppose I shall travel by air, since time is of the essence and I'm sure there are many who will want me to return quickly."

Dena wasn't impressed. For one thing, not even Doug Donkey could fly. But she had to admit that he certainly seemed to be successful. It wasn't unusual for her to feel agitated, stupid, or jealous when he was around.

"I'm taking my children with me again this year. It does them so much good to travel at their age. It gives them a well rounded view that will help them find their own way in the future . . . "

Her mind raced with defensive thoughts. Her yearling was doing just fine, so who cared if his children traveled or what fancy education he gave them! So what if they had a bigger pasture, better feed! She hated making these comparisons, and she tried not to do it, but his loud braying and asinine behavior were simply maddening! When he wasn't one-upping her, he seemed to delight in ridiculing her. "Hey, what do you say we play horse?" he asked. "I'll be the head and you can just be yourself." And then Doug Donkey laughed and laughed, "EE-Aww, EE-Aww. That's a good one, huh?" while Dena said nothing.

"Did I mention, we just got back from a visit to Jack and Jenny's pastures? Mom and Dad are doing great. They just love it when we visit. We all had so much fun together!" The next thing he said felt like a kick in the head. "Dad is sad that you don't ever come home for a visit." Dena's heart sank. They lived so far away, and she couldn't just pack up her foals and travel there. She was barely making ends meet as it was. Her ears drooped, her knees buckled, and she just sat down, feeling like a complete failure. Doug seemed to notice that. "Don't worry," he reassured her. "I told them you can't afford it."

As anger and tears welled up in Dena Donkey, she thought to herself, What a jackass.

The V(ery) I(nsecure) P(erson) boasts, brags, and belittles when needing to feel special.

Understanding the VIP

In our Lens of Understanding, the VIP's behavior originates in the Normal Zone, out of the positive intent to *be significant* (Figure 18-1)

There are two ways that the intent to *be significant* can lead to the VIP's difficult behavior:

1. Threatened intent: fear of not being significant
2. Projected intent: seeing others as less significant

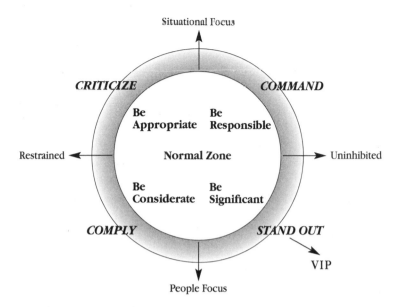

Figure 18-1

The VIP's behavior begins when someone who wants to *be significant* comes to believe that something more than being unique is required to fulfill this intention. Their internal requirement is to live with purpose, and their external requirement is for feedback that tells them they matter. They cannot be satisfied with being in the background if it seems to deny them the impact they want to have. The pressure they place on themselves to matter becomes a need to Stand Out, to somehow go beyond the norm of what everyone else does. That is when the VIP appears and your relative moves from the Normal Zone to the Either/Or Zone.

But the Either/Or Zone is a fork in the road, a choice point out of which comes greatness or danger.

In the Dimension of Greatness, this desire for significance in order to stand out can provide significant advantages to the family. In fact, such desire and willingness are often the motivational drivers for big achievements, significant contributions, and making a meaningful difference in the world. The VIP seeks to be a force of nature. VIPs shine in the light of their accomplishments. The reflected glory gives their relatives bragging rights, and access to resources that otherwise might not be available. Grateful family members admire their courage and drive for mastery. VIPs reward their pride by using their success to improve the lives of loved ones.

When a loved family member is faced with a problem, the VIP brings his or her resources to bear on it. A VIP might motivate siblings to organize a birthday party for a family elder, or give an instrument to a sibling's child who wants to learn to play music. Or the VIP may simply be the life of the party, the enthusiastic relative whose high-energy stories and antics keep the energy going at a family event.

But if they take the other fork in the Either/Or Zone, by polarizing out of fear or projection, the behavior moves into the Danger Zone. Then the VIP seeks to impress rather than influence others.

Regardless of their accomplishments and achievements, the Danger Zone VIPs look to others in the family for validation of their worth and significance. If they find only discouragement, disregard, or disrespect, the internal demand to Stand Out grows in intensity, until the VIP becomes known as someone with a swollen head, an inflated sense of self, and an obnoxious need to show off and be in the spotlight.

Range of Difficulty: From Boring to Condescending

The VIP may be a pompous bore, regaling the family with the same old stories that everyone has heard numerous times before. Their past may have been glorious, but in the present, the only thing that keeps them going is your attention.

The swell-headed VIP is a swaggering showoff whose need to be someone special compels the VIP to brag and boast about anything that makes him or her look good while placing others in the shadows. When challenged, VIPs may engage in a reckless one-upmanship.

The snobbish VIP, in order to feel taller, finds ways to make you seem smaller. VIPs must dress better, travel better, eat better, have better kids in better schools, live in better homes with better gardens, and have better ideas and connections than everyone else. They may prefer to keep company exclusively with people who enhance their status, and avoid being seen with family members who remind them of more humble beginnings. Still, they return home every so often, for the sole purpose of not being forgotten.

Whether boring, swell-headed, or condescending, the difficult VIP can be amazingly petty, taking offense at the smallest thing and then making it into something big enough to be worthy of their disdain. They don't deal well with being less than the center of attention, and spend such time being petulant, prone to pouting, sulking, and moping around until someone notices them again, or yelling angrily for an audience until they get one.

One Bad Turn Deserves Another

The VIP's bad behavior is not without consequence. Their difficult behavior produces difficult behavior in others! It may actually inspire a General to crush this seemingly out-of-control distraction. Or a relative of a VIP may become a Pleaser, listening and watching, nodding and grunting, all the while wanting to be anywhere else. Some relatives react by becoming Mystery people who don't have anything nice to say so they say nothing at all. And if the VIP's acting out draws the critical eye of the Judge, the subsequent fault finding will play right into the VIP's own lack of self-esteem, thus causing the VIP to escalate his or her attention-getting tactics, and giving the Judge even more to criticize.

Damage Done

VIPs harm their own interests, because each time they inflate their own importance, it can cause others to feel resentful and to withhold the very encouragement that VIPs crave. Those concerned with responsibility will view them as distracting and annoying, and discredit them because of their behavior. Those concerned with appropriateness will view them as lacking substance and humility. Those concerned with being nice will find them arrogant and inconsiderate. And those whose primary interest is that which truly matters will likely find them irrelevant and of no consequence. In any case, by pulling in all the light, the VIP puts everyone else in shadow, depriving them of reflected glory. The VIP, in turn, is then denied validation and recognition, and their greatest successes are dismissed or overlooked.

Dealing with the VIP

Attitude

While you may find VIPs to be boring, if their attitude has a diminishing effect on your own, you must get over it! Besides, the behavior of the VIP is not necessarily what it appears to be. VIPs need to feel important because of their drive not to feel unimportant. They want to be admired and respected *in order to feel included and loved!* We would like to think that you are big enough on the inside to humble yourself enough on the outside to humor their fantasy. So if you find yourself in the presence of people who only feel good about themselves by going on and on about themselves, enjoy the show. Applaud occasionally, or save your applause until the end.

Demeanor

The key in your approach to VIPs is a relaxed enthusiasm that tells them they're somehow special. Rather than faking this, it's useful to understand the truth of it. Everyone is unique. It is one of the things all people have in common. Ironic, isn't it? Instead of comparing yourself, become curious, even fascinated, by their fascination with themselves. Laugh at their ability to be entertained by their own humor. And be enthusiastic in your knowledge that their aspirations for significance are to your advantage in dealing with them.

Cautions

Don't be critical. If they exaggerate and you judge them for it, it may embarrass them. Worse, if your criticism is on target, they may doubt themselves, feel insignificant, and hate you as a result.

Don't be the first to get confrontational. Any attempt on your part to put them in their place or reveal them to themselves or others, will only backfire on you. It forces them to save face, to puff themselves up and amplify their point of view even more. On the other hand, if they confront you, it is completely appropriate for you to speak up for yourself.

Don't let them misrepresent you or put words in your mouth. If the VIP says you said something that you didn't say, simply say what you actually said again, to ensure that there is no misunderstanding. This isn't a contradiction. It is a restatement of a statement, or a question that hasn't been answered. "Your characterization of me is your point of view, and it does not reflect my intentions."

Options with the VIP

When dealing with the VIP, your options include (but are not limited to):

◆ Get Out of the Way
◆ Start Something Else
◆ Give Them Something to Be Important About
◆ Turn the Monologue into a Dialogue
◆ Give Them a Glimpse of Greatness

Get Out of Their Way

This option is generally the easiest to exercise. It begins with the recognition that VIPs have recognition needs, and that it does you no harm to let them get those recognition needs met. If they want to be treated special, and you or someone else is willing to give this to them, they'll feel recognized and relax. If they have something they really need to say, and it doesn't hurt you to let them have their say, show a little interest and they'll move through it and relax. If they're offended and need to vent their insecure feelings, and it doesn't hurt you to be with them while they do this, give them a little empathy and they'll feel better and relax. And if they're making a fool of themselves and it doesn't hurt you to watch, you can relax and enjoy the show.

Start Something Else

If the VIP is turning your family into an audience and you can't stand it, but nobody's doing anything about it, don't just sit there, start something! When you see your family members slipping into a trance because of the repetitive nature of the VIP's stories, you can move the energy and change things around. Suggest an activity, call people over to another part of the room or building, or change the subject:

VIP: "The administration is finally acting on ideas you have all heard me talk about for years. It's a shame that it took this long, but then it isn't surprising when you realize what the opposition has been up to! If I could get their attention in the capital, you know what I'd tell them?"

YOU: "Gosh, talking about politics sure makes me hungry. Hey, everybody, who wants ice cream and pie?"

Or start a conversation with someone else at the same time, then stimulate others into joining in by asking specific individuals for their opinions and insights. Once you create a conversation bud, others may feel free to do so as well. In no time at all the gathering will go from dull to interesting, from everyone listening to one person to everyone engaged with everyone else. Just turn to the person next to you and in a normal voice ask any question that starts with a who, what, where, when, or how. Make sure your question is completely unrelated to whatever the VIP is talking about.

In the VIPs' worldview, their world is *the* world, and everyone lives in their world. That doesn't mean you have to. You can always choose to leave the room, or fall asleep on the couch, or go listen to music, take a walk, get some air, or watch TV.

Give Them Something to Be Important About

If you know that the VIP actually has some expertise about something, and you can interest yourself in finding out more about it, then see if you can generate some interest in the VIP to talk about it. It shouldn't be difficult to do, because the VIP will gladly talk about anything when he or she is the center of attention. By facilitating the VIPs' natural inclination to talk and guiding it to something you actually have an interest in, you provide yourself and others with an alternative to hearing about things that are of no interest at all!

Then keep them on the topic. If the VIP starts wandering back to familiar territory, ask a relevancy question: "How does that (what they said) relate to this (what they were talking about a moment earlier)." If they wander off again, remind them of the topic. Hold the focus long enough to get them started, and then get out of the way. This keeps VIPs happy. And who knows? Maybe you'll learn something that you didn't already know.

Once you've done this, you may find that they're more willing to step back and let other people talk.

Another way to do this involves showing appreciation for their significance. If they feel important, they may not try so hard to impress. By identifying those things they have worked hard for, achieved, learned, actually know, or have done, and letting the VIP know that you know about these things, you may help them become more secure in their achievements and knowledge, and therefore less likely to puff themselves up in your presence.

When VIPs express emotions, those feelings are a *big deal* to them. You can let them feel important about their feelings by encouraging them to talk. Believe it or not, it won't last forever. In fact, it will be over sooner if you help them express their special thoughts and feelings. When you say, "That's okay to feel that way," it tells them they're special. When you say, "Tell me about it" and "Tell me more," they feel special. When you say, "You can trust me," you're telling them that they're important to you. The bottom line is that VIPs want to feel special, and it's most important to feel special when they're feeling insecure. That includes their insecure thoughts (hear them as special thoughts), their insecure opinions (hear them as special opinions), and their insecure feelings (hear them as special feelings).

Turn the Monologue into a Dialogue

The challenge with VIPs is, first, to get a word in edgewise, and then to know how to keep your part of the conversation going, even when they try to shut you down. To sustain your part of a dialogue, you have to learn a few simple tactics.

Ask for their help. "Help me with this, would you?" When you ask for their help, it sounds to the VIP like you're offering him or her a moment to be a hero. That's hard to resist when you're only asking for a verbal favor. Then start talking and say what you have to say. If possible, in the end, hand it back to them with a question: "What do you think about that?"

This is also a great option if you find yourself in the difficult position of being condescended to in the course of the conversation. Look confused and ask for their help. "Can you help me understand this?" Then backtrack what sounded like a condescending remark and ask for their intention. If they were trying to put you down, this will likely stop them, as they switch from trying to make you look worse to trying to make themselves look better.

Break the generalizations. VIPs tend to speak in broad terms. So when the VIP says "everybody," repeat the word with enthusiasm and then ask, "Who, specifically?" If they say "always," repeat the word and ask, "When, specifically?" This fills in missing details, allowing you and others to engage with the topic rather than observe it, and it keeps the VIP tethered to the shared reality.

If the VIP makes a huge generalization about you, you can break that one too, by providing extreme counterexamples. For example:

VIP: "I disagree with everything you stand for."
You: "You mean you don't want world peace, you don't want me to love my children . . . "

This forces them to get specific or look foolish.

Use generalizations. When the VIP attempts to shut you down by accusing you of bad motives or lack of knowledge, or makes any comparison that promotes them while demoting you, you don't have to defend yourself. Instead, put yourself in neutral and make a general comment about their comment. Leave out all pronouns (I, you, me, they, us, them, etc.), all emotional words (love, like, hate, sad, angry, frustrated, etc.), and use their words as the basis of your dispassionate response.

VIP: "You would know about this if you spent some of your time keeping abreast of the issue!"

You: "Keeping abreast of the issue can be useful." (Then say whatever you wanted to say before they made their comment.)

VIP: "This would be obvious to a thinking person. Clearly you haven't thought about this."

You: "It is certainly possible that a thinking person would be thinking about this." (Then say whatever you wanted to say before they made the comment.)

You can do this whenever they use insulting or intimidating questions too.

VIP: "What makes you so inept? Are you trying to irritate me?"

You: "Sometimes, people get irritated when they think other people are inept." (Then say whatever you wanted to say before they asked the question.)

VIP: "Have you never read what I've written about that? Is reading a well-thought-out opinion too difficult for you?"

You: "Some opinions are more well thought out than others." (Then say whatever you wanted to say before they asked the question.)

Use information-loaded questions. When the VIP is stating his or her opinion as fact, or dismissing your facts as an opinion, and you know that the facts are on your side, you can ask information-loaded questions to bring the facts to the attention of the VIP (and those held in thrall by the VIP's assertions):

"Were you aware of (*provide the facts*)? Did you know that (*provide the facts*)? Have you read the article about (*provide the facts*)? Did you examine the (*provide the facts*)? How interested were you in (*provide the facts*)? How did your education address this (*provide the facts*)?"

Don't wait for a rebuttal, or even a reply. As quickly and enthusiastically as possible, provide the best information you have in this series of questions that calls into question the opinion of the VIP.

Then, to keep it peaceful and productive, you'll want to complete your questions with a statement that acknowledges the significant role the VIP plays in forming the opinions of other. If you've provided meaningful detail in your questions, the VIP now must contend with the information instead of trying to manage you:

"I ask you these questions because people listen when you talk and value what you have to say. So I think it's important that what you say is based on facts."

Restate the question. In the course of a dialogue with the VIP, you may ask a question whose answer is what you need to proceed.

"What evidence do you have for this? How do you know that what you are saying is true?"

The VIP may realize, consciously or unconsciously, that answering with the facts would undermine the power of their own opinion. The VIP's response is to question you for asking the question:

"How can you possibly ask that? How could you not know that?"

When your question is answered with a question, simply restate your question.

"Actually, my question is, what evidence do you have for this? You haven't answered it yet, and I still want to know!"

Deal with defenders.   Sometimes, the VIP may have a defender or two in the room. People come to the defense of the VIP when their own position in the family is dependent on the VIP and when they're afraid of dealing with the VIP's reaction to being challenged. It's also possible, however, that the VIP has earned his or her position in the family. However it happens, if dialogue is your intent, or you want the facts to be heard, then don't let others run interference for the VIP. Instead, be very clear with defenders that your questions are not for them, but are for the VIP.

"Pardon me, (*name*), my question was for (*the VIP*), not you."

Then turn back to the VIP and restate your question.

Create stumbling blocks.   This is the method of last resort. If you choose this method, be aware that it will likely be a defining moment in your relationship with your VIP relative. Done correctly, they will feel chastised. Done poorly, they'll act out whatever insecurity drama seems most feasible to their fevered minds.

You've been warned. Now here's how it works: If the VIP perceives your questions or efforts at dialogue as a challenge to his or her importance, and views you as a fire that needs to be extinguished, you have the opportunity of making the fire too hot to handle. You do this by using forceful disagreement, which has a riveting effect on the VIP since it makes it difficult for them to dominate the space or control the conversation, and it's disruptive in general to their efforts to promote their self-importance.

For example, if the VIP tries to misrepresent your questions or put words in your mouth, tactfully interrupt and backtrack what the VIP has said. Then say it isn't what you said, and restate whatever you said that got them going. Tell them with conviction what words you actually used, and how you want your words to be heard.

VIP: "Oh, so now we are being told—"
YOU: "We're not being told anything. That may be what you think I said, but it's not what I said. This is what I said . . ." (*Say it again.*)

If they ask a yes/no question, and the answer they're looking for seems to be no, then say, "Yes, absolutely."

VIP: "You don't expect us to believe that, do you?"
YOU: "Yes, I do, absolutely!"

If they demand that you explain yourself, as if it's a big deal that you disagree, then disagree with it being a big deal. Instead, minimize your disagreement by calmly saying it's "just a difference of opinion."

If the VIP is exaggerating, and doesn't seem to notice that you are there (thus making it difficult for you to disagree with them), you can simply communicate your disagreement to anyone else who appears to be listening to the VIP. Do this nonverbally, by shaking your head emphatically as if to say "No way." In this way you can distract the VIP's audience. The VIP notices the distraction and turns in its direction. That's what draws the VIP's attention to you, and before you know it, the VIP has invited you into the conversation.

VIP: "Is there something you want to say?"
You: "Just that what you said is not accurate, and I couldn't disagree more."

The VIP may demand an explanation, realizing that any explanation you give might be used to undermine your credibility. So remember, you don't need to explain yourself unless you want to, and explaining yourself may make you look defensive. You can forcefully disagree with what they said, or when they said it, or where they said it, or how they said it, or that they said it, or what they implied, or what they failed to say, because any of these things throws a stumbling block in their way.

Then minimize your response to their grand reactions and casually say, "It's no big deal." It throws off their timing and interferes with their agenda. By refusing to bow down, and instead speaking up with a forceful disagreement, and then minimizing your response to their reaction to your disagreement, you place verbal stumbling blocks in their way. This prevents them from getting on a roll, from launching into the spotlight and then holding a room hostage to their whims, or getting off the ground, so a conversation isn't possible.

You can use forceful disagreement one on one, with little consequence other than perhaps getting the VIP to avoid you. You can use stumbling blocks in front of the family, if you have the sense that others find the VIP's behavior as tiresome as you do. But be warned. When doing this in front of your family, make sure that others are on your side. Unless you're certain that other family members are with you, creating stumbling blocks will just come across as rude behavior on your part and strengthen the VIP's standing with the family.

Give Them a Glimpse of Greatness

Sometimes you have to draw a bigger line, and tell your problem relative the truth about how their behavior is self-defeating and what you think would work better instead. The overview is the same for honesty with any of the problem behaviors. Plan it, write it, rehearse it, pick your time and place. (See Chapter 8 for more details.) Your goal in being honest is to give them a glimpse of Greatness.

1. Positive intent
2. Be specific
3. Reveal the deeper meaning
4. Suggest something
5. Reinforce behavioral change

However, there's one aspect of honesty specific to the VIP:

4. **Suggest something.** Offer them significance in your life in exchange for a specific change in their behavior.

> "I'd feel a lot better about you if you showed a little interest in me sometimes (*be specific*)."
> "I'd be a lot more interested in hearing about your kids if you showed some interest in hearing about mine."

"I'd have more respect for you if you showed some willingness to consider what I have to say."

"I would think the world of you if you helped me sometimes to deal
with my world (be specific)."

"If you want me to appreciate you and enjoy your company, you have to
back off and give me a little conversational space (be specific)."

Fable Finale: Dena and Doug Donkey

Dena had finally saved enough to travel with her two foals for a brief visit
to her parents, Jack and Jenny. She wished she could stay longer but
couldn't afford to miss work for very long. Doug would be there too. Since
she had a limited amount of time, she was determined and prepared to
not let her brother dominate and spoil it for her.

Jenny had organized a dinner party, and relatives came from far and
wide, even some she hadn't met. She had just started a conversation with
one of them when her brother Doug butted in.

"Yes, I'm back from my Asian tour, working on the extinction problem
with *Equus hemonius*. Of course, I was able to contribute a lot due to my
extensive background in . . . "

Dena surveyed her relatives and noticed their eyes beginning to glaze
over and ears starting to droop. She reminded herself that she didn't
come all this way to listen to another one of Doug's monologues.

"Excuse me, Doug, but I have to say how great it is that you're committed to the preservation of a species."

Doug's ears stood proudly, "Why, thank you."

Then she looked at everyone else. "So let's not ruin Doug's good work
by starving ourselves to extinction. Who's hungry? I think Jenny made
some fabulous hay pie."

That seemed to wake everyone up, because there was a stampede out of the corral and into the barn. Doug was left behind, staring after them.

Sometime later Doug wandered into the barn, where everyone was eating and chatting. Dena looked over at him. He looked so small and alone, standing there in the doorway by himself. Though she didn't want to be dominated or put down by him, she also didn't want him to feel bad about himself either.

"Doug," she said, "I am so glad you are here. Can you help us out?"

His eyes brightened and his ears perked up.

"You've traveled to so many places. Taste this hay. Can you tell what variety it is?"

Doug walked over to the bale and took a nibble. "Hey, that *is* good. I'm not sure where it came from or what variety it is, but it sure is delicious. I did taste something similar in Asia but it had more spice."

Dena smiled, "It must be nice to experience so many exotic places."

Doug said, "Actually, it's really nice to be home," and with that he gave his sister Dena a nuzzle.

The moral of this story is that with a little distraction and a lot of determination, you don't have to let anyone make an ass out of you.

Quick Summary

- ◆ Enjoy Them and Get Out of the Way
- ◆ Start Something Else
- ◆ Give Them Something to Be Important About
- ◆ Turn a Monologue into a Dialogue
  - • Ask for their help
  - • Break the generalization
  - • Use a generalization
  - • Use information-loaded questions
  - • Restate the question
  - • Deal with defenders
  - • Create stumbling blocks
- ◆ Give Them a Glimpse of Greatness

Chapter 19

The
Meddler

Fable: The Life and Loves of Sally Squirrel

Sally Squirrel arrived at the branch where she was supposed to meet the new squirrel guy in her life. She hoped it was sufficiently far from home in order to keep her mother Suzie from finding out.

But then came a demanding voice from a tree away. "Sally, where are you hiding? Show yourself." And just like that, her mother was on the same branch, facing Sally.

"So how's the chipmunk?" Suzie demanded. "I heard you were seen with one."

Sally sat silently stunned, not only at how quickly the news had gotten around, but at how twisted it had become. "Who told you I was seeing someone?" she asked. Someone must have seen her, she thought, because she hadn't told anyone, particularly her mother. She didn't want to have to deal with the relentless questioning she knew she was about to undergo. It was like an interrogation, only without the bright lights.

"A little bird told me," her mother replied. "Why would you give a chipmunk the time of day? Do you plan to live in a hole in the ground? Chipmunks are nothing but hoarders, if you ask me. They never amount to anything."

Sally didn't want to tell her a thing. Yet she felt compelled to say something. "C'mon, Mom! He's not a chipmunk. He's a wonderful southern squirrel, and I'm just getting to know him!"

"Southern? What kind of family does he come from? What are his plans for the future? Did you know that stylish Sammy Squirrel hops by our home every week, asking after you? He is so bright-eyed and bushy tailed. I told him you would have acorns with him tomorrow at the big oak tree.

"You told him what?" Sally screeched.

"You heard me. He looks like a solid provider, not another one of the nutcases you keep getting involved with!"

"But I'm seeing Red tomorrow," Sally squealed, and smacked herself in the head with her tail for revealing his name.

"Red, is it? In which tree does he live? I'll let him know that you can't make it."

"Mother! You will do no such thing."

Suzie didn't even flinch. "Red? What kind of squirrel is named after a color? What does he do, this 'Red'? Does he have any plans?"

Sally was now so off balance from the onslaught of questions that she stuttered out a feeble, "I don't know what he plans to do. I'm just getting to know him myself."

"Don't tell me he's another dropout, or that he's just a gatherer. Anyone can do that. You know what they say. Eventually, even a blind squirrel finds the nuts."

"No, as a matter of fact, he's not a dropout. In fact, he's a flier! He can glide, he's cute, and he's funny. For all I know, maybe he'll go into entertainment. He gets his picture taken every day. He's the most downloaded squirrel on the Internet! He's going to be somebody!"

Suzie twitched her tail in disgust and pressed on. "Not a high-flying dot-com squirrel! And where will you be when he crashes and burns? How do you know he isn't just trying to weasel his way into your nest for a season? After all, why buy the feeder when you can get the seeds for free?"

Suddenly, horror crossed Sally's face as she looked a few branches beyond her mother and saw Red! She covered her face with her tail, hoping he wouldn't see her, but a hop, bounce, and flying jump later he was right there with them.

"Hi, Sally, ma'am." He tipped his head to Suzie. "How ya'll doin'?"

Sally still hadn't uncovered her face. From behind her tail she mumbled, "Hi, Red."

Suzie looked him up and down, "So you're Red. I'll have you know I'm Sally's mother."

With a gentle sweep of his tail and a bow of his head, Red drawled, "A pleasure to meet you, Mrs. Squirrel."

"I hear you and my daughter are dating," Suzie said. Sally was still hiding her face behind her tail, when the situation went from bad to worse.

"So, Red, what are your intentions toward my daughter? Are you going to marry her?"

Red's mouth began slowly to open, but before he could answer, they heard an urgent voice cry. "Mother, Mother!"

It was Sally Squirrel's sister Sarah, who hopped, leaped, dropped when she missed a branch, made a good recovery, then jumped, and joined the three of them on the branch.

"Mother, I think the chipmunks may be raiding our nest."

Without a word Suzie bolted from the branch and was gone.

"Do ya'll need muh help?" Red asked.

Sarah Squirrel gave them a wink of her eye and a shake of her tail, and they realized that she was helping them out.

"Thanks so much, Sarah," her sister said. "I owe you."

"Yeah, you do. But right now you two better get out of here before she gets back."

As the two squirrels leapt, jumped, and scampered off, Sally wondered, Why does Mother have to do that? The last thing I need right now is her interference in my life!

The Meddler thinks they know what's best for you. So they use unwanted questions and advice, to try to manage your life.

Understanding the Meddler

The Meddler's behavior begins when the intention to *be responsible* combines with the intention to *be appropriate* (Figure 19-1).

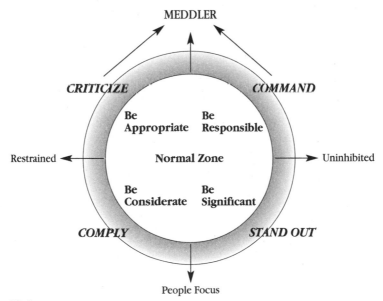

Figure 19-1

When the intent to *be appropriate* is projected, and the intent to *be responsible* is thwarted, this person intervenes to get others to change what they're doing. This could happen in any situation where, according to them, something should or should not happen. They want you to know what needs to be avoided and what needs to take place, and they act as if they have no confidence in the ability of others to make it happen. Good intentions intensify, and become the need to Criticize in order to make others aware, and the need to Command in order to produce the right result. "When are you going to get married?" they'll want to know, and then give you the third degree. Prodding instead of persuading, they find that their attempt to have influence is treated like interference. That's when the Meddler appears, and the behavior moves from the Normal Zone to the Either/Or Zone.

But the Either/Or Zone is a fork in the road, a choice point out of which comes Greatness or danger.

In the Dimension of Greatness, the desire for responsibility combined with critical thinking can be of great service to the family. At his or her best, a person who is meddling is capable of demonstrating the best qualities of both the General and the Judge. The person takes action to prevent problems and asks questions to guide fuzzy thinkers to greater clarity. On occasion, it seems, there is opportunity to meddle. If you see that your child is about to run into a busy street, meddling is completely appropriate and the responsible thing to do. You grab the child by the arm and hold them back, or shout a warning to them before it's too late. Or if a child or a parent or a sibling is getting involved in a relationship with someone of bad character, and you have credible and relevant information about that person's past, indeed it would be irresponsible to say nothing, and it would be inappropriate to ignore the information or keep it to oneself. In the Dimension of Greatness, meddling might involve a careful introduction of missing information or drawing attention to a perceived danger.

But if the other fork is taken in the Either/Or Zone, by polarizing out of fear or projection, the Meddler's behavior moves into the Danger Zone.

Range of Difficulty: From Nosy to Manipulative

There's your basic nosy meddling, where the Meddler looks over your shoulder in order to get a glimpse into your life. This involves poking around in subjects that are no one else's business, in order to find out what you're doing.

There's the controlling Meddler, who looks over your shoulder in order to make sure you do exactly what they want done. Don't do this. Do that. Watch out for that. Don't touch that. Do what you're told or be judged a failure.

Then there's the interfering Meddler, who does things for you, against your express wishes, but for your own good. After all, the Meddler knows what's right for you. And you're obviously not going to take the appropriate amount of responsibility,

Finally, there's the manipulative Meddler, messing with a key detail of your life in order to affect some other part of your life. You, of course, are the last to know. And by the time you find out, the deed is done and you get to deal with it.

From what you wear, to whom you spend time with, to how you talk, to what you do, the Meddler is keeping an eye on you.

One Bad Turn Deserves Another

The difficult behavior of the Meddler is not without consequences. It produces difficult behavior in others! Meddling is one of the fastest ways to create a Mystery, who may believe (rightly!) that cutting off all contact is their only choice to get away from the Meddler's commands and criticisms. Meddling can lead to rebellion, with the Rebel consciously or unconsciously going in the opposite direction to the one the Meddler recommends. Meddling in the life of someone significant is likely to invoke the VIP, who is too important to have his or her life messed with by an amateur. And the Meddler brings out the pushover in the Pleaser, by taking advantage of that person's need to Comply.

Damage Done

Following the law of supply and demand, when there's too much supply of advice, then there is little demand for it. People will go to great lengths to conceal information and protect themselves from unwanted intrusions of the Meddler. You can hear this in the way the Meddler's relatives talk to each other when the Meddler is not around. "Don't tell them about this . . . " and "This is between you and me" are evidence of the intent to keep up the "Keep Out" sign. And it isn't just the advice that relatives want to keep away. It's also the way in which that advice is offered! As a result of past meddling, even if what the Meddler has to say could be helpful, it has little chance of being received. The fight or flight reactions lead to the Meddler being cut off and placed in solitary confinement. This cutting off can be as complete as never seeing or talking with them again, or as limited as keeping every conversation with them as superficial as possible. Whether it's 30 days in the cooler or a life alone, the Meddler winds up losing all influence on the lives of the people the Meddler loves.

Dealing with the Meddler

Attitude

Of all the problem behaviors you could deal with, the Meddler's can be the most perplexing. Meddlers' good intentions, no matter how badly implemented, are evident. Their desire to do the right thing is, for them, an irresistible call to action. You're not going to convince them that meddling is wrong, because in their frame of reference nothing could be more right. Instead, in your behavior and manner, approach the Meddler with caution and a strong sense of responsibility. This blends with their intent to be appropriate and responsible. Enter into the dialogue from a place of commitment, strength, and determination, while knowing that they must do what they think is right and responsible. A little bemusement, kept to yourself, is a plus. It will help you not to take their behavior too seriously, no matter how invasive or personal they become.

Demeanor

Be relaxed and reflective in the presence of invasive and even hostile questions. Just because they ask doesn't mean you have to answer. Instead of answering, ask them a question back, and then be curious enough to look and listen for whatever's behind what they've said. If they ask about your diet or weight, be curious about their food and appearance issues. If they ask about your love life, be curious about their relationship issues. If they ask about your finances, be curious about their money issues. Speak with self-assurance, so that you send the clear signal that you're responsible for yourself and alert to making your best choices. Your nonverbal response must also convey that you're responsible and want to do what's right.

Cautions

Don't answer questions that have not specifically been asked. If they don't ask, don't tell. Just recognize human nature instead of spilling the beans. And if they do ask, you don't have to tell. Rather than deal with the content of their questions, focus on their intentions and the pattern of their relationship with you.

Don't volunteer details or reveal anything that you don't want them involved with. Once the cat is out of the bag, it's difficult to put it back in. (Although why the cat was in the bag is something we've never really understood.) Realize that they may not know where to draw the line and may go further than you want them to.

Don't involve them unless you know they have something to offer. If they do have something to offer, let them know what it is, rather than leaving it open-ended. By exercising some responsibility over their input, you may be able to maintain an appropriate boundary between you.

Options with the Meddler

When dealing with Meddlers, your options include (but are not limited to):

- ◆ Appreciate Their Intentions
- ◆ Give Them a Place to Meddle
- ◆ Meddle with the Meddling
- ◆ Negotiate a Boundary
- ◆ Give Them a Glimpse of Greatness

Appreciate Their Intentions

The behavior of meddling is often adopted as a solution to the problem of loneliness. More often than not, a Meddler is someone older than you, with too much time on his or her hands. Add to this the feeling of being unwanted and unneeded that sometimes comes with age. The result? You have someone trying to have some responsibility by applying to whoever else is around what they think they've learned from their own life. When Meddlers occupy their thoughts with the business of others, they can experience being with others, even if they're alone. When they see you, they can't help but offer you what they came up with for your benefit.

Other times, Meddlers meddle to compensate for the guilt they feel over their own failures. They didn't figure out what to do until it was too late for them, but it isn't too late to help you!

Telling Meddlers that what they're doing is wrong, verbally, or nonverbally, will likely trigger a wave of self-justification and defensive communication that could damage the future of your relationship. Obviously, this is better avoided.

While you may hate what they're doing, there's no reason or value to hate them for doing it. Instead, you can express appreciation to them for their interest and concern. In this way, you meet them where they are. And with a little luck, you may relieve a good deal of the pressure that drives their behavior by receiving it as an intended gift rather than interference or imposition. That's why it's hard to go wrong when you thank Meddlers for their intentions.

If possible, you can even thank them for their actions, based on your understanding of their intentions. Thank them for visits, for gifts, for advice, for time spent, for interest. Let them see you as someone who respects their desire to be responsible and appropriate, and they will remain open to your influence down the road.

Give Them a Place to Meddle

Sometimes people meddle because they have nothing else to occupy their time. With all that time on their hands, they get to thinking about ways to meaningfully contribute to the people they love, and they arrive at the idea of making their relatives' lives their hobby. They'll offer their good advice, keep an eye on things, and watch out for preventable problems, trying to make sure that nothing goes wrong.

If they're determined to meddle, put the behavior in context and give the Meddler a place to meddle. Ask their advice on an issue of lesser consequence. This may create a diversion from the subject you would prefer them to leave alone. Pick an area where their meddling is harmless and possibly constructive. Invite their assistance. Let them help you with something, even if it's something you can do more easily without their help. This gives them the feeling of being responsible and appropriate, and may satiate their need to be involved in your life.

If the Meddler is meddling with your wedding preparations, put him or her in charge of something, even if it's just making the place cards. Count your blessings that you have someone willing to help, and take advantage of the Meddler's offer!

Meddle with the Meddling

There are many ways to meddle with the meddling, like taking control, having a canned response, or creating a diversion.

Take control. You can stop being a victim by taking control of the meddling. Become fascinated with it, and try to find out everything you can, from the source—the Meddler, of course! Find out their interests. Find out their behavioral definitions. Find out by asking questions! Ask enough questions and you may even reveal to them that they know less about the subject than they thought. If that's the case, they'll back off and get out of your way. Let their behavior be your cue. The next time they ask about your private life, ask them what they want to know and then ask more questions about their answers.

MEDDLER: "Are you dating?"
YOU: "What is it you want to know about that?"
MEDDLER: "Well, I want to know what kind of person you're seeing."
YOU: "What kind of person would you like me to be seeing?"

MEDDLER: "You shouldn't wear that. It makes you look fat."
YOU: "It makes me look fat to whom?"
MEDDLER: "People."
YOU: "What is it about looking fat that matters this much to you?"

MEDDLER: "All that butter will raise your cholesterol."
YOU: "How much will this butter raise my cholesterol?"
MEDDLER: "I mean in general."
YOU: "How much butter in general will raise my cholesterol?"

Have a canned response. If your Meddler meddles in predictable ways, and you can anticipate the kinds of things they'll say, then having predictable responses to say in response may be all that's needed to derail the meddling. For example:

MEDDLER: "Dear, when are you going to get married?"
YOU: "Aunt Ellen, I'll get married just as soon as I find someone to love me as much as Uncle Harry loves you."

This one is particularly effective, because it has two possible reactions. If Aunt Ellen is unhappy with Uncle Harry, she isn't going to keep rushing you into something you might regret. And if she is happy with Uncle Harry, she's going to want you to wait until you find the right person.

Predictable responses are best thought of ahead of time. The next time your Meddler meddles in that predictable way, what do you want to remember to say? Write it down, practice it, and then when the opportunity presents itself, use it!

Create a diversion.   You can also use Junk O'Logic to create a diversion. Junk O'Logic makes an artificial connection between what Meddlers say and what you say in response.

MEDDLER: "That coat is not going to keep him warm. Why don't you buy him a decent coat for the winter?"
YOU: "Thanks for mentioning the winter. I was in town the other day, and I saw this lovely window display that you would have enjoyed so much!" (Then just keep going, for at least a minute!)
MEDDLER: "If you get fat, no one is going to like you, and you'll end up alone and miserable, like your father's brother. Is that what you want?"
YOU: "I'm so glad you mentioned him. Have you talked with him lately? The last time we spoke, he . . ."

Once you start talking, keep going, for at least 30 seconds to a minute. This may be enough to distract them and make them forget their attempt to meddle. You can also employ a visual distraction.

MEDDLER: "I can't believe you wasted your money on that car. What were you thinking?"
YOU: "Look! Over there!"

Then point somewhere, suddenly, and start talking about what you see at the end of your finger. Watch them get confused! On the phone, say, "Oh my! Amazing!" And then start talking about anything else. This sort of sudden and strange behavior is called a pattern disruption. If you do it regularly in the presence of a behavior you want to discourage, your Meddler may find it harder and harder to remember to bother meddling at all.

You can do this for your other relatives too! One woman told us of the time her mother demanded to know of her boyfriend, "When are you going to marry my daughter?" Her sister jumped in just then with a distraction. "When are you going to pass the potatoes?" Then she quickly changed the subject to something else, and they made it through the rest of the meal without any further meddling.

Negotiate a Boundary

What's usually missing with meddling is a clearly defined boundary between you and the Meddler. When you find that the Meddler in your life is working toward an apparently different life for you than the one you're living, it may be time to negotiate a boundary that you both can live with.

Plan a meeting. Set a formal appointment to talk with your relative about the role he or she is playing in your life. Agree together on a time and place where you can talk, preferably someplace neutral where you can both feel relaxed and free of your normal day-to-day responsibilities—like a restaurant or a walk in the park. By making this a planned conversation instead of a casual one, you're more likely to bring the problem behavior into focus:

> I appreciate all your efforts to look out for me over the years. I have a problem that I would like to discuss with you. Could we make a lunch appointment to discuss the role you play in my life? I have some ideas that I think will make it less stressful and more productive for both of us. I'd like you to bring your ideas about this to our meeting too.

Be prepared. Know yourself. You have to know your own limitations going in or you'll wind up with a boundary you can't live with. Then there's the problem of being so determined to get your relative to agree to your terms that you wind up alienating them. If you're in a hurry to get the conversation over with, your anxiousness works against you. And this isn't a "have to" situation, either. If it doesn't work out, you still have power. If the relative continues to interfere in your life, you can always walk away. Knowing that you aren't trapped, that you have a tenable fallback position, gives you some breathing room to hang in there and work your way through the process, even when the going gets tough.

Examine the problem and determine what your issues are. Is it about time? Does the Meddler spend too much time around you and your family? Is the problem unsolicited advice? Do you feel you're being treated like a child? Does the Meddler actually interfere in your life, doing things expressly against your will? In any case, to make your case, you'll need to know what the specific issue is for you. What is your interest? How do you want it to be if it changes from the way it is? Clarify this in your mind so that when you communicate, you communicate clearly.

You also want to know something about your relative's needs and interests. If your relative doesn't want you to get hurt, that is valuable information. If your relative thinks there's some way you should improve, understanding why this matters to him or her gives you valuable information. If he or she thinks you'd be happier if you only did as you're told, that's valuable information. And the more you know, the more you can do. Information is power, and as in any negotiation, it makes the difference in how well it turns out for you.

Behave wisely. On the day of your conversation, be pleasant throughout. If you're feeling frustrated and stuck, take a break to regroup, then come back fresh and start again. Keep your conversation focused on behavioral definitions (see Chapter 7) and interests, instead of talking about your relative. Be looking and listening for a solution that gives your relative something to feel good about when he or she gives you what you want.

If you can identify your relative's motivation, and then show how helping you get what you want will help the relative to get what he or she wants, you will have closed the deal and redefined the boundary in your relationship.

The rest of the process will be covered below, under *Give Them a Glimpse of Greatness*. But there are a few more pointers to bear in mind here.

Open with a Positive. Though it's only an opening phrase, it serves the purpose of placing a positive framework around a potentially difficult conversation: "I know you care about us, and that you really mean well when you . . . " Then give a specific example of the meddling problem.

Describe the problem. This is where you state your position. If your relative is demanding too much of your time, be honest about it. If your relative is doing things against your wishes, like spoiling your children or talking to significant people in your life without your permission, be honest about it. Always preface your honest statement with the words "I know you mean well when you . . . " or "I know you're trying to be helpful when you . . . "

Talk about the effects. This is where you tell your relative the part that's hardest on you, and this therefore is the hardest part of the process. Do it in a pleasant manner, but do it well, because everything depends on you providing an accurate understanding of your problem with his or her behavior. Make sure your description includes yourself, so that your relative is hearing about the effect on you rather than your opinion of them.

I felt so angry and frustrated, I could barely talk to you. It really bothered me that you went ahead and did something that I asked you not to do. The result is that I feel afraid to trust you, and anxious about having you spend time with the kids. And I feel awful about that, so it's getting worse for me, not better. Though your intentions are good, it's your actions I'm having trouble with.

You can also talk about what might happen if the behavior continues. Many people are motivated to change out of fear of negative consequences. This may prove to be the missing piece in your relative's understanding of the situation.

Let your relative reply. This is where you listen to your relative's position. Let the relative explain, defend, and justify as much as he or she desires. Look and sound like you completely understand, while listening for possible interests that could give you some options. When you give your relative the chance to account for his or her own behavior, you may be surprised to learn that the underlying reasons were actually better than the ones you had thought to be applicable.

Describe a desired boundary. If you've been listening well, chances are you've now thought of a way to have it work for both of you. But even if you draw a blank on options, you have to tell your relative what it is that you want. If you ask for more than you expect to get, you have room to back down a bit and let your relative feel that something has been won. If you like, you can ask your relative for a solution before you offer yours. But you must get some option on the table in order to draw the line somewhere.

Say what you would like to experience around the issue. What works for you? What doesn't work for you? Are there subjects where you would welcome the relative's interest? Indicate what those subjects are. Is there another way your relative could show an interest? Tell your relative what it is. Be as specific as possible, and communicate in a calm, responsible way so that you are setting a good example of how you want your relative to respond.

Establish a signal. Once you've agreed upon a new boundary in the relationship, it would be nice if you could walk away from the conversation knowing that it was firmly in place. But that isn't likely. The Meddler's behavior was automatic and unconscious, at least in part. You can expect some backsliding. It helps both of you to have a signal system in place so if the behavior reoccurs, you can bring it to your relative's attention without creating a conflict. The signal could be something small, like holding up your first finger and slowly moving it from side to side. Or if the problem happens on the phone, a word or phrase may be helpful. When you have a way to keep the boundary defined, your relationship can improve through time.

Reinforce the boundary. Catch your relative in the act of doing it right and show some appreciation. Make it your responsibility to pay attention in order to reinforce the behavior you want.

Give Your Relative a Glimpse of Greatness

Sometimes, your best choice is to tell problem relatives the truth about how their meddling behavior is self-defeating. The overview is the same for honesty with any of the problem behaviors. Plan it, write it, rehearse it, pick your time and place. (See Chapter 8 for more details.) Your goal in being honest is to give them a glimpse of Greatness.

1. Positive intent
2. Be specific
3. Reveal the deeper meaning
4. Suggest something
5. Reinforce behavioral change

However, three of these items are specific to the Meddler:

1. Project positive intent.   "I appreciate that:

. . . you care about my relationship."
. . . you want me to be happy."
. . . you care about my personal hygiene."
. . . you care about how I look."
. . . you care about how I dress."
. . . you want us to have a nice wedding and get the right gifts."

3. Reveal the deeper meaning

"I feel put down, I feel ashamed, hopeless, and discouraged. And I want to protect myself from feeling that way so I ignore you. It doesn't have to be that way. This is something I can't change right now. I'm not married, I am fat, and I'm working on these things."

4. Suggest something

"You can help me, and here's how it would work. If you see clothing that would work for me, I would be interested in hearing about where to find it. If you know someone who you think would be a good partner for me, I would be willing to consider them, but only if you tell me and not them. Showing an interest in my life is not off limits to you. But this is the way in which you can be successful with your interest in helping me with my life."

Fable Finale: The Life and Loves of Sally Squirrel

Sally Squirrel sat on a branch shyly sharing some nuts with Red. She knew it was only a matter of time before her mother showed up. Sure enough, a leap, a scamper, and a jump later, and her mother was on the same branch with them, suspiciously checking them out.

"Hello, ma'am," Red said politely.

"Hi, Mom," said Sally.

Sally turned to Red and said, "I'll see you later." Red took the hint, but no sooner had he turned tail, hopped, bounced, and leaped away than Suzie began the interrogation.

"So, you're still seeing that Red!" she said intensely. "What are your plans? Where is this relationship headed?"

This time, Sally was ready. She chuckled inside, and reminded herself that just because her mother asked a question, that didn't mean she had to answer it. Instead she said, "Thanks for wanting the best for me! I appreciate how you're willing to use valuable nut-gathering time to check in with me."

Suzie just twitched her tail and said, "That doesn't answer my question."

Sally had spent a lot of time mentally preparing for this. She spoke calmly and directly. "Mom, I really do appreciate that you want me to have a good relationship. But we have a problem here."

"Really?" her mother said. "What is it?"

"I know you mean well, but when you follow me around and snoop on my relationship, it drives me nuts! I feel like running away from you. Sometimes, I even consider doing something nutty just to spite you, like seeing a squirrel that really *is* no good for me. You don't want that, do you?"

"Of course not! But—"

Sally was determined not to let her mother control this conversation. "No buts, Mom. I have found that by getting to know different squirrels, I am able to better define what I'm looking for in a relationship. This is my business, not yours. If I tell you about any of my relationships, it will be when I'm ready to do so. Now, if you like, there is a role for you to play. If you want to tell me about squirrels that you think I might find interesting, I'll consider them. But I don't need a matchmaker, and if you insist on trying to be one—by setting up meetings with them or prying into my affairs—I will ignore you and scamper off the other way. Do you understand?"

Suzie was taken aback. "But I'm simply looking out for what is best for you," she replied defensively.

"I know you are, and I appreciate your intentions. I'm telling you how you can do that successfully. You may not hunt me down and intrude when I'm with someone. But you may ask questions privately. I may choose not to answer them. If you think there's someone I ought to meet, you can tell me. But whether I chose to act upon your suggestion is entirely up to me. All right?"

Suzie looked at the branch beneath her, then said, "You know, I was young once. And my mother did the same thing to me. I can' t believe I am doing it to you. I used to hate it."

"Then you agree to these conditions for your involvement in my love life?"

"Agreed. I promise to do my best to change. But it's so automatic, what if I forget?"

Sally smiled, "Then let's have a signal. If I swish my tail from side to side, real fast like this," and Sally demonstrated, "that means you are crossing the line. Okay?"

"Okay," her mother agreed.

Then Sally said, "There is one area where I really would like your advice."

"Oh, Sally, nothing would make me happier. What is it?" Suzie asked, excited about an opportunity to help her daughter.

"How do you get at those seeds in the bird feeder? I've seen you do it, and you're quite good at it!"

"Yes, I am. Come on. It's not hard. I'll show you."

And with, a leap, a scamper, and a bounce, Suzie and Sally were happily on their way.

The moral of this story is that when you're feeling nuts and seeing Red, take the leap and build a boundary.

Quick Summary

- ◆ Appreciate Their Intentions
- ◆ Give Them a Place to Meddle
- ◆ Meddle with the Meddling
- ◆ Negotiate a Boundary
  - Plan a meeting
  - Be prepared
  - Behave wisely
  - Open with a positive
  - Describe the problem
  - Talk about the effects
  - Let them reply
  - Describe a desired boundary
  - Establish a signal
  - Reinforce the boundary
- ◆ Give Them a Glimpse of Greatness

Chapter 20

The Martyr

Fable: The Three Bears

Winter was in the air. Hibernation day was tomorrow. But tonight all Papa Bear could think about was his final meal of the season. As he sat in his big chair, his mouth watered at the enticing thought of his favorite food, fresh hot porridge.

Mama Bear brought her bowl to the table first, so her porridge would have a chance to cool off. Baby Bear was served next, so that by the time everyone was served and they started eating, his would be just right. Papa Bear liked his porridge piping hot, so his was served last.

As he took the first whiff of his porridge, Papa Bear was distracted by the antics of his bear cub, who was rocking back and forth in his chair with glee. He gently reprimanded Baby Bear. "Sit still or you'll break the chair!" Then he turned to Mama Bear, "That chair is barely holding together. Grampa Bear doesn't know how to make furniture! He should stick to gathering honey and leave the carpentry to the beavers."

Mama Bear nodded knowingly. Then she remembered. "Speaking of your dad, he stopped by earlier. He wants you to come over to help with some last-minute projects."

Papa Bear's jaw dropped. "Help him with projects? 'Honey-do' time is over. Tomorrow is hibernation day!"

Just then, the phone rang. Mama Bear pushed her chair back and reached behind her to answer it. Papa Bear and Baby Bear listened as she said, a little loudly, "Grampa Bear! Yes, yes! I gave him the message."

Papa Bear mouthed, "Tell him I'm already hibernating!"

Mama Bear tried to smooth this over before it got out of paw. "Well, I'm sure there's a very good reason . . . tomorrow *is* the beginning of hibernation and—"

"He's going to hibernate without stopping in to see his parents?" They could all hear his depressed voice coming through the phone's earpiece. "All right. If he can't spare a few moments to help me out or have a meal with us, tell him I understand. Me, I'm not ready to hibernate, because I spent all that time making that nice chair for Baby Bear and those big beds for you and my boy. But if he's too busy . . . "

Papa Bear rolled his eyes, bared his teeth, and then, in an exasperated whisper to Mama Bear, said, "I didn't ask him to make that furniture! Not to mention that my bed is too hard and yours is too soft."

"Mine is just right!" Baby Bear laughed and jumped up and down in his chair with delight.

Papa Bear turned and whispered loudly, "That's because I made it! Now quit jumping around, that chair your grampa made is falling apart!"

Mama Bear, didn't want to be in the middle of this, so she gestured to Papa Bear to come to the phone. "He's your father," she mouthed.

Papa Bear reluctantly rose from the table, knowing his hot fresh porridge would soon be cold stale mush. Feeling grumpy, he grasped the phone in his paw and said, "Hello, Dad. Listen, we're just sitting down to eat—"

"Hey there, big bear! " said Grampa Bear, as if he hadn't heard a word. "Ready for a nice winter's hibernation in that new bed I made you? Must feel good to be able to hibernate in your own home. That's why I worked so hard all those years doing tricks at the circus, traveling from town to town, living life on the road, so my cubs could have it better than me. Now, if it isn't too much to ask, why don't you all come over here, right now? Your mama prepared a special meal for you—fresh fish."

"Aw c'mon, Dad!" Papa Bear said. "You know I don't like fish."

Grampa Bear said, "It would kill your mother to hear you talk that way after she went to so much trouble. Here, your mother wants to talk to you."

Grammy Bear's voice was sweet as honey. "Hi, my favorite teddy bear. I went fishing all day today and caught some fresh salmon, and it's all ready for you when you get here."

Papa Bear groaned, "Aw, Ma . . . "

"Don't 'Aw, Ma' me! Last time I saw you, why, you were nothing but fur and bone. Not to mention that I spent the whole day fishing, even though I just had my fur done. But of course if you're too important to spend a little time with us, or our food isn't good enough for you, we'll understand. Don't feel obligated just because we won't see you for months, and we haven't seen Baby Bear all season. He probably doesn't even know who we are at this point anyway!"

Papa Bear sighed, "Okay, Ma. We'll be there shortly." He hung up the phone and looked longingly at the porridge. "Grrrrr. I love porridge. And I hate fish. I was so looking forward to one last bowl of piping hot porridge before we go into hibernation!"

Mama Bear tried to reassure him. "Don't worry, the porridge will still be here when we get back."

Papa Bear whined, "Well, that's easy for you to say. You like your porridge cold. But I like mine hot. It's not the same when it's reheated. And besides, I haven't even fixed the lock on the door yet. I was planning on doing that after my porridge."

"Oh, don't be a worry bear." Mama Bear replied. "The forest is safe. Besides, we're bears! Nobody will come into our home uninvited!"

And with that the Three Bears left the house and lumbered down the path, with Papa Bear grumbling every step of the way.

The Martyr is a needy giver, giving gifts whether you want them or not. Each one comes with an obligation.

Understanding the Martyr

The Martyr's behavior begins when the intention to *be considerate* combines with the intention to *be significant* (Figure 20-1).

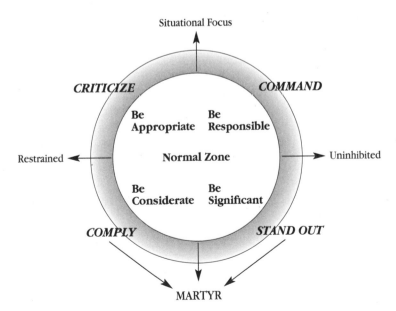

Figure 20-1

When the intent to *be significant* is thwarted, and the intent to *be considerate* is projected onto someone else, the person tries harder to matter in your life in order feel loved, and becomes a needy giver. This could happen between people when there is competition for affection, or the person feels ignored or taken for granted. Then their good intentions grow in intensity and become a need to Comply with what they think you want, or what you say you want, along with a need to Stand Out and be recognized for doing so.

Needing to Comply, they don't ask for what they want, and needing to Stand Out, they fail to find out how to do so. That's when the Martyr appears and the behavior moves from the Normal Zone to the Either/Or Zone.

But the Either/Or Zone is a fork in the road, a choice point out of which comes Greatness or danger.

In the Dimension of Greatness, the desire to be helpful to others—because of the significance of such service—can be a source of great good. In fact it is a powerful cultural reference point, the very stuff of which legends are made. Books, comic books, and movies tell tales about heroes, people who are significant enough to be known and loved for their good deeds. The villains in these stories typically think they're more significant than they actually are. They are seriously lacking in their ability to care about others, and thus are despised by all. At best, the Martyr demonstrates the better qualities of the Pleaser and the VIP. The Martyr will care for the parents when the parents can no longer care for themselves, or care for the child of their child, if their child is not ready for parenthood. And at family gatherings, the Martyr will go to great lengths to make sure everyone gets what they need and has a good time.

But if the Martyr takes the other fork in the Either/Or Zone, polarizing out of fear and projection, the behavior moves into the Danger Zone.

Range of Difficulty: From Obligation to Self-Pity

There are a number of ways for a Martyr to distress and disturb other family members.

First, there's the Mild Martyr approach. Mild Martyrs start with the obligation inherent to any family relationship and build on that as a base. They do what is asked of them, just as most people would. And then they do more, and without question. They also do what is not asked of them, and without asking questions. They observe a need and fill it, thinking, *I'm doing you a favor.* In this way they gain favor by their efforts and build the expectation of their help.

There's also the Muttering Martyr. The pattern is the same, with one exception. Muttering Martyrs do everything obviously and begrudgingly, saying, "Yeah, sure, why not, it isn't like I have anything else to do." They complain out loud, yet they do as they are asked, and over time this builds up their sense of entitlement, of *quid pro quo*. The muttering Martyr says, " I'm doing you a favor, you owe me."

On occasion there's the Martyr Meltdown. Maybe it's the result of doing the other approaches for too long, or maybe it just occurs spontaneously, after the Martyr has had a particularly bad day. Or maybe the Martyr is dealt a reversal in the game of life and it all seems so unfair. They scream, "WHAT ABOUT ME?" and turn into a puddle of self-pity, which pulls hard on whatever obligation is available.

As family members tire of the unsolicited help, bouts of self-pity, and guilt, the Martyr winds up doing more and getting less in return.

One Bad Turn Deserves Another

The Martyr's behavior is not without consequence. Such difficult behavior is likely to produce difficult behavior in others! The General tires quickly of the Martyr's self-pity and wants to confine the Martyr to quarters. The VIP looks down on the Martyr as a VIP wannabe, unable to gain significance without obligation! "Instead of feeling sorry for yourself, why don't you do something with your life like I did!" Pleasers go along with it, trying to fix it and winding up caught by it. The Judge finds the Martyr guilty of inappropriate behavior. The Rebel refuses to be manipulated, the Meddler thinks the situation is an invitation to meddle, and the Mystery gets away as fast as possible.

Damage Done

Martyrs harm their own self-interest in at least two specific ways. First, the unasked-for gifts and service usually go unappreciated. Some relatives decide, "If they want to do it, let them!," and even take advantage of them. Others simply feel no pity because Martyrs provide enough pity for themselves on their own. This locks the Martyr into a try/fail loop from which there is no exit. The harder Martyrs try, the more they fail. The more they fail, the harder they try. The more they give, the less they are appreciated. The less they are appreciated, the more they give. And no one stays around long enough to give back, because being excessively needy and annoying are such unattractive qualities in a person. Attempts by Martyrs to tap into obligation and invoke guilt practically ensure that no one will want to give them anything ever.

Dealing with the Martyr

Attitude

A Martyr is likely to play on any vulnerability he or she finds in you, so keep your shields up! Keep reminding yourself that the Martyr's need for significance is the drive behind the moaning and struggling, rather than someone else's failure to appreciate the Martyr, as he or she claims. Keep some emotional distance on the inside, so you don't get hooked or roped into feeling guilty.

Demeanor

Martyrs' need for validation is so intense that you *must* feel some appreciation for them if you hope to gain their trust and influence their behavior. Approach them as if they deserve gratitude for something, and if you can't think of anything for which to be grateful, then be grateful that their impact on your life has its limits. Appreciate them for all that they *don't* do. Or appreciate them for all they "try" to do. Or appreciate them for all they "want" to do. One way or another, your demeanor must come across as genuinely considerate and appreciative. At the same time, you must empathize with how unappreciated they feel.

Cautions

Don't call them "a Martyr." This is a guaranteed recipe for starting a conflict. Martyrs want your gratitude and empathy, not a label for their behavior.

Don't defend yourself. It serves no valid purpose when the problem is with them rather than you. When you're being held to account for the feelings of insignificance in others, you need only thank them for being honest, or for bringing the feelings to your attention. You don't have to have a "dialogue" about what is and isn't true regarding you. Any defense you offer will sound like you're making excuses, so you might as well excuse yourself from this futile exercise.

Don't try to fix the problem. When the problem isn't yours, or exists only in the mind of the Martyr, any attempt you make to fix it simply affirms and strengthens the Martyr's commitment to having the problem.

Don't let them carry the entire burden. If you see Martyrs taking on all kinds of things about which they can complain later, get engaged, and insist that they should only do their fair share, and that if they take on more, they'll have no one to blame but themselves. By letting them know this in the moment, you create something to refer back to when the guilt trip starts again.

Options with the Martyr

When dealing with the Martyr, your options include (but are not limited to):

◆ Look for a Chance to Give
◆ Disrupt the Guilt Trip
◆ Hit the Reset on the Upset
◆ Say No to Unreasonable Requests
◆ Give The Martyr a Glimpse of Greatness

Look for a Chance to Give

By handling the Martyr's need for significance preventively, you might be able to avoid the latest episode of "Poor me!" While it may or may not cancel an ongoing soap opera, it can give you welcome relief. And it very well might change the foundation of your relationship with one or more problem relatives. Such things have happened before.

Danny told us:

It started about five years after I moved out on my own. My father used to call my sisters whenever Mother browbeat him. He'd say, "I can't do anything right for her. Everything I do is wrong. She's never happy no matter how hard I try. I don't think we're going to make it." But when they asked him why he kept trying, his answer was always the same. He felt like he owed it to her. It's easy to understand why he felt that way, because she was always at him about what she'd done for him. Why did she do all those things for him? I asked her, and she said it was because she owed it to him! And he was always on with my sisters about what he had done for them. And why did he do those things for them? I asked him, and he said it was because he owed it to them! And my sisters were on with me about what they had done for him! I asked them why they did all those things for him, and they said because they owed it to him! One day it occurred to me that here are all these people that I care about, and they all do wonderful things for each other, and yet they don't give each other any real appreciation, because everyone feels so unappreciated. And so they're all driven by guilt! So I make it my work to give all of them the appreciation they deserve. And why do I make that my work? Because I love them, and it is my pleasure to appreciate them. And they do deserve a lot of appreciation! My appreciation may not mean that much to them, but at least this way they're all getting some. And maybe someday they'll follow my example. You never know! In the meantime, I get to enjoy all of them, and they seem to enjoy me too.

Let Martyrs know you don't take them for granted, and they'll be less likely to assume that you've forgotten them. You can do so in the following ways:

Tell them what you love. When they do things or say things that you don't appreciate, tell them that you appreciate their positive intentions. Then tell them what they could do that you would appreciate even more. By directing them to an area where they can know it matters, they learn how to play a role in your life that truly matters to you.

Take their side. If you do something that crosses them, and they blame something you said or did for their hurt feelings, there is no amount of explaining that will change the way they feel. But if you apologize or acknowledge their view of the situation, they may let go of their hurt and choose love.

Harry told us:

> My mother, Sybil, learned from my wife's sister that I had not told her about a significant event involving my daughter. Sybil was so furious that she stopped talking to me completely. Whenever I called, she would shout at the phone, "You don't care about me!" and then hang up. If I came to her door, she would yell from the other side, "Go away. You don't care about me!" This was difficult for me, because I had withheld the information initially in order not to upset or worry her. But after the fact, it was having the opposite effect. One day, I sent her a huge bouquet of flowers with a note that read, "I see your point. I was thoughtless. I love you. Please forgive me." The result? She called me and thanked me for the wonderful flowers, and told me that she loved me too.

Speak to the child within. Like a child going to extraordinary lengths to win approval, the Martyr often tries harder than anyone to win your love and appreciation. When you see this behavior as childlike, you can speak to the child within. Using the same facial expressions and voice tones that you might use with a child, give the Martyr the attention he or she desires. When the Martyr says a pathetic "Poor me," you can lift the burden from the Martyr's shoulders by saying, "Oh, you poor baby! You need a wittle woving wight now, don't you?" Such a playfully loving communication may be just what is needed to soothe their soul. Several of the people we interviewed described how effective this playful approach is. Perhaps doing this makes you come across to them as "wovable and iwwesistable!"

Disrupt the Guilt Trip

The Martyr is visiting you. The phone rings, and as you excuse yourself and reach to answer it, the Martyr says, "That's all right, take the call. Though I'm only here for a little while, don't worry about me. I'm sure whoever it is has something more important to tell you than what I was talking about." That's your invitation to go on a Guilt Trip, a field trip into the fantasyland of If/Only, If/Then, Shoulda-Coulda-Wouda, and I Wish! The feeling of guilt is your ticket to ride. Board the bus and away you go. But you don't have to get on the bus. When you understand the dynamic of guilt, you can avoid it.

Strip it. When you understand the nature of guilt, you can strip away the veneer of obligation to see exactly how the Guilt Trip works.

So what is guilt? It is the emotion that you feel when you do something that violates your values. If you value family but your job keeps you away from them, you feel guilty. If you value loving kindness but yell at your child, you feel guilty. If you see someone suffering and do nothing to help, and

you value being of service, you feel guilty. Even if the action or inaction that
violates your values is your best choice under the circumstances, you still feel
guilty. Guilt is not inherently a bad thing. People who don't feel it at all tend
to end up as criminals. When it doesn't debilitate, it can motivate. Guilt helps
us moderate bad behavior, it induces introspection and even contributes to
the process of creative thinking. You can resolve guilt feelings by taking
action or refraining from action. So the feeling of guilt has the power to make
us consider our actions and change our behavior in order to restore our values to their rightful place in our lives. How does guilt hook into your sense
of obligation? When you feel in the wrong, you want to set things right! A
person who grows up with constant criticism, or who gets blamed for things
they did not do, may feel in the wrong even when they are not. Intentionally
do something "bad" as an act of rebellion and live with the fear of being
found out. They are ready to go on the Guilt Trip. People brought up to
believe that doing nothing is the worst thing they can do may feel guilty
every time they try to relax. Such guilt feelings are the price for an E-Z Pass
on the Guilt Trip Turnpike. All that remains is to punch your ticket, and they
oblige you. They create a link between your sense of regret/obligation and
you doing what they want. In effect, they say, "If you were more responsible, you would do as I want." "If you were more caring, you would do as I
want." "If you were more appropriate, you would do as I want." "If you were
more significant, you would do as I want." Or they might use the negative
corollaries: "If you weren't so irresponsible, you would do as I want." "If you
weren't so inappropriate, you would do as I want." And so on.

Flip it. When the Martyr directly says something intended to make you
feel guilty, you can flip it around to make the Martyr feel guilty for saying it.
Flipping the guilt requires you to notice it and turn it around. If Martyrs
accuse you of not caring, tell them they aren't caring about your caring. If
they tell you that you don't appreciate them, tell them they must not appreciate your appreciation. By refusing to accept their explanation of your
behavior, and calling their behavior into question, you flip the guilt back
where it belongs, and thus free yourself of any obligation to do or not do
what you do or don't want to do.

MARTYR: "You don't appreciate all I've done for you."
YOU: "I do appreciate all you've done for me. But I don't think you
         appreciate my appreciation!"
MARTYR: "That's not true."
YOU: "Well, it isn't true for me either."

MARTYR: "If you really loved me, you would help me with this."
YOU: "If you really loved me, you would understand why I can't."
MARTYR: "But I do really love you!"
YOU: "And I do really love you too."

Snip it. Another way to take you on a Guilt Trip is to encourage you to do what you want to do, and to feel bad while you do it! Martyrs attempt to attach the consequence of guilt to your determination to make your own choices. Why? Because guilt becomes obligation. By building the sense of obligation over time, they can invoke it at a future time to get what they want, or to stop you from doing what they don't want you to do. Obligation, even when it's manufactured in this way, can be just the kind of access they need to keep you in check on the larger issues of the relationship. The best protection is to snip the connecting cord they've attached that ties your choice to guilt. First, snip the cord inside yourself. Then thank them for their support, as if support was what they had to offer. This disconnects their access and frees you to move on without any chains of obligation to bind you.

MARTYR: "Go ahead. Don't worry about me."
YOU: "Okay. That's great. Thanks!"

MARTYR: "Here, let me get the check. I'll find a way to cover it."
YOU: "All right, if you insist!"

Sometimes the Martyr assigns value to your choices, and makes a negative comparison to the Martyr's own value in your life, in either caring or significance:

"You care more about him than you do about me."
"You care more about yourself than you do about me."
"You think that is more important than me."

The best response is to snip the connection between doing what you want and the motives assigned to it by the Martyr. You can easily do this by assigning a different value of either being responsible or being appropriate. Then appreciate their understanding.

MARTYR: "Go ahead. You obviously care more about that dog than you do about me."
YOU: "Actually, I'm taking care of the dog because I gave my word, just like you would if you were in my place."

MARTYR: "Go on, if your husband and children are more important to you than your own mother."
YOU: "Actually, I have a responsibility to attend to my family's needs, just like you attended to ours."

MARTYR: "You don't have to come visit if you have more important things to do."

You: "You're right. It would be wrong to spend the money to make the trip right now."

Nip it in the bud. What is the hook that obligates you with the Martyr? What do you feel guilty about and how does the Martyr use it? To stay off the trip, you have to free yourself of the guilt that isn't yours, and act on the guilt that is.

If someone gives you feedback in an honest and nonmalicious way, and that feedback makes you feel bad about yourself, then there is no Martyr involved, and the Guilt Trip is your own. Identify the undermined value in your life, do something to restore it, and the burden of guilt will evaporate. If you feel obligated because of something someone has done for you, balance the equation and be done with it. Take an inventory of what you've done in return for what your difficult relative has done for you, and see how it looks on the balance sheet. If you owe a debt and haven't repaid it, come up with a plan and implement it. Or identify how you're repaying the debt and give yourself credit for it by knowing what it is. Then, if a Martyr pulls on the obligation string, it will be attached to nothing and come off in the Martyr's hand.

Hit the Reset on Their Upset

Sometimes, people are upset because they keep upsetting themselves! Dr. Albert Ellis,[*] the founder of Rational-Emotive Behavioral Therapy (REBT), noted a key distinction between emotionally healthy people and emotionally unhealthy people. It all comes down to what he calls "rational self-acceptance." He observed that acceptance of life's difficulties and one's own human frailty leads a person to greater patience, perseverance, and happiness. Emotionally healthy people do not determine their intrinsic value by external measures. No matter their accomplishments and possessions, or the opinions of others, such people accept themselves as they are, and so have nothing to prove. It is enough just to be alive, do their best, and enjoy themselves.

Emotional problems, irrational thoughts, and difficult behaviors, on the other hand, are often the result of taking external events personally. The best thing you can do to improve a family member's sense of self-worth, is to see and treat the family member as an intrinsically valuable human being and then help your relative to find the place where the event is not about him or her, even if it has his or her name attached to it. Your point of access is in the kind of things your relative says. When the Martyr expresses self-pity, hit the reset on this upset in the following ways:

---

[*] More about Dr. Albert Ellis and his insights on unhealthy emotions and their treatment can be found at *www.rebt.org*

Respond to exaggerated badness. Have you ever had something bad happen to you, and you played it over and over in the privacy of your mind so you wouldn't miss out on any aspect of the badness of it? While everyone does this at some point in life, the Martyr tends to make a habit of it. A glass of wine is spilled at an otherwise wonderful family gathering, and the Martyr says, "The whole evening is ruined." If there isn't enough food, or some detail was inadequately planned, the Martyr says, "This evening is a disaster!" But was the whole evening ruined? Or was believing so what ruined it for the Martyr? Was the gathering a disaster, or was the Martyr's response the disaster? When people exaggerate the badness, you can exaggerate their exaggeration and then ask for a counterexample.

MARTYR: "Nothing could be worse!"
YOU: "Nothing? You can't think of a single thing that could be worse?"

Counter the frustration. Martyrs tend to express frustration with generalized self-pity, even though the are referring to specific external circumstances outside of their control. They say always, never, everybody, and nothing. If you have a specific counterexample (and there are probably plenty for you to draw on), here's how to use it:

MARTYR: "You never come over to visit"
YOU: "Remember last week when we stopped by?"

MARTYR: "I know nobody cares about me."
YOU: "Then why did we throw that birthday party for you last year?"

Upgrade to preferences. Life is change, and it cannot be controlled. Preferences work better than rigid demands in dealing with people and events in a healthy way. People with preferences have some control over their own thoughts and feelings. People with rigid demands of life try to control events and people, and when their demands are not met, they become miserable. They could find a way out of their misery if they upgraded their demands into preferences, so that instead of focusing on how something "should" work out, they could focus on how they prefer it to work out, based on how it is. While the Martyr may be unable to make this shift, you can offer an upgrade:

MARTYR: "You could have been more thoughtful about my request."
YOU: "You would have preferred me to be more thoughtful about your request?"
MARTYR: "I would have done anything for you, if you would have just asked."
YOU: "You would have preferred to do whatever I asked?"

When this kind of pattern is repeated over and over, it may make an impression on the way the Martyr thinks about the woulda-coulda-shoulda's.

Say No to Unreasonable Requests

Saying a clear *"No"* is an important skill, particularly for people with a well-rehearsed Pleaser approach to conflict avoidance. Saying no can help you to be a more authentic person, because you're letting people know how you actually feel about things. And when you agree to help or be helped, they'll know it's sincere and meaningful, not grudging or given with hidden, ill feeling. Saying no does not make you selfish either, so long as you're not focused on your self-interest to the exclusion of others. When it comes to saying no, it isn't what you say—it's how you say it that makes the difference. Say it calmly and simply, like it's the most normal thing to say in all the world. Repeat it if you have to. Keep it simple. If you encumber it with excuses, out of concern that the Martyr might get upset with you, your no is easier to challenge and undermine. And if you become aggressive in saying no, the Martyr will get very upset and will only remember how he or she felt when you said it, rather than focusing on what you were talking about.

To add some power to your "No," shake your head no at the same time. This makes it a congruent message and carries more force than the mixed message of saying no while looking tenuous, uncertain, or confused. To make your refusal more palatable to the Martyr, you can preface it with a cushioning phrase, like, "Thanks for asking, but no" or "I'm sorry but I have to say no" or "Unfortunately, the answer is no." If you like, finish with another cushioning phrase, like, "Thanks for asking" or "Thanks for thinking of me" or "Perhaps another time."

If you're uncomfortable with saying no, practice on empty elevators. At each floor, act as if you're being asked to get off before it's time and say, "No, not here" and "No, not now" and "No, it's too soon." Then, when it is time to get off, say, "Yes, here it is!" and feel how great it is to say yes only when the time is right.

Give Them a Glimpse of Greatness

Sometimes you have to draw a bigger line, and tell your problem relative the truth about how his or her behavior is self-defeating, and what you think would work better instead. The overview is the same for honesty as with any of the problem behaviors. Plan it, write it, rehearse it, pick your time and place. (See Chapter 8 for more details.) Your goal in being honest is to give your relative a glimpse of Greatness.

1. Positive intent
2. Be specific

3. Reveal the deeper meaning
4. Suggest something
5. Reinforce behavioral change

However, there are two aspects of honesty specific to the Martyr:

1. Project positive intent. Tell them, "Thanks for:

. . . taking care of things."
. . . putting all that work into it."
. . . making such a wonderful dinner."

2. Be specific. Remember to use language like, "I am sure you can appreciate," before showing them the self-defeating nature of their behavior.

Fable Finale: The Three Bears

It was one week before hibernation day when Papa Bear announced to Mama Bear and Little Bear (who wasn't a baby anymore!) that they were going to visit Grampa and Grammy Bear. Mama Bear looked at Papa Bear curiously, and he answered the unspoken question, telling her, "I don't want any last-minute calls ruining my prehibernation day porridge, like last year."

Papa Bear entered the secret code into the new alarm system he installed, double-checked the locks, and off they went. A short while later they arrived at his parents' den.

"Hi ya, Dad!" he called.

"Hello there, son! To what do we owe this pleasant surprise?"

"Well, I felt bad that last year's hibernation good-byes were rushed and last-minute. I thought we'd come earlier this year to see if you need help with any projects. At the least, we can have a nice visit and wish you a good winter's rest."

"Well, that's darn nice of you," said Grampa Bear.

Then Grammy Bear came out of the cave. After exchanging hugs with everyone, Mama Bear gave Grammy Bear a freshly collected jar of honey. "Here," she said. "Just a little thank-you present from all of us for all you do."

"Isn't that special!" said Grammy Bear, holding up the honey so her honey bear could see it.

Grampa Bear slapped Papa Bear on the back and said, "So what should we do, sonny boy, build some more furniture?"

"Ah no, no!" Papa Bear replied quickly, adding, "I mean you already made us plenty of furniture, which we appreciate. But I think the time would be better spent if you played with your grandcub!"

So Grampa Bear showed Little Bear some of his famous circus tricks. Meanwhile, Papa Bear decided to handle the dinner issue with his mom before it became a big deal. "Mom, can we talk about dinner?"

But before he could go further, Grammy Bear said, "Don't tell me you're not going to eat salmon. You never appreciate the good food I make for you." Papa Bear growled, which stopped Grammy Bear short. Then Papa Bear softened and said, " I don't think you appreciate just how much I appreciate you."

Grammy Bear's eyes widened. She was clearly confused by Papa Bear's relaxed posture and caring tone. Papa Bear continued, "I love you, Mom. I know you go to a lot of trouble to get salmon. You also prepare it with such love, and everyone else loves it. So I don't mind if you serve it. It's just that I don't care for salmon, no matter who makes it, and that's why I'm not going to eat it. Still, I can enjoy everyone else enjoying your wonderful salmon, and I'll enjoy all the other delicious dishes that you have on the side."

After a moment's pause, Papa Bear added, "However, there is one area where I would love the help of your culinary expertise."

Grammy Bear was feeling the love. "Sure, my little cubby, what is it?"

"Well, I love porridge so much. And if you could figure out how to reheat it and still have it taste good, it would mean a lot to me."

"Figure it out? That won't be necessary. Tonight while everyone else eats salmon, you're going to be eating a bowl of fresh, hot porridge, made the way your mama makes it"

And with that, they gave each other a big bear hug.

The moral of this story is that a firm no, a big hug, and a jar of honey make for a happier hibernation.

Quick Summary

- ◆ Look for a Chance to Give
- ◆ Disrupt the Guilt Trip
  - • Strip it
  - • Flip it
  - • Snip it
  - • Nip it in the bud
- ◆ Hit the Reset on Their Upset
  - • Respond to exaggerated badness
  - • Counter the frustration
  - • Upgrade to preferences
- ◆ Say No to Unreasonable Requests
- ◆ Give Them a Glimpse of Greatness

Chapter 21

The Mystery

Fable: The Ant and the Grasshopper

The Ant and the Grasshopper were as unlikely a couple as you will ever meet. Yet they could not deny the love that drew them to each other. Greta Grasshopper often remembered the day Andy Ant crawled into her life. She was hanging on a blade of grass when she looked down and saw him. He was all black and shiny, and he was carrying a boulder that must have been 20 times his own weight, though he could have been out for a stroll for all the difference it seemed to make. She dropped down and introduced herself, and that was that. Their eyes met, and they both knew they were meant to be together, differences be hanged. She believed they could get past them, and they did. Love bloomed, and Greta was gloriously happy.

For a little while, anyway.

Andy couldn't wait to introduce her to his colony. And that's when all the trouble began. You see, lost in the mushy emotion of infatuation, Greta had failed to consider the size of Andy's family. Andy's aunts alone numbered in the tens of thousands, and then there were all his uncles, cousins, and siblings. She still shuddered at the memory of the first family picnic she attended with him. They ate everything in sight! And they were so rigid and structured! It seemed that everybody had to do things exactly the same way, and in the same style. They went so far as to walk in single file! And talk about boring conversation! Some of the uncles were real drones. It was "The colony this" and "The colony that," everything, it seemed, for the colony.

She had so many judgments about them as a family, but she tried to keep them to herself. After all, if you don't have something nice to say, don't say anything at all. At the same time, she worried about what they thought of her, and was afraid they would undermine her love relationship with Andy. They certainly couldn't help but notice her. She stuck out in a crowd, because of her bright color and tremendous size. And she was certain they were talking behind her back, because they had so little to say to her front. So she kept to herself at his family's gatherings, and once they got used to her, nobody seemed particularly interested in finding out much about her.

Now, it was five years since the marriage, and Greta had kept her own last name, Grasshopper, because it was obvious, for one thing. For another, G.G. was the logo she used for her various ventures, and that's how other insects knew her. And, most important of all, her last name was an important part of her self-concept and self-esteem. Just because she loved an ant didn't mean she had to become one! But her new relatives refused to acknowledge this, addressing the two of them as the Andy Ants. And Andy's mother, the Queen, had yet to get her first name right. She called her Galina, Gladys, Gertrude, Godzilla, but never Greta.

One day, Greta decided enough was enough. They didn't want to know her for who she was, and she no longer wanted to know them either. More often than not, she refused to go to his family gatherings. On the rare occasions when she did go, she kept her antennae down and her mouth shut, biding her time until it was time to leave. Only a few thousand Ants seemed to notice this, asking Andy, "What's her problem?" To which Andy Ant could only shrug.

When someone feeling like an outsider gets far enough outside, they become a Mystery to those on the inside.

Understanding the Mystery

The Mystery's behavior begins when the intention to *be appropriate* combines with the intention to *be considerate* (Figure 21-1).

When the intent to *be appropriate* is projected, and the intent to *be considerate* is thwarted, this person withdraws from the futility of a failed relationship. This could happen in any situation where a Danger Zone family member is critical of how they live their life, or tries to control them, or refuses to recognize them, or needs too much from them. Then their good intentions grow in intensity and become the need to Criticize the bad behavior of others, held back by the need to Comply with that bad behavior. It is an impossible situation of pointless engagement in a difficult relationship, and there seems to be no way to get the problem to stop.

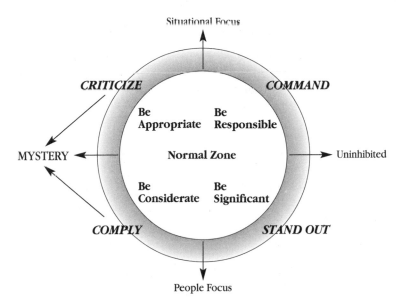

Figure 21-1

That's when the Mystery's behavior moves from the Normal Zone to the Either/Or Zone.

But the Either/Or Zone is a fork in the road, a choice point out of which comes Greatness or danger.

In the Dimension of Greatness, the desire to be appropriate and the desire to be considerate at the same time have great value to the family. The greatness of the Mystery is not in what they do, but in what they don't do. And when it comes to the Mystery, this is no great mystery. They don't issue orders. They don't interfere. They don't disagree. They don't show off. They don't say one thing while meaning another. They don't give gifts with strings attached. In fact, the Mystery is in many ways an ideal relative, except for one problem: They are nowhere to be found.

Any relative can become a Mystery to their own family when these two desires combine and no relatives take an interest in keeping them involved in the family. Perhaps the greatest mystery about the Mystery person is how other family members fail to notice their gradual disappearance.

Range of Difficulty: From Minimal to Missing

The range of Mystery behavior can be from totally withdrawn to totally missing.

There is the minimal Mystery. This is the type you see at family functions. Mysteries' responses are minimal. They hold back. They don't reach out to others. If you reach out to them with questions or conversation, it's like talking to smoke. You get short answers, conversation abruptly ends, or your questions are turned back to you. You know no more after talking with them than you did before the "two" of you spoke.

Then there is the partial Mystery—those who keep attention off themselves by avoiding contact. They show up, but only rarely, maybe once every year, or every few years.

Finally there is the total Mystery. This is the family member who disappears. You may not hear from total Mysteries for years. Your knowledge of them becomes limited to the snippets of gossip and rumor provided to you by other family members, who learned their information in much the same way.

One Bad Turn Deserves Another

This behavior is not without consequence! The Mystery person's silent avoidance leaves more space for the General to command, the Judge to judge, the Meddler to meddle, the Martyr to wallow, the VIP to boast, and the Rebel to rebel. Everyone else gets to deal with the worst behaviors of everyone else. Then the Mystery uses all the amplified difficult behavior to justify his or her final decision to be missing in action.

Damage Done

Though some family members may not be worth being around, other family members might serve the important role of support and protection. But when the Mystery person disappears, both the Mystery person and their family completely lose these advantages. And by the nature of the Mystery's decision to leave, neither will ever know what they missed.

There may be an even more important advantage denied to the Mystery by the decision to go away and stay away: the advantage of self-awareness and self-actualization. Cutting off family is actually like cutting off a part of your self. The Mystery loses the part that could teach him or her how to be courageous instead of afraid, or to be knowledgeable about the interpersonal realm. Instead of protecting themselves from family, Mystery people may have to live with their judgments and their reactions, and never develop the strength to get beyond them.

Finally, if the Mystery cuts off the in-laws, it could cause a rift in the home, in the form of problems for the spouse. When the spouse visits family, they may feel embarrassed and unsupported, having to offer explanations to justify the missing person.

Dealing with the Mystery

Attitude

The attitude you must have if you hope to end the mystery of a Mystery person is one of curiosity, of wonder, and of a willingness to be surprised at what you learn and how things turn out. Dealing with a Mystery is like a voyage of discovery. Be curious about who the Mystery is. Be eager to find out what you haven't discovered before.

If you're dealing with an angry Mystery person, there are attitudes that will not only help you, but also help the Mystery person move through the anger.

The first is a clear line of responsibility. Know that you are not responsible for the Mystery person's feelings, and the Mystery person is not responsible for yours.

Second, when Mysteries express their anger, you don't need to fix them, change their mind, alter their opinion, or convince them of anything. That makes it easier for them to face their anger openly and honestly with you.

And third, think of anger as a signal, built into the human emotional system, to indicate that something is wrong. Beneath the anger, you're bound to find pain. If you speak to that pain instead of reacting to the anger of the Mystery person, the anger may very well disappear on its own.

Demeanor

With the Mystery, your patience truly is a great virtue. You can demonstrate your patience with a slow approach, and a gentle pace that keeps a buffer zone of space and time between what the Mystery says and how you respond. Any attempt to rush forward will push the Mystery away. Relax, take it easy, and welcome any sign of engagement as a first step in a long process. Handle a Mystery with care.

Cautions

Don't argue. The Mystery will withdraw.

Don't get intense. The Mystery will run away.

Don't say too much. The Mystery uses silence as a shield. The more you say, the less the Mystery has to say. So keep your statements very simple, and once you've made them, wait a while for a reply.

Don't give advice without permission. Mysteries withdraw from relatives with whom they have no rapport. Advice bounces off a person with no interest in hearing it. If you want to make a suggestion, ask for permission: "May I make a suggestion?"

Don't talk about yourself. The Mystery is always willing to let someone else have the attention, because it helps him or her stay out of the limelight. If you refuse to make yourself the focal point of interaction, you increase the chance of bringing something valuable to light.

Options with the Mystery

In dealing with the Mystery, your options include (but are not limited to):

◆ A Healthy Respect for Distance
◆ Check In
◆ Draw Them Out
◆ Reach Out
◆ Solve the Mystery Healthy Respect

A Healthy Respect for Distance

There has to be a healthy respect for distance in all relationships, and this is particularly true in families. Relatives may not care to talk too much about their personal experiences with other family members. They still do it, and they often regret it. They understandably want to avoid judgment, meddling, and opposition. Especially from people they will know the rest of their lives. People put boundaries in place in order to protect their space, so they can have a life of their own. Relatives aren't automatically granted a license to dig for dirt or look for problems needing to be solved. Besides, sometimes it just isn't a good idea to go where you haven't been invited.

It isn't an all or none situation. But favored relatives are mindful of space/time. They don't overstay their welcome, nor do they occupy too much space or time in each other's lives. This is in service to one another, yet self-serving at the same time. Call it enlightened self-interest, but think about it. When people spend too much time minding each other's business, who's minding their own? Then each person thinks, "There ought to be a law," without applying that law to themselves. Maybe there is a law, and it governs family relationships. If there was, it would be called the "Healthy Respect for Distance" law and it would go something like this: Keep personal stuff personal and private stuff private, and let everybody else do the same. Some family problems aren't for the whole family.

Check In

Sometimes, private stuff isn't really meant to be private. It's just that way because the person is shy. Nature hates a vacuum. The open and outgoing person might find the shy Mystery person hard to understand, but this is the easiest Mystery to solve.

Why are some people shy? It could be that they never learned good communication as children, because their parents didn't talk much with them or respond when they asked for insight and input. Others are self-conscious, because they're afraid of being judged, or afraid of saying or doing something that might lead to mistreatment or rejection. Some people are shy whenever they're in a social situation where they feel conspicuous (just married into the family, for example) or psychologically vulnerable (like when personal information becomes public). Sometimes people feel socially awkward and prefer to keep to themselves until they can determine how to fit in with others at an event. That kind of shyness is usually a pleasant though tense mixture of interest and fear, approach and avoidance. It is a transient condition, and it ends when the person feels safe, or identifies a comfortable way to engage with others. Many families address and resolve this kind of awkwardness during get-togethers by organizing games in which everyone can participate, whether it's a golf scramble, horseshoes, or a board game.

Shyness isn't inherently bad. In fact, some degree of shyness is healthy and normal, and most people experience it at least once in a while. But the downside of shyness is that inherently shy adults tend to be lonelier than people who are comfortable being themselves around others. Perhaps that is why shyness can also be a symptom of depression. When people are depressed, afraid about their lives, and not knowing how to ask for what they need, they may become socially disengaged and disappear off your radar unless you occasionally check in on them. Here are a couple of ways to check in on the shy people in your family:

Activities. One possible approach to resolving the mystery of a shy person is to engage them in a nonthreatening activity, like folding laundry, or drying dishes, or delivering a message to the group. By giving them a designated role that requires them to interact with others, they have an alternative to keeping to themselves, one that doesn't require much of them.

One on one. Another approach is to talk privately with them before talking publicly with them. When no one is looking, pull them gently aside and say, "So, tell me about your life" or "What have you been up to?" or "What's happening in your life these days?" If you can get them to start talking, and refrain from interrupting, they may quickly get past the awkward stage and warm up to their environment. When you're initiating that first contact, the inhibiting presence of company could make all the difference between no response and a great response.

It's important to allow the shy person to warm up, instead of getting in their face. A little nonverbal blending may be all that it takes to establish some connection before initiating a conversation. Then, asking permission to have a conversation can draw out a shy person and engage them in a relationship.

Ginny told us:

My husband Frank and his brother Bill are boyish and boisterous. They love to laugh, they love spending time with their parents, and they always have a good time when they get together. But when Bill got married, he picked someone very unlike himself. Bernie, his wife, is shy, soft-spoken, and when Bill dragged her to family events, she always kept to herself. I think the fact that she was uncomfortable with them made them all uncomfortable with her, and they seemed to want to avoid her just as much as she avoided them. They gave her a lot of space, which I'm guessing was the only thing she liked about them. It got pretty bad for a while. I remember telling my husband that Bernie was like a ghost against the wall most the time. No one noticed her if she didn't move. The part that bothered me most about this was that Frank and his family talked about Bernie when she wasn't around, and most of it was fault finding and nit-picking. And Frank was always teasing Bill about her. "Hey, Bill, what's with Bernie? Doesn't she like to have fun?" I imagine that this put some pressure on Bill, and he then turned around and put that pressure on Bernie. So the situation got worse over time. I got tired of the tension and hearing everyone's judgments, so I decided to see if I could do something about it. What I did wasn't any big deal, but it made a difference. I always said hello to Ginny and pulled her aside to talk with her. I showed an interest in her life. When I found out that she taught special education at the local grade school, I used every conversation with her to learn more about her work. The difference this made is that, while Bernie is still uncomfortable with the rest of the family, she's always happy to see me now, she hugs me back, and even wants to sit with me during meals. That may not sound like much, but she's happy to see me and I'm happy to see her too. And the family seems to be warming up to her, because they see that it's possible.

Ginny's story is an excellent example of dealing with the Mystery's shyness. All that's required is to tone down your own assertive behaviors, show an interest in the Mystery, listen to what he or she has to say, and be patient and persistent.

Draw Them Out

Do you have an angry Mystery to solve? Drawing them out works better than keeping them out or barging in.

If the Mystery is suppressing anger, or denying it altogether, you will recognize it in his or her avoidance of certain topics, people, places, and the things with which it's associated. Left unattended, suppressed anger chokes the life out of more positive emotions. The beliefs and attitudes that create the anger can then hold it in place, so that each time it rises to the surface, it gets pushed back down again. In time, suppressed anger can turn into bitterness and hostility that colors experiences and creates self-fulfilling prophecy. To surface and release suppressed anger, it must first be expressed.

The Mystery could be angry about almost anything. Some family members may be angry too, blaming the Mystery for damaging the relationship and going away. Such anger tends to reinforce the Mystery's decision to disappear. If you're angry at the Mystery, you have to deal with your anger before you can deal with that of the Mystery. Even if you're not angry, any discomfort you have around anger can undermine your effectiveness, particularly if the anger is directed at you.

You can explore the world of suppressed feelings if you have a flashlight and you know what you're looking for. Here's a brief list of things to look and listen for when drawing out an angry Mystery:

Seek the cause. Remember, the point of asking is to stop the suppression of emotions blocking the relationship. So rather than squandering any opportunity that opens to you in response to your outreach, go for the source immediately. What is the cause of the problem? What's going on? Ask your questions in an open-ended way, and then wait for an answer. That is the first step to solving the Mystery.

Keep the focus on them. Though the Mystery may name you and blame you, your language and attitude must continuously reflect the fact that the Mystery's feelings are his or hers, not yours. So instead of personalizing what the Mystery has said, you reflect the ownership back to the Mystery. For eample:

MYSTERY: "You are so frustrating to deal with!"
YOU: "I am frustrating for you to deal with?"
or
YOU: "So you're frustrated with me?"

To help you keep your focus, make it your purpose to learn something about the Mystery that you did not know. For example, once a Mystery person has told you the truth about the hurt behind the anger, you might learn something that changes the way you think about that person in a significant way. Tell the Mystery person about it, about what it means to you and how it affects your view of the Mystery. That's what happened to Lynn:

> When my dad finally told me what was wrong, why he'd stopped talking to me for so long, the first thing that occurred to me was how insensitive I had been to his needs and interests. Looking at what I did from his standpoint, I could clearly see how he did the only thing that he could do. He withdrew, and kept his peace. He refused to interfere, even though my choices were offensive to him! I never wanted him to feel any of those things that he went through. If I'd known what the problem was, if he and I would have had open lines of communication, maybe together we could have come up with some other way of dealing with it. But we didn't. I thought I knew what was going on for him, but I really knew nothing at all. So I just kept doing the very things that troubled him the most and caring about it the least.
>
> His being honest with me meant a lot to both of us. Once I knew what the problem was, I did the only thing I could do. I apologized. Not for what

I did. But for how my choices had affected him. It was such an eye opener that I don't think I'll ever quit apologizing!

Identify some options. Sometimes, knowing how the Mystery person feels isn't enough, particularly if the problem still exists. The Mystery's option was to withdraw. You want to help this person to discover that he or she has other options. Find out: Does the Mystery think that withdrawing somehow solves the problem? How is this solution contributing to the problem, maintaining it, or worsening it? In other words, how is what this person is doing self-defeating? What was the road less traveled? What options are now available that they didn't have when they first withdrew? What options were available then that have not yet been considered? Finally, and importantly, what would they be willing to do differently now?

If you recognize yourself as part of the problem, this is the time when your personal participation is required. What options are available to each of you? What will you each do? What will you both do? Developing options through dialogue is one way to work the Mystery out.

Reach Out

Some people don't go away mad, they just go away. It's safe to say that their silence speaks volumes. And when someone stops communicating, doesn't return messages, or doesn't answer the door, a family has cause for alarm. If a relative of yours stays silent and unresponsive, it could be a sign that the relative is in some kind of trouble. Some people respond to trouble by wanting to be left alone. Whether it is a health challenge or a financial problem, the last thing a troubled person may want to deal with is the family's "stuff."

Obviously, the most desirable response of a family member when a relative is in trouble would be some reassurance, and maybe a hug: "I love you. I'm here for you. I support you. I'll help you in any way I can. Just let me know what you need from me." Just about everybody would love to feel they have support when going through a difficult time.

Perhaps the Mystery needs help but does not want to acknowledge or accept it. If it's a difficulty that he or she has decided to deal with in isolation, and you get wind of it, what is the best response? Is it sympathy? We think not. Sometimes, showing sympathy to a person in trouble simply reinforces that person's sense of victimization and consequent inertia. Empathy has more value. It comes from the humbling awareness that "There, but for grace, go I." And sometimes you do a greater service telling people to quit feeling sorry for themselves, get off their duff, and do something, than telling them how badly you feel for them.

We heard from one woman who was going through a divorce, and her whole family was in an uproar about it. They were crazy about her husband, had built strong relationships with him, and thought he was an all-around great guy. They kept demanding to know how she could do this to him, instead of listening to her explanations. Here, their own relative had made a choice that affected them all, and none of them could do anything about it. The situation reached the boiling point, and she took an unusual step. She had a special sweatshirt made up at the mall. She wore it home on her next visit. Emblazoned across the chest were the words, IT'S ABOUT ME! But their failure to make the connection was the last straw for her. She gave up on them and went away, because she interpreted their self-interest as selfishness.

So rather than telling a Mystery how difficult it is for you to hear about his or her troubles, reach out to the troubled Mystery. This alone invites engagement, and the possibility of giving help when requested to do so.

Solve the Mystery

Solving the Mystery is what you may want to do when a sibling or parent stops talking to you, or a young adult leaves home and doesn't look back. If you experience their silence as a mystery, then you'll want to get to the bottom of it.

If you want them back, or if you just want a chance with them, you have to solve the mystery of why they left. But there is no single way to handle the disappearance of a person into Mystery. Each family's situation is unique, and it's up to each family member to work out how they'll respond to someone going away. Emotionally healthy people tend to recognize that relationships are reciprocal. To paraphrase a saying about friendship, "In order to have loving relatives, you have to be a loving relative." Let the Mystery know that you're available and that your support or assistance is only a phone call or e-mail away. Let the Mystery know what you're willing to do, through a card, a phone message, or a brief e-mail. Be consistent about this through time, give it enough time, and you just might be able to solve the biggest Mystery in your family.

Give Them a Glimpse of Greatness

Sometimes you have to draw a bigger line and tell your problem relative the truth about how his or her behavior is self-defeating, and what you think would be better instead. The overview is the same for honesty with any of the problem behaviors. Plan it, write it, rehearse it, pick your time and place (see Chapter 8 for more details). Your goal of honesty is to give the relative a glimpse of greatness.

Here's what's involved:

1. Positive intent
2. Be specific
3. Reveal the deeper meaning
4. Suggest something
5. Reinforce behavioral change

The good news is you probably won't be interrupted by the Mystery while you speak honestly to him or her. More important than what you say is how you say it. Intensity, frustration, and strong emotion will work against you, forcing the Mystery to back off further or withdraw deeper into the fortress of solitude that is the Mystery's thoughts. Instead, pick a time to talk when you have time to talk. Then slow down, relax, take your time, allow for long pauses and silences, and get into a rhythm with your Mystery relative.

The Mystery, by saying nothing, may believe that saying nothing is the same as doing nothing. But that nothing *is* something, and when you show Mystery relatives how being a Mystery impacts on others, you reveal a deeper meaning that may meet them where they are and bring them out into the open where a real relationship is possible.

Fable Finale: The Ant and the Grasshopper

Greta hadn't gone to a gathering of Andy's colony in three years. But this was a special occasion, because the Queen of the hill was going to appoint her successor. Andy, in his small way, made a big deal out of Greta coming along. "I'll just keep to myself until it's over," Greta promised herself.

As they approached, they could see that this was no ordinary event. Everyone was there for the big picnic that preceded the naming. There were ants as far as Greta could see, every one of them seemingly engaged in some kind of activity. Yet no sooner had Greta and Andy arrived than Andy Ant's 100 aunts pulled Greta aside to have "a private conversation," as they put it. (While 100 ants seemed like a lot to Greta, from the ants' point of view, any gathering of under 1000 ants was a private one!) At first Greta found that having 100 ants staring at her all at once was a bit disconcerting. She wanted to hide, but clearly that wasn't going to be possible. "I'd be hard to miss in this crowd," Greta said to herself regretfully.

But it didn't take long for Greta to realize that something was different in the way they were relating with her. For the first time since she married Andy, they seemed to actually be curious about her, instead of just going about their business. They quickly and efficiently formed a neat line in front of her that stretched as far back as she could see. They stood in perfect order and took turns excitedly asking her questions.

"So what is it that grasshoppers eat?"

"Which of those is your favorite food?"

"Do you have any predators that you worry about?"

"How are humans affecting your habitat these days?"

It used to be that they were not interested in me at all. Now, they're too interested! Greta thought. At this rate I'll be answering their questions all day!

That's when she noticed that something large and yellowish at the back of the line was moving in her direction. She couldn't believe her compound eyes! There was a whole corncob coming toward her, and it seemed to be moving on its own! It wasn't until it got closer that Greta saw the ants underneath it, each doing his or her part to carry it forward. Then they placed it on the ground in front of her and said in unison, "Here's a little something we hope you will like!"

Greta was amazed at this family effort to make her feel welcome. How did they manage to find out her favorite food, communicate it to one another, find it, harvest it, and deliver it to her in so little time? She had to admit that this family was incredibly industrious and efficient.

"Mmmm, sweet corn, it's my favorite!" said Greta between munches. "Thank you so much!" Then Andy Ant's 100 aunts began asking her questions again. Now they were speaking to her in perfect unison, which was quite disconcerting until she got used to it.

"So how high can you jump?"

Greta replied, "Oh, most grasshoppers can jump 20 times our body length."

Andy Ant's aunts exclaimed, "There's something we have in common! We ants can lift 20 times our own body weight! Of course we can do more together than we can apart, but it's a place to start!" They seemed to all be smiling at her. "Is that how you get around? By hopping?"

"Well, yes," Greta answered, "but I also have these wings, and I can fly."

All as one, Andy Ant's 100 aunts said in unison, "Oooooh, she can fly!" Then the first one in line turned to the one behind her and spoke, who then turned to the one behind her and spoke, and so on down the line. Greta thought she heard the words, "Greta" and "fly" over and over again, though she couldn't be certain as she was not completely fluent in Antonese. But before she knew it, her husband's 100 aunts were joined by his uncles, cousins, siblings, and who knows who else. There must have been thousands of ants swarming around her.

"Fly, fly, fly, fly," they started to chant, quietly at first, then louder and louder. Their excitement grew, as Greta helped them climb aboard her back. Then, as she took off, a hush fell over the crowd, leaving only the sound of Greta's vibrating wings as she soared above them! They watched in wonder for the next two hours, each waiting their turn. Greta enjoyed giving her newfound family the ride of their lives, 100 at a time. The Queen went last, all by herself. She whispered to Greta, "You've made quite an impression on everyone! Welcome to the family! If you don't mind, I would be delighted to have you lead the March of Succession, with me upon your back!"

Andy came running up, a quizzical look on his face. To which Greta exclaimed, "They like me! They really like me!"

The moral of this story is that when you get someone to jump for joy, they're likely to land in the center of the family.

Quick Summary

- ◆ A Healthy Respect for Distance
- ◆ Check In
- ◆ Draw Them Out
  - • Seek the cause
  - • Label the feelings
  - • Keep the focus on them
  - • Identify some options
  - • Reach out
- ◆ Solve the Mystery

Chapter 22

The Rebel

Fable: The Black Sheep

Sean Sheep was the black sheep of the family. When everyone went one way, he had to go the other way. If you told him what to do, even if you were joking, he had to do the opposite. If you offered a suggestion, his standard answer was, "Baaahhh." He refused to get his wool cut, because he liked to wear his fleece all wild and long. He even changed his name from Sean Sheep to Mike Sheep. Why? Because, as he put it, "I know the authors are using an alliterative naming pattern in their stories. But they are not putting that on me, just for their own amusement!"

On this particular day he had good reason to be moody. He could have gone home for the holidays with his wife Sherry Sheep, but hated the thought of "standing around with a bunch of sheep while the old rams play their stupid butt-head games." And without an excuse, he felt obligated to go to his own "stupid family gathering" down at Mother Goose's barnyard. "Baaahhh."

He saw some familiar faces as he entered the barnyard, and his mood brightened. Jack and Jill were usually fun to hang out with. "Hey Jack, how's it going?" Jack worked for Jill's father, in the water transport business.

"Hey, Mike Sheep! Not too great, I'm sorry to say. I injured myself again." Jack replied.

"Oh, don't tell me. The hill and the water?"

Jill nodded as Jack said, "Yeah, I fell down and broke my crown."

Then Jill added, " And I came tumbling after."

Mike wandered into the gathering and looked around. There was already a crowd. He thought to himself, Nothing's changed. Same old relatives, having the same old conversations and doing the same old things. There were the three visually challenged mice. The cat was playing the fiddle, and hadn't improved a bit in two years. And, of course, that other Jack, showing off by jumping over candlesticks. Then he saw old King Cole, a merry old soul who was always trying to give Mike unsolicited advice.

"Oh no! He sees me!" thought Mike.

"Say there, Sean Sheep! What's this I hear? It's *Mike* now, right?" King Cole pounded Mike on the arm. "How's it going, big shot? I've been meaning to give you some advice. I hear tell things aren't working out with your—" But Mike cut him off with a sweep of his hoof. "If I want your advice, I'll ask for it!" Then he turned abruptly and walked away. The old king stood there shaking his head, mumbling, "Why does he fight everyone who wants to help him?"

Mike thought he was over his anger with Mother Goose for that stupid rhyme about him, but being here just brought all that up again. "If one more person says to me, 'Baa, baa, black sheep,'" he muttered, "I'll—" and then he bumped right into the grand matriarch herself.

"Sean, so good of you to join us. We're about to start the annual reading of our nursery rhymes. Why don't you get us started?"

"The name's *Mike*! And forget it. It's a stupid tradition! I'm not reading anything!"

"Baa, baa, don't be such a black sheep!" cried the Three Blind Mice in unison, and collapsed into giggles on the ground. Mike's head began to throb as he thought, Never a farmer's wife around when you need one.

Suddenly Little Bo Peep screamed, "Look everyone! Up on that wall! It's Humpty Dumpty! He's going to jump!"

Little Boy Blue exclaimed, "Not the wall thing again." Old Mother Hubbard sighed, "He does this every year." For Mike, it was the last straw. He yelled, "Hey, Humpty. You, up there on the wall. Yeah, I mean you, egghead! Can't we have one year where you spare us your pathetic narcissistic plea for attention?"

Mary's little lamb nudged Mike with her nose. "Be nice to him. He's fragile."

Mike looked at her with disgust. "I am tired of walking on eggshells around him. And as for you, don't even start with me. You are such a wimp, you don't even have a name of your own."

"I do too have a name," she bleated. "My name is Mary's Little Lamb."

"Your so-called name makes you a possession of Mary. You represent everything that is wrong with sheep. All you do is follow Mary, wherever she goes. You call that a life? When are you going to stand up for yourself?"

Mary's Little Lamb stamped her feet and said, "*I do too* stand up for myself." Then she looked at Mary sheepishly and asked, "Don't I?"

But Mike didn't hear it, because he was on a roll. No more holding back! "And look at Jack Horner, he just sits in a corner. When are we going to admit that our family has some problems and get him some help?"

"He is perfectly normal," said Miss Muffet.

"Yeah, you would think so, Miss Arachnophobia. I knew I shouldn't have come here!" And with that, Mike turned and walked out, leaving everyone in stunned silence. After a time, Mother Goose broke the spell. "If he wants to be the black sheep of the family, that's his business. Let's go on with the reading of the rhymes."

When Mike was a half mile away, he leaned despondently on a fence, angry, embarrassed and depressed about his outburst. As he pressed his throbbing head against the fence post, he mumbled, "What kind of family is this? How am I even related to these characters?"

Feeling insignificant, the Rebel holds others responsible.

Understanding the Rebel

The Rebel's behavior begins when the intention to *be significant* combines with the intention to *be responsible* (Figure 22-1).

When the intention to *be significant* is thwarted, and the intent to *be responsible* is projected onto someone else, the Rebel holds others accountable for the Rebel's own feelings of insignificance. This could occur in a sit-

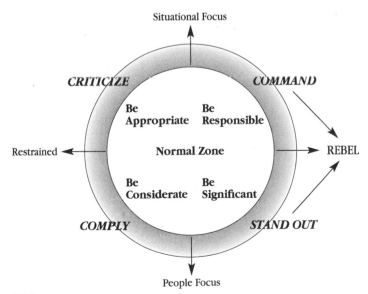

Figure 22-1

uation where people believe they are responsible, it matters, and yet they cannot gain compliance. Or someone else is in charge and demands their compliance, no matter how they feel. In either case, if it seems that they're not being treated with the respect they think they deserve, or someone else is being treated with more respect than they are, their good intentions grow in intensity and become a need to Stand Out by taking Command. If they can't be in charge of what others are doing, they can at least let others know they're in charge of themselves. That's when the Rebel appears, and behavior moves from the Normal Zone to the Either/Or Zone.

But the Either/Or Zone is a fork in the road, a choice point out of which comes Greatness or danger.

In the Dimension of Greatness, the desire for significance and self-determination can be a boon to the family's well-being. At their best, Rebels are capable of demonstrating the best qualities of both the General and the VIP. Not bound by tradition, the Rebel speaks for change in a family that is out of step in a rapidly changing world. The Rebel draws attention to counterexamples and meaningful shades of gray that help others develop a broader perspective when there are problems in the family. The Rebel goes first when others are resistant or afraid, and then comes back with a report, which helps others gain options they might otherwise have overlooked. The Rebel helps weaker members stand up to stronger ones, and holds stronger ones in check by questioning undeserved authority. And perhaps most important, the Rebel provides an example to younger family members of speaking up with personal truth, thus greatly increasing the likelihood that the younger people will learn to speak up for themselves.

But if they take the other fork in the Either/Or Zone, by polarizing out of fear and projection, the behavior moves to the Danger Zone.

The Rebel, when acting out of fear and projection, demonstrates the worst of both the General and the VIP in combination. The internal demand to Stand Out and at the same time take Command keeps growing in intensity, until the Rebel becomes known to the family, either in the situation or in general, as a disrespectful problem child, or an emotionally irresponsible maniac with serious control issues and self-esteem problems.

Range of Difficulty: From Frustrated to Furious

The range of Rebel reaction is a wide one, from frustrated to furious, from irreverent to seemingly insane. Whether it's an argument, a torrent of verbal abuse, or a full-scale tantrum, it puts the Rebel's needs squarely in the center of everyone's attention.

There's the Rational Rebel, sometimes known as a brooder. Even if they respect you, Rational Rebels are likely to question your directions. No generalization goes unchallenged, every example you offer gets a counterexample in return, and everything is open to debate.

There's also the Ridiculing Rebel, who mocks you with innuendo and sarcasm. This Rebel's cruel laughs and pointed barbs are aimed squarely at your self-esteem or your authority.

Then there's the Radical Rebel. Command them and they go the other way. Trap them and they go on the attack. Ignore them and they get in your way. And if you get in their way, they'll organize a resistance. If you frustrate their agenda, they'll fly into a rage. They want you to back off, or cave in out of fear of the force of their anger. Their behavior may seem out of control to you, but it works well to frighten others into submission.

Finally, there's the Undercover Rebel, who works behind the scenes to undermine your authority. If they know the family secrets, they'll use your fear of public shame to control you. They want you to know they're to be reckoned with.

One Bad Turn Deserves Another

The Rebel's difficult behavior is not without consequence. Rebellion usually turns into a contest of wills with the General, who perceives the Rebel as irresponsible and even a danger to others. Rebellion feeds into the judgments of the Judge, which may then spread to other family members who willingly agree about the worst characterizations of the Rebel's behavior or motives. Or the Rebel may bring out the Pleaser in the nicest people in the family, those who fear emotional volatility and wish to avoid it at all costs. But Pleasers resent the bad behavior, and while they may forgive it, they'll remember it for years. And to get away from the seemingly irrational behavior completely, a Mystery may develop. Eventually, the Rebel is unwelcome whenever the family gets together.

Damage Done

The problem behavior causes real harm to both the Rebel and to those who must deal with him or her. For one thing, the Rebel's health may suffer. Flying into a rage tends to drive up the blood pressure and increase nervousness and poor digestion. When Rebels oppose you, they stand out, but they may also stand alone. The Rebel uses blame to gain significance, but is marginalized in the process, as their angry rebellion alienates potential allies and infuriates those they respect the most.

As a result, Danger Zone Rebels tend to cut themselves off from their environment, withdraw into their cave, and evaluate the unfairness of their world: all the places where they feel unrecognized for their good intentions or best efforts, all the times when someone else gets the credit or gets to decide. But brooding doesn't bring clarity. It only strengthens their belief in the reality of their point of view. They may keep this to themselves for a time, try to hold it in, but when they feel pent up, they act out, challenging authority at every turn, and shouting down the opposition that their position creates.

Ironically, they don't mean to be mean, and they are never nicer than when they feel bad for behaving badly. That's because they do know that their behavior isn't winning them any friends in their family.

Dealing with the Rebel

Attitude

The problem with people who identify themselves by what they're against is that if you pander to it, you make it worse. Remember, they hold others responsible for their feelings of insignificance because they're trying to get rid of those feelings. They are looking for a way to escape from self-imposed feelings of insignificance. They think that by pinning the blame for these feelings on something outside of themselves, they can get some relief from the bad feelings.

So take none of it personally, because it isn't about you. If they're mocking you, laugh with them. If they try to start an argument, say, "You could be right" or "That's one way of looking at it." If they're yelling, say, "I don't want you to feel that way." If they threaten to do something out of anger, say, "You don't have to do that." If they escalate beyond that, tell them you love them, and that because you love them, you can't stay around as a witness when they behave like "that." (The less you say about "that," the better!)

Demeanor

You will need to create a calm and nonthreatening atmosphere in which to learn the cause of the rebellion. In other words, you must maintain a sort of practiced neutrality, neither comforting nor disagreeing with anything they say. Noncommittal grunts and head nods are sufficient. Be ready to acknowledge all feelings, those you like and those you don't like, while handling your own reactions in order to set a good example of responsible behavior. Perhaps you recall the proverb, "A fool gives vent to his anger, but a wise person keeps himself under control."

Cautions

Don't get defensive. If you try to defend, explain, or justify yourself, you wind up making yourself look guilty of all charges. If you reject the Rebel, you encourage his or her worst thoughts. If you withdraw your love, Rebels will get louder, or you will lose all influence while inciting them all the more.

Don't box them in or trap them with threats and ultimatums. Backed against the wall, their only option is to lash out. And trying to crush the rebellion only serves to deepen the polarization and to damage future efforts to improve the relationship.

Don't direct them. A detailed question is more valuable than a detailed assertion. All of your communications should have the effect that you are simply "running it by them," rather than telling them what they should do, must do, or will do. "What do you think about doing this . . . " would be better than saying, "Do this." Their willingness to act has to come from inside them, and external demands impede that willingness. Rebels will heed your counsel but not your demands.

Don't talk down to them or negatively compare them to others. Negative comparisons infuriate the Rebel and spark more anger and rebellion.

Don't run away. If you must leave, look them in the eyes, take a deep breath, say, "I don't think continuing to talk about this right now can be constructive," then take aim at some other activity and walk away slowly, head held high. Your leaving is not meant to punish, but to protect them from having a witness to behavior for which they will likely be ashamed later.

Options with the Rebel

Whether a rebellion will be constructive or destructive depends on your response to it. When dealing with a Rebel, your options include (but are not limited to):

◆ See Your Part
◆ Hear Them Out
◆ Propose a Solution
◆ Draw the Line
◆ Give Them a Glimpse of Greatness

See Your Part

Own up to the part you've played in past conflicts. If possible, ask for their forgiveness. Unresolved, these things will become a wedge between you and give the Rebel an excuse for further rebellion and continued conflict.

You can go even further than you might think. While the problem may not be your responsibility, you can take responsibility for it anyway. If you approach Rebels with statements that take ownership, you may find that it calms them down and makes them more receptive to moving in a new direction. You can counter their accusations by telling them that you want what they want. This puts you both on the same side and makes rebellion more difficult to launch or sustain.

REBEL: "You don't spend any time with me."
YOU: "I want to do better."

REBEL: "You don't understand me."
YOU: "I want to understand you."

REBEL: "You're wasting my time."
YOU: "I want to value your time."

REBEL: "You don't listen!"
YOU: "I want to listen."

Hear Them Out

Brooding Rebels are deeply disturbed by the way life doesn't conform to their wishes or expectations. Talking helps them to figure out what's going on. It gives them a way to process their anger and disappointment, and make sense of it all. So when the Brooding Rebel starts to talk, don't interrupt, and do ask questions when you get the chance. This conveys to the Rebel that you value his or her concerns, and it gives the Rebel the experience of being drawn in instead of shut out. A brooding rebel will jump at the chance to clear the air. But the only way the air truly gets cleared is through listening and understanding. That doesn't mean you agree, disagree, or can do anything about it. But it does mean you do your best to put yourself in the Rebel's shoes to see things the Rebel's way. And it does mean that you offer reassurance that talking is a good choice:

No matter how bad this seems, I know we can work it out. Your feelings are important to me. Your problems will not be dismissed. I won't get angry at you for being angry.

Deal with feelings. The Rebel may use strong emotional tactics to support an emotion-based point of view, like justifying rage, pouting, and calling people names. When you speak to your relative's feelings, you disrupt these tactics. You can let him or her know that you have an open mind, an interest in understanding and solving the problem. In this way, you penetrate the emotions and bring the Rebel to a place of reason.

I have my own point of view, but if you see this another way, I'm open to being persuaded.

Instead of defensively denying the problem: "You don't understand . . .," let them know that the solution is more important to you: "I want to work this out."

Instead of claiming not to care: "I don't care what you think, so deal with it!" tell them they can talk with you about it: "Something is going on here that I don't understand. Tell me what you think about this, I'm interested in your view."

If Rebels attack you personally, disrupt the attack by asking questions about their opinions. Ask them to tell you when they formed that opinion of you. What made them draw that conclusion? Where did they get that idea? Such questions change the Rebel's trajectory and may provide you with valuable information.

REBEL: "If you really cared, you would . . . "
YOU: "When did you decide I don't care?"

REBEL: "You're a meddling old fool . . . "
YOU: "What made you draw that conclusion?"

If the Rebel gets into ridiculing you, you can always ask for intent. A simple "What are you really trying to say?" should move them beyond the put-down and toward making sense.

If they defend their emotions, acknowledge them:

REBEL: "I have every right to feel this angry!"
YOU: "You certainly do."

Sometimes your best response to an emotional diatribe is an internal one. If they try to shame you, affirm yourself. If they call you a name, call yourself a nicer one. If they say something that is patently untrue, tell yourself the truth.

The reactive hormones released by your brain linger in your system for only a few seconds. If you can learn to do anything else with your mind for just those few seconds, your brain will be released from reactivity and you will again be able to think clearly. Think about that: Just a few seconds makes the difference between an overly emotional reaction and a reasonable response.

Before trying to make a case or propose a solution, make sure that you confirm what you've heard. "If I understood what you just told me, you are upset with . . . " Say it back, and then ask if you got it right.

Heed the warnings. Have you heard the sound of distant thunder? It tells you when a storm is getting near. Likewise, there are usually rumblings before a rebellion. Heed the warning signs, and you may be able to take the action that eliminates the need for rebellious reaction. Think back to the last time your relative polarized. What set him or her off? What happened right after that? If you can use the last time to identify, in advance, the signs and symptoms of surging emotion, you can be ready for them when they appear.

When you hear, "Nobody cares who I am!" or "That cuts it!" or "That's the last straw!" it's usually a sign that the Rebel is about to go off the deep end. It's also a good time to get involved and let the Rebel know that you're on his or her side.

REBEL: "Nobody cares who I am."
YOU: "I don't want you to feel that way."
REBEL: "That cuts it!"
YOU: "This is a misunderstanding. We can resolve this."
REBEL: "That's the last straw."
YOU: "Let me see if I can help."

When you notice the rumblings, immediately put yourself on the same side as the Rebel. This is the time for making it as important to you as it is to the Rebel, so that the signals you're sending tell the Rebel that you're on the same side of working something out.

Propose a Solution

If you don't like the way things are going, or where they've already gotten to, you can be an agent of change instead of a victim of circumstance. Influence requires a direction, which means you'll need to come up with an alternative to what is happening or about to happen. Anyone can point to blame. But taking aim requires the art, and the science, of persuasion.

Appeal to interest. Speak to the interests of the Rebel, as well as to the interests of any family members who are caught up in the situation. Appeal to reason, appeal to their feelings, or appeal to their character. If you anticipate an objection, bring it up first, to eliminate it before it can get in the way.

For example, imagine that your family's self-concept is one of intelligence and political engagement. Your brother Jon thinks of himself politically as a champion for the underdog. At a family gathering, Jon gets angry about something his grandfather says which is incredibly mean-spirited and shortsighted. To make matters worse, Grandpa says that anyone who disagrees "is basically an uninformed idiot." Jon takes the bait, rebels against such narrow-mindedness, and turns it into an argument. Soon the accusations are flying, and Dad tries to shut the argument down, by pounding on the table with his fist. His attempt to crush the rebellion backfires, by adding to the volume and intensity of the turmoil. Jon's rebellion now involves two fronts, Grandpa's narrow-mindedness and Dad's control trip. Jon tries to simultaneously shame Grandpa while putting a chink in Dad's armor. Gramps thinks it all very funny, and keeps it going by egging Jon on. Dad is screaming for compliance, and being ignored. Meanwhile, the Pleasers (a handful of cousins and siblings) sit with baited breath, hoping the noise dies down soon. But that's unlikely, because the VIP takes Grandpa's side and throws some support into the mix to further polarize the subject. The Mystery gets up and leaves the room. And you're sitting there talking to yourself. Well, you think, I hate to meddle, but this is no fun, and I'm getting indigestion. You decide that you have to take action, or the whole gathering will turn into a painful memory. What do you do?

First, you get everyone's attention, using the tactful interruption on Jon or Dad (whoever is the loudest), and then you make a proposal that speaks to the family's self-concept of intelligent and political engagement.

> Hey, I have an idea! We're an intelligent family, so why not apply our intelligence to talking about this? How about postponing this discussion until dinner is over, and then making it a debate? We all seem to have definite ideas about this issue. If we have an open debate, everyone will get a chance to offer proof for his or her point of view [*appeal to reason*], and nobody will have to leave with a painful memory [*appeal to emotion*]. Besides, we're good people, and we're better than this [*appeal to character*]. How about it? Table the discussion until after the meal is over and then have a debate? All those in favor, raise your hand!

If you've been persuasive, you'll get support for ending the fighting, and that will be the end of that. The debate may or may not happen, but that wasn't the point, right?

Rebel's choice: But what do you do when Rebels are angry at you for trying to control them, meddle in their lives, dismiss their concerns, or some other perceived injustice? Then offer a choice to address their grievances:

> I have an idea, and I wonder what you think about this. What if we were to start over, and you were to tell me how I've upset you, and then give me a chance to respond?

Then leave it up to them. If they say no, they're defeating their own interests. By saying no they demonstrate to themselves that their problem is their own anger rather than your behavior. Let it go, the storm will pass. If they say yes, you have already influenced the situation for the better. And if they have another idea, hear it out. Ask questions about it, to demonstrate an interest and to learn what the idea represents to them.

Draw the Line

When feeling inadequate and insecure, put down, or shut out, the Rebel may lash out with intense anger. It could be pointed sarcasm, building themselves up by putting others down. Or, if they feel ignored, they could start yelling. Oppose them and they go off the deep end into what appears to be a state of uncontrollable rage. In every case, there's a hidden threat that if you just do what they say or say what they want, they won't be angry or sarcastic, and they won't hurt you anymore. But it ain't necessarily so. Giving in to the Rebel is unlikely to protect you the next time they go off. In fact, it's likely to encourage them to do the same behavior again. And backing off won't help you either. When you walk away, you leave them seething, and when you return, they'll come at you again. Instead, you have to draw the line. You can do this in a number of ways.

Be the example.   The most compelling way to draw a line is through your own example. It takes two to tangle, so refuse to get into a shouting match, and demonstrate self-control and clear communication. Be respectful, even when they're not, and avoid embarrassing them in front of other people.

Resist temptation.   Assigning blame does not draw the line on anything, and nothing gets better as a result. You only succeed in making a victim of yourself. You cannot effect change when you are the effect of what is changing. You can only effect change by being the cause of an effect. To draw the line, be the cause, not the effect!

Speak from strength.   Say that their behavior stops here or the interaction is over. You can let them know this verbally, telling them your expectations, and establishing specific consequences for specific behaviors. You have to speak up, and speak out, but not shout, so that your behavior is assertive enough to take seriously but not so assertive as to be taken as an attack.

> REBEL: "@#$# you big *&()*, and I'm *&*&^ had enough of your constant @#$#*, aaaaaahhhhhh yip, yip, bla-BLA!"
>
> YOU: "You have the right to my attention, but only when you communicate your grievances to me in a respectful manner. I have the right to walk away if you persist in yelling."

Once you've drawn the line in the sand, do not back away from it! Doing so sends the wrong message, and you wind up with a worse situation on your hands than if you had done nothing at all. Following through may be the only way to let them know you mean business. And knowing you mean business will impact on the way they interact with you the next time.

Hold them accountable.   Don't assign blame and don't accept blame that doesn't belong to you. When Rebels blame you for their choices, remind them that they make their choices and they are accountable to themselves for what happens to them as a result. Accountability is different from blame, in that it defines the standard by which you will measure behavior. That's why it's so important to make sure that expectations around behavior and actions are clearly defined, proactively rather than reactively. Then, when performance doesn't measure up, you have a reference point by which to identify the difference between what was said and what was done. This helps you account for your own actions in response.

Restore and reconcile.   This is particularly important with the Rebel who is living with regrets. When something awful has actually happened, forgiving the people involved is not the same as forgetting that it happened. Instead, remember what happened, restore the relationship a little wiser, and reconcile yourself to the fact that you're dealing with a Rebel. Restitution is likely to help the Rebel remember. Replacing what was broken, restoring what was taken, and in particular restoring goodwill, means bringing a gift whose meaning is "I apologize. I've learned. I'll do better next time." If you find yourself talking with a regretful Rebel, instead of telling the Rebel to come bearing gifts, ask how he or she might make amends for his or her part in what happened.

Give the Rebel a Glimpse of Greatness

Sometimes your best choice is to tell your problem relative the truth about how the rebellious behavior is self-defeating. The overview is the same for honesty with any of the problem behaviors. Plan it, write it, rehearse it, pick your time and place. (See Chapter 8 for more details.) Your goal in being honest is to give your Rebel relative a glimpse of greatness.

1. Positive intent
2. Be specific
3. Reveal the deeper meaning
4. Suggest something
5. Reinforce behavioral change

However, there is one aspect of honesty specific to the Rebel:

1. Project positive intent. "I appreciate that:

. . . *you're ready to stand up for yourself."*
. . . *you're willing to speak your mind."*
. . . *you won't let yourself be controlled or pushed around."*

Fable Finale: The Black Sheep

Mike Sheep couldn't believe he was going back to Mother Goose's place so soon. He had hoped to stay away for a very long time, but the family was celebrating Old King Cole's retirement, and Mike felt obligated to attend. Although he found the old guy's advice annoying, even Mike had to admit that Old King Cole was a merry old soul. And, more important, he was family. But Mike was still feeling embarrassed about the last time he'd gotten together with his weird relatives, so he was determined not to lose his temper this time.

He didn't see anyone in the barnyard, so he figured everyone was inside the barn. As he got nearer to the door, he heard the sound of fiddling and laughter coming from inside. He had just about made up

his mind to enjoy himself, when Old Mother Hubbard accosted him at the entrance.

"Well, if it isn't Miiiike," she sarcastically said, "the black sheep in the family. I didn't think you would dare show your face around here again so soon. Come to ruin Old King Cole's party?"

Mike was taken aback by the insult. Who does she think she is? he thought. He could feel his blood pressure rising and his temper starting to flare. But he controlled the urge to give her a piece of his mind, and mentally commanded himself to relax.

Old Mother Hubbard, on the other hand, was just getting started. She dished out another helping of scorn. "You ungrateful sheep. You think your rhyme is so bad? At least you have some wool, three bags full! I can't even give my poor dog a bone. Every time I hear my rhyme, I cry for my poor dog."

Mike felt the waves of anger starting to build. He wanted to bleat at the top of his lungs. But Mother Goose, hearing the commotion, came over to where they stood and spoke softly to Old Mother Hubbard. "Dearie, please be so good as to leave me alone with Mike for a few minutes. Little Miss Muffet has some extra curds and whey for your dog, and she's waiting to give them to you!"

Hubbard turned and walked away.

Mike was shaking. He took a few more deep breaths as he and Mother Goose stared silently at each other. When at last she spoke, she said, "I know you've always hated your nursery rhyme. I apologize for trying to get you to read it each year."

This sudden apology took Mike by surprise. It was the last thing he expected to hear. "Bah, you don't care!" he said defiantly.

"I hear that you don't think I care, Mike, but I do!"

"Bah, how could you ever understand?"

Mother Goose was prepared for this reaction. Instead of expressing frustration, as she would have in the past, she calmly said, "I want to understand. And I have an idea. What if we were to start over, right now? Tell me how I upset you, and I'll listen. Then, when you're done, I'll ask you to let me respond. Does that seem fair?"

Mike wondered what was in that trough he drank from earlier in the day. His head felt like it was spinning. The things she was saying were throwing him off balance. He liked them and hated them at the same time! I'll just play along, and see what her game really is, he thought.

"Bah. You want to know how you upset me? Well, for one thing, I don't see how you could make up that dumb rhyme about me! No one else has a dumb one. Just 'cause I'm a sheep doesn't mean I'm stupid!" He ranted on for several minutes.

When he had stopped his bleating, Mother Goose replied, "Well, Mike, I hear that you hate your rhyme. I have a different perspective about the rhymes, but I'm open to being persuaded if there's something better you have in mind"

Mike wasn't buying it. "What's this? A technique you got out of some self-help book? You don't care, you don't care what I have to say, and you know it!"

Mother Goose reminded herself that Mike's anger wasn't about her, even though it sounded like it was. She didn't need to take it personally. Then she calmly but firmly said, "Mike, I want to listen, and I do care. But you wouldn't want me to talk to you the way you're talking to me. If you want me to listen, you're going to have to communicate with me in the same way that you'd like me to communicate with you. I can't work it out with you, unless you're willing to work it out too."

That got Mike's attention. He stared at her, not knowing how to respond.

She continued, "So, you think you're the only character who's unhappy about their rhyme? Did you ever stop to think that there are over 300 rhymes attributed to me and only about 15 percent are well-known? Did it occur to you that there are far more characters with unknown rhymes than there are famous ones? I know a number of creatures who would love to be as famous as you. They're unhappy because they're unknown and unappreciated as a result."

They stared at each other in silence for several moments. Then Mother Goose said, "Mike, I am sincerely sorry that you don't like your nursery rhyme. You have a right to your opinion, just as I do. It isn't right for me to force you to read it if you don't like it. I can't do anything about what is already published and famous, but I can do something about family gatherings. Your feelings matter to me, and I will not ask you to read your rhyme ever again, if that's how you feel about it."

Mike was speechless. What she was saying was completely unexpected, but it was music to his ears.

"Listen, Mike, you like to look at things differently and you like to do things differently. How about coming up with some new ways for all of us to interact at these get-togethers? Maybe everyone could get to know each other a little deeper, beyond the rhymes? I'm not kidding. Between you and me, some of these rhymes and stories are getting a bit old. A change would be good for us. Come on. What do you say?"

Mike took a deep breath, but this time it wasn't to suppress his anger. He just didn't want to cry. And for the first time in a long time, he didn't want to say "Baaahh" either. Then he smiled, and for the first time Mother Goose could remember, he looked contented! Together, they turned and walked into the barn to celebrate Old King Cole's retirement.

The moral of this story is that when someone gets angry and defensive, it's time to be flexible about making a change.

Quick Summary

◆ See Your Part
◆ Hear Them Out
  • Deal with feelings
  • Heed the warnings
◆ Propose a Solution
  • Appeal to interest
  • Rebel's choice
◆ Draw the Line
  • Be the example
  • Resist temptation
  • Speak from strength
  • Hold them accountable
  • Restore and reconcile
◆ Give Them a Glimpse of Greatness

Chapter 23

The Dimension of Greatness:
Top 10 Qualities of Great Relatives

When conducting our interviews in the research stage of this book, we asked questions like: "If one of your family members was an ideal relative, what characteristics would they embody? What would they be like? What would they do?"

Some of the people we talked to replied that they did have such a relative. Some said they had a whole family of them! Others told us they could only dream, so that's what we asked them to do. What follows are the top 10 composite responses about what constitutes a great relative, in descending order of frequency.

1. A Great Relative Values Communication

"I am interested in what you have to say." Ideal relatives are good communicators, and one of their greatest skills is the ability to listen. An ideal relative listens to what's being said. He or she does not pretend to listen or talk over you, but really listens.

"I want you to be able to hear what I have to say." Ideal relatives pay attention to what they are communicating, how they are communicating, and the effects their communications have on you. When they start to say, "You should do this" and "You should do that," they catch themselves and rephrase it so that what they want to say expresses what they think rather than what someone else "needs" to do. They take your feelings into consideration before they give you advice or offer to help. They are tactful in what they say, yet they don't lie or skirt the issue. They approach sensitive subjects with both love and tact.

"I won't impose my opinions on you." They provide feedback when asked to do so, but in way that is supportive and loving; never damaging to anyone's self-esteem or put in a way that could build walls. They get permission before offering feedback. They're able to talk openly and constructively about past conflicts without anyone assigning blame. They communicate directly with you about their own needs and requests, instead of using other people to manipulate a situation just to get what they want.

"I value what we talk about." When you see them again, it seems like they pick up with you where you left off last, and begin sharing as if you've never been apart. And they maintain a sense of humor in their communications, even when what they discuss with you is serious.

2. A Great Relative Loves Unconditionally

"You can count on my love." The ideal relative loves you no matter what you do or what kind of trouble you get yourself into. If they have a problem with you, they talk about the actual problem instead of having opinions about it or about you. Their love is constant. They are nonjudgmental. They don't point out flaws, but instead they understand that no one is perfect, so they simply accept you. Their unconditional love also extends to your spouse or partner and your kids.

"I won't make what you do more important than who you are in my life." If you do something they don't like, they forgive you instead of holding on to a grudge or blaming you forever. They accept the imperfections that make us all human, and they don't need you to fulfill their expectations in order to be happy with you or to love you. They don't take things you say or do personally, like when you can't make it to a family event. They maintain perspective in the relationship and understand that the lifelong connection of family should not be derailed by petty short-term conflicts or disagreements.

"I am here for you." You could be anywhere in the world, day or night, in any kind of trouble, and the ideal relative would be there for you without question. Ideal relatives are loyal to you in their love for you, and appreciate you exactly for who you are instead of for what you are not.

3. A Great Relative Is Accepting and Respectful

"You are someone special to me." Ideal relatives accept, respect, and appreciate your individuality. They recognize the unique characteristics of other family members and don't need you to be the same as they are.

"**I respect your right to your own point of view.**" They understand that people will have differences of opinions, and they can respect your opinions, even if they don't agree with them. If they think that a topic might polarize the family, they avoid it altogether. They are not threatened by nor are they a threat to anyone's political or ideological or religious opinions, because they have no need to convince you of their point of view or oppose you for your own.

"**I recognize that times and styles change.**" They are flexible enough to realize that times change, so they can be open to the social norms and lifestyles of today instead of holding you to standards from other eras. They don't impose their expectations on you to be a certain type of person, or fit a certain picture or stereotype, and they don't require you to have a certain type of relationship with them.

"**I mind my own business.**" They don't impose their dreams on you, and are considerate of your own dreams and aspirations. They're able to work out their relationship with you so it speaks to your needs as well as their own. They know when to keep their opinions to themselves about how you run your life, trusting you to guide yourself and navigate through your own life without their interference. They can accept your choices and decisions, so they don't try to manipulate or sway you to see things their way. They can have a discussion that is inclusive of your feelings and views instead of exclusive to their own. They allow their adult children to raise their children in their own way, without offhanded remarks about nutrition, clothing, grades, and the like. They're not demanding, they do not try to make decisions for you. They show compassion and empathy while respecting your individuality.

"**When I'm with you, I'm responsible for myself.**" They are respectful of your personal space, so they call before they come over. They don't overstay their welcome. They attend to their own needs. They accept your help when offered, but don't wait for you to offer. If they need something, they let you know. They exercise their parental responsibility with their own small children, and make sure they behave properly when in the homes of their relatives.

4. A Great Relative Offers Support

"**I'm on your side.**" The ideal relative finds out what kind of support you need and then supports you in that way. They are respectful and considerate of other family members' feelings and can express concern or joy for your life and allow you to do the same with them. They're sensitive to offer advice only when asked, knowing when to step back and allow you space, and yet they are there when you need them. They don't feel a need to remind you of your mistakes or shortcomings, but will be a consistent source of praise and encouragement for your accomplishments. You know you can rely on them and that they will still be there even if it all goes wrong. They never say

"I told you so." They're honest and trustworthy in this, so you feel safe and encouraged when they are around.

"I won't put you down behind your back." They don't participate in gossip about you or put you down behind your back or get into competition with you. You know they'll stand up for you if others try to gossip about you. They say nice things about you when you're not there.

"Tell me what you need from me." They provide emotional support when needed. They don't withdraw their love, even when they disapprove of what you say or do. You can be honest with them, because you know they won't abandon you. They view your mistakes as learning opportunities. They offer reassurance. They don't give unsolicited advice.

5. A Great Relative Is Helpful

"I'm here if you need me." They will help you when you're sick, pitch in when you're overwhelmed, provide guidance if you want them to, and coach you if you ask for direction. You trust them and count on them with one of the most precious of jobs—helping you with your children when you need it. At family functions and gatherings, such as dinners, parties, reunions, the ideal relative contributes to a group effort to make the event a success. They don't always wait for you to ask, and will offer their help if they think you need their assistance. They care but are not overbearing, they offer advice and experience if you ask, and there are no shades of disapproval accompanying their advice. Their help comes without strings attached; they do not act as if you "owe" them. They feel comfortable asking you for help when they need it, and want you to feel the same. They're not too busy to help you. They only give you the help you ask for, and don't impose their idea of "help" on you "for your own good."

"If you give me your word, I expect you to keep your word." The ideal relative is masterful at loving accountability. When you break a promise or don't do what you've said you would, ideal relatives lovingly remind you of what you've promised, describe what you did, and ask you to account for yourself. They express their concerns in a nonjudgmental manner, allowing you to take responsibility for your own mistakes. If they see that you may be harming yourself or others by your behavior, they will respectfully bring it your attention. They're able to give honest feedback and can accept honest feedback from you, even if it sometimes hurts.

6. A Great Relative Keeps in Touch

"I will stay in touch." The ideal relative finds the perfect balance of staying in touch. Ideal relatives are there when you want them, and not there when you don't. They don't pressure you to call, or expect you to feel obligated. They don't try to make you feel bad if time passes between contact. They don't wait to hear from you and then get angry when they do. They'll reach out to you if they haven't heard from you. They take responsibility for the continuity of the relationship.

"Let me know how you want to stay in touch." They make efforts to stay in touch with you in a way that values your time, relationships, and other commitments. They take the time to learn how keeping in touch best fits into your life, whether through phone calls, e-mails, or occasional visits.

"You have a right to some privacy." They are interested in you and your life, but not too much. You can genuinely be open with them about what's going on with you, but you don't have to keep them informed of every development. You know they care because they ask questions about your life before talking about theirs. And though they're interested in your life, they're also sensitive about areas you would prefer not to share. When they come to visit, they also know when to leave, finding that perfect balance in frequency and time. The time you spend with them is valued, instead of clocked.

"I want to share some of my life with you." They're willing to share their lives openly with you, providing you with the chance to celebrate with them in times of joy and victory, or for you to offer compassion or empathy when they're going through a hard time. But they don't lean on you to make their life work. They share both the good times and the bad, and invite you to do the same.

7. A Great Relative Is Wise with Money

"I'll do what I can." If they loan you money, they don't ask for it back right away. If they borrow money, they always repay it! If you're in need, they open their wallets, promptly forget that they loaned you money, and then act surprised when you pay them back. Also, they won't mention it to anyone else, and you won't keep hearing about it from them. At the same time, the ideal relative doesn't ask for your financial help. On family trips they offer to pay their own way, and do their part to share in expenses.

8. A Great Relative Is Also a Friend

"I don't just love you. I like you too!" Because of mutual respect and support, the ideal relative can also be your friend. A "good relative" is a "good friend," to whom you happen to be related. As you each get older, the ideal relative looks to build common ground and nurture it. The rules of friendship are applied, so they don't get privileges that are unacceptable in other relationships.

9. A Great Relative Doesn't Hold On to the Past

"I don't define you by what you've done in the past." The ideal relative realizes that people can change and evolve, and they don't limit their idea of you to the past. They don't keep reminding you of your mistakes or tell stories about your past that make you uncomfortable. If there are any negative patterns from the past that concern them in the present, they address them straight on with you, and work with you to identify the evidence or actions they require of you to let it go and move on. They have no doubt that you have the capacity to grow as a human being. They treat you as an intellectual equal, not a son or daughter of 15 when you're over 30 years old. As your adult child, they're willing to forgive you for the past and discover who you are in the present as a person, rather than limiting you to the role of parent.

10. A Great Relative Is Fun, Optimistic, and a Positive Influence

"I love life." The ideal relative is someone you just want to be around because he or she makes you feel better about yourself and life in general. Ideal relatives help lighten your emotional load instead of adding to it. You can go to them, depressed or concerned about something, and they laugh, smile, and let you know that everything is okay and will work out. They help you put your troubles in perspective by their sense of optimism. They're positive people, and they laugh and smile a lot. They find reasons and opportunities to laugh with you, and organize activities that family members can enjoy together. Their presence in the room tends to bring out the best in everyone.

Be a Great Relative

And there you have it, the top 10 qualities of an ideal relative. We don't know what your personal list looks like, but we're fairly certain that many of these qualities, if not all of them, would appear on it. Turn it around and you can know how it's possible for you to be a great relative to your own family members. In the long term, this is likely to accomplish more for you than wishing one of them was a better relative to you. If there is truth to the aphorism that "We get what we give," then giving greatness should get you greatness in return.

In the deepest sense, your family, our family, is the whole of humanity. Descended from common ancestors, sharing a common destiny, each of us has a part to play in building a world that works, a world worth sharing, a world in which our children and our children's children can look back at us and admire our willingness to choose greatness over pettiness and love over difficulty. Peace in the world begins with peace in our hearts, then peace in our homes and with our families. This book represents our contribution to the betterment of the human family. The next step is yours. Will you take it?.

Appendix

In our exploration of family relationships, we have chosen to steer clear of serious familial pathology caused by severe and persistent mental illnesses. That is why, with the exception of this chapter, you'll find little if anything in these pages for dealing with child abuse, narcissistic personality disorder, alcoholism, bipolar disease/manic depression, obsessive compulsive disorder, anxiety disorders including panic disorder, post-traumatic stress disorder, or phobias. We also chose not to focus on codependence.

Nevertheless, we must acknowledge that these problems produce a wide variety of difficulties in families, many of which are personalized and internalized, and then reacted to with hurt and anger, essentially because of a lack of understanding and information. If you believe you're dealing with serious pathology in your family, you do not need to go it alone. Get help! Reach out, access the resources in your community, and learn about your options. Sometimes the best way to love your family is from anywhere else in the world.

Resources

See the "Community Service Numbers" in the front of your telephone directory. Or call the 800-directory to get a listing of toll-free numbers (800–555–1212).

Organizations

NAMI
National Alliance for the Mentally Ill
200 North Glebe Road
Suite 1015
Arlington, VA 22203-3754
Website: www.nami.org

NAMI is a nonprofit support and advocacy organization of consumers, families, and friends of people with mental illness, which emphasizes the biological view of causes and treatments. Their website has an excellent section on illnesses and treatments.

NIMH
National Institute for Mental Health
5600 Fishers Lane
Rockville, MD 20857
301–443–4513; TDD 301–443–8431
e-mail: NIMHPUBS@nih.gov

Provides a list of free publications on depressive and other mental disorders, including a comprehensive listing of resources for help.

SPAN
Suicide Prevention Advocacy Network
5034 Odin's Way
Marietta, GA 30068
886.649.1366
e-mail: act@spanusa.org
Website: www.spanusa.org

National advocacy organization for the development of a proven effective suicide prevention program, and network for legislative initiatives and public action.

Peer Counseling Groups

Re-Evaluation Counseling, www.rc.org
Co-Counseling International, www.cci-usa.org

An Invitation
from the Authors

If you would like to find our more about our other books, audios, and videos or tell us your success stories, then visit our Web sites at:

www.DealingWithRelatives.com

www.TheRicks.com

www.DealingWithPeople.com

or e-mail us at:

Dr. Rick Kirschner: *dr.rick@talknatural.com*

Dr. Rick Brinkman: *dr.rick@rickbrinkman.com*

About the Authors

Dr. Rick Kirschner and **Dr. Rick Brinkman** are world-renowned professional speakers and authors. They began their careers as holistic physicians whose specialty was the mental and emotional aspects of healing and wellness. They are the coauthors of the bestselling audio and video tapes *How to Deal with Difficult People,* as well as six other audio and video training programs. Their previous book, *Dealing with People You Can't Stand,* is an international bestseller with translations in 10 languages. They have also coauthored the book *Life by Design, Making Wise Choices in a Mixed Up World.* They now present their entertaining keynote speeches and training programs worldwide. Their client portfolio includes AT&T, Hewlett-Packard, Texaco, the Inc 500 conference, Young Presidents Organization, the U.S. Army, and hundreds of other corporations, government agencies, and professional associations.

For information about the authors' keynotes and seminars, visit www.TheRicks.com.